Virginia Woolf and the Materiality of Theory

Virginia Woolf and the Materiality of Theory

Sex, Animal, Life

Derek Ryan

EDINBURGH
University Press

© Derek Ryan, 2013, 2015

Edinburgh University Press Ltd
The Tun – Holyrood Road
12 (2f) Jackson's Entry
Edinburgh EH8 8PJ

www.euppublishing.com

First published in hardback by Edinburgh University Press 2013

This paperback edition 2015

Typeset in 10.5/13 pt Sabon by
Servis Filmsetting Ltd, Stockport, Cheshire

A CIP record for this book is available from the British Library

ISBN 978 0 7486 7643 9 (hardback)
ISBN 978 1 4744 0234 7 (paperback)
ISBN 978 0 7486 7644 6 (webready PDF)
ISBN 978 0 7486 7645 3 (epub)

The right of Derek Ryan
to be identified as author of this work
has been asserted in accordance with the
Copyright, Designs and Patents Act 1988,
and the Copyright and Related Rights
Regulations 2003 (SI No. 2498).

Contents

Acknowledgements		vi
Abbreviations		viii
Introduction: Virginia Woolf and the Materiality of Theory		1
1	Materials for Theory: Digging Granite and Chasing Rainbows	26
2	Sexual Difference in Becoming: *A Room of One's Own* and *To the Lighthouse*	58
3	Queering *Orlando* and Non/Human Desire	101
4	The Question of the Animal in *Flush*	132
5	Quantum Reality and Posthuman Life: *The Waves*	171
Bibliography		203
Index		220

Acknowledgements

My first 'thank you' is to Jane Goldman for her generosity and guidance as I undertook the doctoral research which has led to this book. Without her boundless energy and passion for Woolf studies, and her friendship, *Virginia Woolf and the Materiality of Theory* would not have been possible. I also owe a huge debt of gratitude to John Coyle and Vassiliki Kolocotroni for all their support throughout my time at Glasgow, and to Alison Thorne and David Goldie for encouraging me to pursue my interest in Woolf's writing several years ago. For generously giving their time to read earlier drafts of this study and for providing invaluable comments and suggestions I would like to thank Jessica Berman, Bryony Randall, Laci Mattison, and my two anonymous readers for Edinburgh University Press. Thank you to Jackie Jones and her team for helping me to bring this book to publication.

I am extremely grateful to have been introduced to the Woolf community over the past few years and to have been welcomed so warmly: thank you for inspiring conferences, events, and conversations, and especially to Judith Allen, Suzanne Bellamy, Pamela Caughie, Kristin Czarnecki, Claire Davison-Pégon, Jeanne Dubino, Gill Lowe, and Kathryn Simpson. Thank you to Mark Hussey and Pam Morris for allowing me to read and quote from forthcoming essays. It was a privilege to co-organise the 21st Annual International Conference on Virginia Woolf in Glasgow (2011), and I thank everyone who attended for making that such a memorable occasion. This book has also benefited greatly from conversations I had with my fellow researchers and friends, whether in our 'Theory at Random' reading group, over an afternoon coffee, or in the pub. In particular, I thank Rebecca DeWald, Andrew Eadie, Erik Fuhrer, Ruth Hawthorn, Henry King, Lil Rose, and Mark West. A very special thank you to my dear friends Laura Gilmour, Vhairi Gilmour, and Kevin Wilkinson.

I am especially grateful to my Mum, Pauline Barrington, to William

Barrington, to my brother, Chris Ryan, and to my late, beloved Gran, Margaret McConnochie. The love and unwavering support I have received from them over the years has been a constant source of inspiration.

Finally, my deepest thanks to Stella Bolaki for her love, encouragement, and patience as I spent many long days and nights completing this book.

Earlier versions of portions from Chapter 1 appeared in '"Nature, who has played so many queer tricks upon us": Digging Granite and Chasing Rainbows with Virginia Woolf', in Kristin Czarnecki and Carrie Rohman (eds), *Virginia Woolf and the Natural World: Selected Papers from the Twentieth International Conference on Virginia Woolf* (Clemson: Clemson University Digital Press, 2011), pp. 202–7, and in 'Woolf's Queering of Granite', *Virginia Woolf Miscellany* 82 (2012): 20–2. An earlier version of a part of Chapter 4 appeared as 'From Spaniel Club to Animalous Society: Virginia Woolf's *Flush*', in Derek Ryan and Stella Bolaki (eds), *Contradictory Woolf: Selected Papers from the Twenty-first Annual International Conference on Virginia Woolf* (Clemson: Clemson University Digital Press, 2012), pp. 158–65. An earlier version of a part of Chapter 5 appeared as 'Woolf and Contemporary Philosophy', in Bryony Randall and Jane Goldman (eds), *Virginia Woolf in Context* (Cambridge: Cambridge University Press, 2012). I am grateful that this material could be reprinted with permission from these publications.

I would like to acknowledge the financial support of the Arts and Humanities Research Council and the University of Glasgow for funding the doctoral research on which this book is based.

Abbreviations

Works by Virginia Woolf

BA	*Between the Acts*
CR1	*The Common Reader Vol. I.*
CR2	*The Common Reader Vol. II.*
CSF	*The Complete Shorter Fiction of Virginia Woolf*
D1–5	*The Diary of Virginia Woolf*
F	*Flush: A Biography*
L1–6	*The Letters of Virginia Woolf*
JR	*Jacob's Room*
MB	*Moments of Being*
MD	*Mrs Dalloway*
ND	*Night and Day*
O	*Orlando: A Biography*
PA	*A Passionate Apprentice*
RO	*A Room of One's Own*
E1–6	*The Essays of Virginia Woolf*
TG	*Three Guineas*
TL	*To the Lighthouse*
VO	*The Voyage Out*
W	*The Waves*
WF	*Women and Fiction: The Manuscript Versions of* A Room of One's Own
Y	*The Years*

Editorial Note

For translations, the date given in parenthesis on first mention of the text is the first publication date in original language.

Introduction: Virginia Woolf and the Materiality of Theory

> I reach what I might call a philosophy; at any rate it is a constant idea of mine; that behind the cotton wool is hidden a pattern; that we – I mean all human beings – are connected with this; that the whole world is a work of art; that we are parts of the work of art. *Hamlet* or a Beethoven quartet is the truth about this vast mass that we call the world. But there is no Shakespeare, there is no Beethoven; certainly and emphatically there is no God; we are the words; we are the music; we are the thing itself. (*MB* 85)

When Virginia Woolf, in this famous passage from her unfinished and posthumously published memoir 'Sketch of the Past' (1976), outlines her 'philosophy' or 'constant idea', she presents us with a 'conception' of life that is embedded in materiality: a 'pattern', 'hidden behind the cotton wool of daily life' (*MB* 85). It is, as Mark Hussey has recently put it, a form of theorising that is 'grounded' and 'embodied',[1] and other critics have placed emphasis on Woolf's formulation of human communality through language and art: Lorraine Sim, for example, writes of 'a connective principle' in Woolf's 'pattern' which is revealed through art and society;[2] Emily Hinnov claims, more explicitly, that 'Woolf views aesthetics as a vehicle for social action that might bring about humanistic unity [. . .] coherence and interconnectivity, she speaks to the web-like linkage between all of humanity, accessible through our participation in art';[3] Bryony Randall suggests that 'far from being a unified, self-sufficient, self-explanatory temporal unit', Woolf's 'moment of being' is an experience inextricably tied to reading and writing;[4] and Jane Goldman, aligning this passage with a Habermasian 'intersubjectivity' and a Bakhtinian 'social origin' of language, argues that 'Woolf positions herself as part of a community of subjects, accessible through language but with no transcendent position outside it; [. . .] she understands language to be socially constructed and present only in its material utterances.'[5]

Woolf's focus here does indeed appear to be primarily on the question of art and particularly writing ('I make it real by putting it into words') as well as of the human communality behind this writing ('we – I mean all human beings – are connected with this') (*MB* 85), but there is an additional ontological inflection to this excerpt from 'Sketch of the Past', one which extends the non-transcendent interconnectivity beyond a concern solely with the human and language or art, and which therefore speaks to key issues in this book concerning theory and materiality (and the materiality of theory).[6] That is, the 'philosophy' reached in the above passage hinges on a conceptualisation of the collective pronoun 'we' that expands as it intensifies through each clause. In the first instance 'we' is clearly intended as representative of 'all human beings', yet the *connection* Woolf emphasises is one between this human 'we' and the 'pattern' or 'vast mass we call the world': 'We' are not only 'the words', but also the 'music' and, crucially, the 'thing itself'. We find, then, a communality that is extended beyond a purely human concern and where language is not the only immanent feature (to single out language in this way would be precisely to see it as, in some way, transcendent); in other words, we might say here that Woolf is concerned with world-making, not simply subject-making or word-making. This is further elucidated by the instance of 'shock' created by the embedded flower at St Ives:

> I was looking at the flower bed by the front door; 'That is the whole', I said. I was looking at a plant with a spread of leaves; and it seemed suddenly plain that the flower itself was a part of the earth; that a ring enclosed what was the flower; and that was the real flower; part earth; part flower. (*MB* 84)

It may be that it is only through the human act of writing down (and indeed verbalising, as Woolf notes here) an instance such as this that Woolf feels she can 'make it whole' and find 'satisfaction' and 'reason', but the conceptual model of a non-hierarchical, intricately interconnected whole is suffused with the vitality and materiality of the 'dominant' sensation (over her 'passive' self) of the 'real flower' that was 'part earth; part flower' (*MB* 84–5). To be sure, both the event of writing and the event of the flower itself are immanent, creative processes.

What is emphasised by Woolf, then, is 'intuition'[7] that is 'given to me, not made by me' (*MB* 85) and which 'refers to her idea that there is a pattern behind things, and in telling us the origin of this idea, she suggests that it comes from the pattern itself'.[8] As Woolf writes in a letter to Vita Sackville-West on 16th March 1926, contemplating 'rhythm' this time rather than pattern, 'a sight, an emotion, creates this wave in the mind, long before it makes words to fit it', and therefore through writing 'one has to recapture this, and set this working (which has nothing apparently to do with words)' (*L3* 247). And in the two paragraphs following the 'we are' refrain in 'Sketch of the Past', Woolf undercuts the notion of language as primary event. She at first appears to outline the 'far more necessary' importance of writing over other activities by 'spending the morning writing' rather than, as one example she gives, 'walking'. Following this, however, Woolf states that it was precisely whilst on her 'walk yesterday' that she was 'struck' by the realisation – 'these moments of being of mine were scaffolding in the background; were the invisible and silent part of my life as a child'. She goes on to describe the 'people' who were at the 'foreground' in her childhood, but these people, and therefore this foreground, are merely 'caricatures' (*MB* 86). What is left in the foreground of the reader's mind is the 'scaffolding', the fact that 'one is living all the time in relation to certain background rods or conceptions' (*MB* 85). What I am suggesting here is the sense that Woolf's writing is not so much concerned with a 'materiality [. . .] which blots out the light' of being,[9] as it is with illuminating materiality as precisely the possibility of being: the becoming of the material world.

This book explores how materiality is theorised by Woolf long before she started to write 'Sketch of the Past' in 1939, through the various connections she makes in her writings between human and nonhuman, embodiment and environment, culture and nature, life and matter. My title, *Virginia Woolf and the Materiality of Theory: Sex, Animal, Life*, points to three interrelated aspects of this study. Firstly, I engage with Woolf's writings in the context of theoretical debates which, broadly speaking, have marked a shift in the past fifteen years or so from the focus on language and discourse to questions concerning materiality and ontology; or, put another way, from the primacy of culture to its entanglement with nature. The debates I place Woolf within are all concerned with various aspects of materialism and immanence rather than abstraction and transcendence, forming part of a turn towards new materialisms in contemporary theory. This entails reading Woolf alongside the philosophy of Gilles Deleuze – a prominent figure throughout the book and someone who cites Woolf as exemplary of some of his most important concepts – as well as eminent contemporary theorists of materiality including Donna Haraway, Elizabeth Grosz, Karen Barad, Jane Bennett, and Rosi Braidotti, the latter of whom demonstrates at various points how Woolf's modernist aesthetics and feminist politics are influential on her thought. Secondly, moving away from the human- and subject-centred analyses more prominent in Woolf (and modernist) scholarship, each of my chapters engage, both seriously and I hope playfully, with a diverse range of nonhuman objects and materials that provide the impetus for Woolf's reconceptualisation of materiality – or, we might say, the materials for her theories. These include granites and rainbows (Chapter 1), paint and grass (Chapter 2), wedding rings and a motor-car (Chapter 3), fur and flesh (Chapter 4), and matter itself, that productive yet elusive fabric of our material world (Chapter 5). It is the recognition of Woolf's particular form of embedded theorising that underpins my efforts in the first half of this book to shed new light on widely recognised discussions of Woolf in relation to feminism, sexual difference and sexuality, but that also leads in the second half of the book to open up her writings to emerging and less familiar critical paradigms which foreground the question of the animal and posthumanist conceptualisations of life. Thirdly, I seek to unsettle the perceived opposition between historical and theoretical approaches to Woolf's writings. Whilst the so-called 'turn' (or return) to the archive and historicism in modernist studies coincided with the diminishing influence of postmodernist or poststructuralist theory (based on the largely misguided premise that this theory was anti-historical and not concerned enough with the material contexts), there are crucial questions concerning materialism in relation to those terms in my subtitle – 'sex', 'animal', and 'life' – that are currently being posed in literary studies and contemporary theory, and which have still to be fully explored in Woolf's writing. Taking seriously the ways in which Woolf *theorises* materiality throughout her work, rather than focusing only on how she alludes to, or comments on, the material context in which she lived, demonstrates that the material world is not purely a concern for archivists or historicists, and that the way we historicise is affected by how we theorise materiality and how theory is materialised. In other words, to conceptualise is also to contextualise.

Working through these three stated concerns, my central argument will be that throughout her writing Woolf theorises the creative, immanent materiality of human and nonhuman life; that is, wary of the philosophical, ethical, and political pitfalls of individualism, binary oppositions, and transcendence, Woolf's writing offers new conceptualisations of the material world where the immanent and intimate entanglements of human and nonhuman agencies are brought to the fore. By focusing on wide-ranging but interrelated issues across five thematic chapters, and by reading Woolf alongside but also *in*side theoretical writings (and *vice versa*), I hope to offer a new perspective on Woolf's writings and to demonstrate the ways in which her texts help elucidate the subversive potential (and limitations) in these current theoretical contexts – therefore exploring in the process some of the aesthetic, political, ethical, ontological and conceptual links between modernist literature and theory. More specifically then, and building on the premise reached by poststructuralist and postmodernist criticism that Woolf radically destabilises essential differences based on binary oppositions, I go on to ask: what precisely are the modes and models of materiality made possible by Woolf's texts and by the complex theoretical and critical contexts her writing has so clearly affected?

Woolf, modernism, and theory

The broader links between the modernist aesthetics, and cultures, that emerged in the first half of the twentieth century and those theoretical debates that proliferated in the second half have recently been emphasised in Stephen Ross' edited collection, *Modernism and Theory: A Critical Debate* (2009). In his introduction, Ross argues that while scholars (re)turning to the archives over the past two decades have widened the scope of what we now think of as the new modernist studies, it is unfortunate and somewhat puzzling that this has often coincided with the marginalisation of theory:

> The ironies attending this elision verge on modernist absurdity: theory's challenge to predominant notions of the literary, canon formation, disciplinary formations, high and low culture, progress, civilisation, and imperialism helped make the new modernist studies possible. Also, theory's concern with globalization, imperialism, gender and sex roles, race and racism, reason and superstition, enlightenment and benightedness, sovereignty and slavery, margins and peripheries, and ethical complexities continues, albeit in a different register, modernism's already articulated concerns. Modernism's critique of modernity animated theory's invention of postmodernity, while theory's anti-foundational stance extended modernism's indeterminacy, linguistic complexity, and reflexivity.[10]

Despite the temporal gap, theory dating roughly from the mid-1960s to the mid-1990s – whether phenomenological, psychoanalytic, poststructuralist or ('third wave') feminist – is, according to Ross, 'integrally bound' to modernism precisely because of shared aesthetic and political concerns but also because its philosophical roots are 'either modernist (e.g. Heidegger, Husserl, Sartre, Wittgenstein) or shared by modernism (e.g. Kant, Hegel, Schopenhauer, Nietzsche, Kierkegaard)'.[11] Where our readings of Woolf are concerned, it is particularly important to add Henri Bergson to this list, especially considering that in one of the earliest monographs on her writings, Ruth Gruber suggests that Woolf was 'living in the Bergsonian atmosphere' and was 'too innately creative, too inherently Bergsonian to be called Bergson's imitator', and several critics have followed in forging links between Woolf and Bergson.[12]

Indeed, in the years since theory's prominence in modernist studies began to wane in the mid-1990s, a renewed interest in the philosophical roots of Woolf's modernism has been evident in important studies which have considered her writing alongside the likes of David Hume, Emmanuel Kant, Bertrand Russell, Walter Benjamin, Martin Heidegger, and Maurice Merleau-Ponty.[13] These considerations of 'Woolf among the philosophers'[14] thoroughly contradict Michael Lackey's view that to properly understand Woolf's work we must 'banish philosophy';[15] rather, they reinforce Goldman's reflection that 'contextualising Woolf is not simply a historical turn. It entails a simultaneous return to theoretical and critical contexts, in which the processes of historicising and contextualising are always already placed.'[16] In recent years then, the philosophical contexts in which Woolf was writing have combined with historical analyses, and have helped shape the way we engage with Woolf's modernism.

But where the aforementioned studies are primarily concerned with philosophical contexts contemporary to when Woolf herself was writing (and therefore sensitive to the risks of decontextualisation), a central tenet of Ross' argument is that it is also important to rearticulate the links between the modernist literature and the theoretical debates of the latter decades of the century, and as I aim to demonstrate in this book into the twenty-first century, so that we might begin to theorise modernism anew (and, we might even say, to modernise theory) in our own contemporary moment. This is itself a matter of contextualisation: the connections between modernism and theory are strengthened by reading literary and theoretical texts alongside one another in ways that involve not simply using theory to provide a particular methodology for readings of modernist texts or using modernism to provide examples of theoretical concepts; rather modernism and theory might, as Ross puts it, be thought of as 'mutually sustaining aspects of the same project' where 'modernist writing thinks theoretically and theory writes modernistically'.[17] The extent to which this is true of all modernist writing, and indeed theory of the kind Ross focuses on, is of course contestable, but I want to take from his argument the emphasis on bringing together or intercepting modernism and theory, themselves a multiplicity of historical movements and moments, which need not be thought of as a flight from, rather a rethinking of, material realities. As Fredric Jameson states in his 'Afterword' to the same volume:

> it is a reinvention of the historical situation alone that allows us to grasp the text as a vibrant historical act, and not as a document of the archives. And this is why even those texts which seemed to have become documents in a

now distant past, like the one-time masterpieces of the modern, suddenly come alive as living acts and forms of praxis – aesthetic, social, political, psychoanalytic, even ontological – which imperiously solicit our attention.[18]

As a theorist of the modern on her own terms, and someone who prompts us in 'How it Strikes a Contemporary' (1925) to 'scan the horizon; see the past in relation to the future' (*CR1* 241), Woolf provides with her writing the ideal context 'to ask not just what modernism can tell us about theory and what theory can tell us about modernism, but also what the nexus modernism/theory can tell us about the twentieth century's preoccupations, tendencies, triumphs, and failures'.[19]

In Woolf studies, the influence of poststructuralist and postmodernist readings of Woolf in the 1980s and 1990s testifies to the previous connections made between modernism and the kind of theory Ross claims is now marginalised, but also shows the limitations of approaches where 'theory' was largely synonymous with deconstructive readings which focused on the de-centring of (human) subjectivity, language, and discourse. Whilst my argument in this book will depart in important ways from such readings by turning to questions concerning the nonhuman as much as the human, objects as much as subjects, materiality as much as language, my approach to Woolf undoubtedly owes a debt to these studies, and in particular four well-known texts by Toril Moi, Makiko Minow-Pinkney, Rachel Bowlby, and Pamela Caughie. Firstly, the introduction to Moi's 1985 book *Sexual/Textual Politics*, though not the first poststructuralist reading of Woolf,[20] is commonly referenced as a turning point in Woolf criticism where Moi introduces her wide-ranging analysis of Anglo-American and French feminisms by placing Woolf as a forerunner of feminist theory.[21] Advocating a Derridean and Kristevan approach to Woolf, Moi argues that she challenges realist aesthetics and humanist formulations of identity, and she makes her often-cited and important assertion that Woolf's modernist aesthetics and feminist politics are not to be seen as mutually exclusive, that her feminist politics are located '*precisely in her textual practice*'.[22] Following this, in *Virginia Woolf and the Problem of the Subject* (1987), Minow-Pinkney provides the first book-length study to adopt this approach, offering a more detailed focus on Julia Kristeva and Jacques Derrida, and reading with and against Jacques Lacan, in her feminist poststructuralist psychoanalytic account of Woolf's writing which seeks to find a new deconstructive understanding of subjectivity. Echoing Moi, Minow-Pinkney argues that Woolf's modernist experimental aesthetics can 'best be seen as a feminist subversion of the deepest formal principles – of the very definitions of narrative, writing, the subject – of a patriarchal social order'.[23] Published a year later, Rachel Bowlby's *Virginia Woolf: Feminist Destinations* offers a broadly poststructuralist reading of Woolf's feminism – albeit that it departs from the more technical analysis provided by Minow-Pinkney – to suggest that 'issues of literary representation, historical narrative and sexual difference are inseparable throughout Woolf's work'. Bowlby argues that this is precisely what makes Woolf a feminist writer, one that questions 'the very notion of straightforward directions and known destinations'.[24] Finally, in the wake of these feminist poststructuralist and psychoanalytic readings of Woolf, Caughie's 1991 study, *Virginia Woolf and Postmodernism*, focuses on how various strands of postmodernist/poststructuralist theory and literature challenge the motivations and reading strategies with which we approach Woolf's texts. Caughie does not seek to claim Woolf as a postmodernist *avant la lettre*, but to challenge orthodox modernist and feminist readings of her writings which fail, she argues, to move past various binary oppositions between 'conventional and modern, masculine and feminine, appearance and reality, the external and the essence'.[25]

Reflecting on these poststructuralist and postmodernist approaches to Woolf and to feminism, and acknowledging that self-identifying as either is now considered to be unfashionable (indeed, according to Moi's own recent comments, 'the poststructuralist paradigm is now exhausted' and postmodern feminism is 'an intellectual tradition that has been fully explored'[26]), Caughie today maintains that there is still important work to be done concerning the relationship between modernism, poststructuralism and feminism:

> If I continue to ride that dead horse, it is because I believe that 'things may stay true longer than they stay interesting.' There remains the need for a feminist intervention informed by the insights of poststructuralist theory that would have us question notions of collective identity or action, end-oriented narratives, or the past as redeemable. Where a notion of progress returns in our history of theory is not in the notion of ends, as if there is a goal to be realized, but in the realization that feminism is what cannot pass, or become passé.[27]

Theory may well have been, to some extent, marginalised over the past fifteen years or so in the expansion of modernist studies, but there is little doubt that by opening up readings of Woolf to various critical and theoretical contexts (including fields recognised today as cultural studies, gender studies and queer theory) these postmodernist and poststructuralist readings continue to be important in challenging our assumptions – whether from a theoretical, historical, or cultural perspective – about the stability of intentionality, language, meaning, and identity.

Yet if poststructuralist or postmodernist readings of Woolf remain important in drawing attention to some of the continuities between modernism and theory, helping us to reassess, as Ross puts it, the 'preoccupations, tendencies, triumphs, and failures' of the twentieth century, they also lead us to new theoretical concerns and conceptual paradigms which impact on how we think about the relationship between modernism and theory at the beginning of the twenty-first. As such, this book departs from the above approaches to Woolf's modernism and feminism where they placed emphasis on language and discourse and on psychoanalytic structures of (human) subjectivity and desire. This is precisely to take account of the changing nature of 'theory' since the predominance of poststructuralism and postmodernism in the 1980s and early 1990s, where materiality has become the grounds for important debates that seek to re-evaluate how we think of the relationship between culture and nature, human and nonhuman. That this is still linked to poststructuralism rather than a complete break from it is emphasised by the fact that the work of Deleuze (solo and with Félix Guattari) is crucial to these new theories of materiality. As a key figure of what is often seen to be 'high' (poststructuralist) theory and someone who was profoundly influenced by modernist literature, Deleuze, as I will explain in more detail below, has only recently come to prominence in modernist studies and Woolf studies, much later than other poststructuralist thinkers such as Derrida, Lacan, Kristeva, and Foucault. But as well as aiming to fill a gap in Woolf studies where her work has yet to be systematically considered alongside Deleuzian philosophy, my reading of Woolf is placed in the context of contemporary dialogues on materialist theories of 'sex', the 'animal', and 'life' that have been inspired by, expanded upon, and produced challenges to, Deleuze's thought (for example the reactions of feminist theorists to the concept of 'becoming-woman', discussed in Chapter 2, or the conflicting ways that theorists have responded to Deleuze and Guattari's writings on animals, discussed in Chapter 4). When I focus on important materialist theorists of the following generation(s), including Braidotti, Grosz, Haraway, Barad, and Bennett, I do so not to suggest that what is revolutionary in contemporary theory can be characterised simply by the shift from one set of thinkers to another, but to situate my readings of Woolf in the context of ongoing and contentious theoretical debates concerning nonanthropocentric conceptualisations of our material world.

Following poststructuralism, there may well be a 'contemporary theoretical astuteness', as Claire Colebrook puts it, 'consisting of acknowledging the provisional status of one's position' and an awareness of 'some textual mediating condition – there is no sex in itself, race in itself, history in itself', but the way in which this awareness passes through diverse fields and disciplines sometimes 'avoids the problem of theory'.[28] In this book I am not concerned with imposing a theoretical framework onto Woolf's texts so much as I am in addressing the act of doing theory itself, focusing on the ways in which Woolf's texts are themselves theorised and theorising. Such an approach entails, of course, choosing to read Woolf in certain ways and in particular contexts, foregrounding certain critical frameworks and debates rather than others. But in making such choices I am keen to avoid the limitations in the kind of postmodernist approach Caughie advocates in her earlier book, where her polemical critique of dualisms too easily falls back on a 'refusal to choose', a phrase that recurs throughout *Virginia Woolf and Postmodernism*,[29] as itself a subversive act rather than exploring the ways in which specific choices – whether made by or for us – can lead us to find heterogeneity and multiplicity affirmed in Woolf's texts. Whilst not wishing to reduce Woolf's writings to any one theoretical framework, then, in this book I have chosen to focus on specific thematic concerns and commit Woolf's texts to particular theoretical alliances. As I demonstrate in Chapter 1, rejecting totalising and binary models of language and thought does not take us into a space of noncommitment, of a postmodernist 'refusal to choose' where we nonetheless remain within a system of language, vacillating there but never reaching beyond or outside the text, and each of the following chapters are concerned with committing language to something more than itself. Any theoretical approach to Woolf will, to some extent, be partial, but what interests me is the ways in which recognising, accounting for, and experimenting with Woolf's own mode of theorising does not entail suspending or deferring commitment to careful and sustained analysis of her texts; rather it is to conceive of committed, close readings that are nonetheless changeable and open, remaining aware, as Woolf writes in 'Craftsmanship' (1937), that 'the truth they try to catch is many-sided', and so will require change, revision, and future perspectives (*E6* 97).

Despite premature obituaries then, theory has far from disappeared (just as, conversely, historicism is hardly a nascent activity). As Jane Elliott and Derek Attridge's recent intervention in *Theory After 'Theory'* (2011) suggests, the role of theory itself is at an exciting stage, 'returning' in new and unexpected forms:

> Since the mid-1990s, the story goes, theory has continued to diversify, drawing on the work of a range of new figures and examining a host of new archives and arenas, but its newer incarnations offer at most a kind of afterlife of the once vital object that was 'Theory', a diluted form lacking in both intellectual substance and institutional prominence. [. . . But] where theory

continues to thrive, it increasingly adopts positions that challenge some of the fundamental intellectual stances that once defined 'Theory' [. . .] new work is being produced that mounts such challenges from within theory's now much wider institutional and discursive boundaries.[30]

If we are to consider the relationship between Woolf and theory today, it has not simply to be a return to the poststructuralist or postmodernist readings of Woolf that were influential in the 1980s and 1990s but a turn towards new theoretical paradigms that seek to address the limitations of those approaches whilst building on their subversive potential. My own efforts in this book are to forge creative links between Woolf's modernist/feminist aesthetics and politics and contemporary theories of materiality, locating theory within Woolf's writing, as well as Woolf within theory, so as to bring her modernism and her own theorising firmly into the foreground of current debates in fields such as feminist philosophy, queer theory, animal studies, and posthumanities. It is at the intersection of these two concerns – on the revitalising of the relationship between modernism and theory and of theory after 'Theory' – that my reading of Woolf and the materiality of theory can be situated.

Woolf, new materialisms, and Deleuze

Considering the relationship between Woolf's writing and materialism is itself nothing new to Woolf studies. Michèle Barrett, in her 1979 introduction to *Virginia Woolf: Women and Writing*, makes clear that Woolf was both a literary theorist[31] and concerned with the material conditions of women and men: 'She argued that the writer was the product of her or his historical circumstances, and that material conditions were of crucial importance', and 'she claimed that these material circumstances had a profound effect on the psychological aspects of writing, and that they could be seen to influence the nature of the creative work itself'.[32] Barrett cites a famous passage from *A Room of One's Own* (1929) to support her argument, where Woolf writes that 'fiction is like a spider's web' and that 'these webs are not spun in mid-air by incorporeal creatures, but are the work of suffering human beings, and are attached to grossly material things, like health and money and the houses we live in' (*RO* 53). Importantly, and contrary to other feminist Woolf critics such as Jane Marcus,[33] Barrett is uncomfortable with claiming Woolf's 'materialist' argument as a Marxist one.[34] Writing many years later in *Imagination in Theory* (1999) – and having noted the 'intimate blow' dealt to many of the 'working assumptions' of a humanist and historicist

Marxism by poststructuralism's anti-humanism, its critique of teleological thought, and its insistence on the constructed nature of linguistic meaning[35] – Barrett reinforces the 'ambiguity' she finds in Woolf's materialism.[36] Intriguingly, she at the same time notes the ambiguity in Woolf's relationship to humanism, claiming that she displays an 'agnostic kind of not-humanism' in contrast to the more pointed 'anti-humanism' of Louis Althusser or of the poststructuralists.[37] But whilst Barrett is hesitant to go beyond agnosticism and ambiguity, partly as a result of her worries over the political impotence that she fears for such a position, my own reading of Woolf places her in the politically and ethically charged context of debates on materiality which have emerged in more recent years and mark an attempt to unsettle anthropocentrism and to foreground the mutual interdependence of culture and nature, human and nonhuman, meaning and matter.[38]

Virginia Woolf and the Materiality of Theory seeks to more closely and comprehensively explore the relationship between Woolf's writing and nonhumanist or, to use a term I discuss more fully in Chapter 5, 'posthumanist' conceptualisations of the material world. This is not to be concerned with what comes after or without humans, but to better account for the material entanglements of humans with nonhuman objects, animals and environments, in order to reassess the human and the nonhuman both in themselves and in their relationality. By focusing on the ways in which materiality matters to Woolf in relation to the natural world, sexual difference, sexuality, animality, and life itself, this book therefore follows those theoretical approaches that have radicalised our understanding of subjectivity and of language but crucially takes seriously the growing claims of the need, as Diana Coole and Samantha Frost argue in *New Materialisms* (2010), 'to subject objectivity and material reality to a similarly radical reappraisal'.[39] In *Vibrant Matter* (2010), Jane Bennett shows that a radical and nonanthropocentric reappraisal of materialism, coupled with an immanent vitalism, involves an engagement with the material world which is not limited by a humanist and historicist Marxist model:[40]

> How did Marx's notion of materiality – as economic structures and exchanges that provoke many other events – come to stand for the materialist perspective per se? Why is there not a more robust debate between contending philosophies of materiality or between contending accounts of how materiality matters to politics?
>
> For some time political theory has acknowledged that materiality matters. But this materiality most often refers to human social structures or to the human meanings 'embodied' in them and other objects. Because politics is itself often construed as an exclusively human domain, what registers on it is a set of material constraints on or a context for human action. Dogged resist-

ance to anthropocentrism is perhaps the main difference between the vital materialism I pursue and this kind of historical materialism.[41]

These growing attempts to reconceptualise materiality are concerned with the move towards an affirmative (rather than dialectical) materialism which 'sees its task as creating new concepts and images of nature that affirm matter's immanent vitality', therefore complicating how we conceive of causation and emphasising multiple entanglements of human and nonhuman agencies.[42] Coole and Frost outline three central themes of these 'new materialisms': the view of matter as itself having agency, a view that is tied to posthumanism; the status of 'life' and related bioethical and biopolitical issues; and a 'nondogmatic' critical reengagement with 'the material details of everyday life': 'An important characteristic shared by all three components is their emphasis on materialization as a complex, pluralistic, relatively open process and their insistence that humans, including theorists themselves, be recognized as thoroughly immersed within materiality's productive contingencies.'[43] Clearly, this is a far cry from the from the Edwardian materialism of Arnold Bennett, H. G. Wells, and John Galsworthy that Woolf finds so insufficient to capture 'life itself' in 'Character in Fiction' (*E3* 436), and considering Woolf in light of these new materialisms also points beyond the more classically 'materialist' arguments she puts forward in texts such as *A Room of One's Own* and *Three Guineas* (1938), vitally important though that these are.

'New materialisms' are necessarily pluralised, and throughout this book I consider Woolf's wide-ranging reconceptualisation of the material world alongside various nuanced contemporary materialist theories. I begin in Chapter 1 with Woolf's own theory of 'granite and rainbow' which, I argue, is entangled in a vibrant, multiple and creative engagement with, and conceptualisation of, the material world. The subsequent chapters go on to consider Braidotti's materialist nomadic feminism in relation to *A Room of One's Own* and *To the Lighthouse* (1927), Braidotti's 'polymorphous vitalism' and Colebrook's 'queer vitalism' alongside *Orlando* (1928), Haraway's 'mud philosophy' and *Flush* (1933), and Barad's quantum-inspired, material-discursive 'intra-action' alongside Bennett's theory of 'vital materialism' in relation to *The Waves* (1931). All these theories are in one way or another influenced by Deleuze who is engaged with closely in each chapter, and who presents in his philosophy an expressive materiality,[44] 'a kind of supersaturated materialism' as Elizabeth Grosz describes in *Becoming Undone* (2011), 'a materialism that incorporates that which is commonly opposed to it – the ideal, the conceptual, the mind, or consciousness'.[45] It is Deleuze's interest in a 'material vitalism',[46] in the intertwined relation between materiality and life, and therefore his interest in what is outside of language, or rather 'the outside of language'[47] – what goes beyond a concern purely with discourse, representation, and signification – that partly accounts for the fact that within literary studies interest in his theories developed later than other important poststructuralists.[48] This is seen in the way that Deleuze is almost entirely absent from consideration in those poststructuralist readings of Woolf outlined above. When he is briefly referred to by Minow-Pinkney, it is to dismiss his non-dialectical viewpoint and refusal to place language as the primary concern of subject-formation; Deleuze and Guattari are disregarded as 'one-sided theorists' who 'fetishise the moment of de-structuration and a-signification'.[49] Yet in recent years Deleuze and Guattari have been hugely influential in new theories of materiality precisely because, unlike some other poststructuralist perspectives, they do not fetishise language. Linguistic signs do not, for Deleuze, take a higher status than other types of signs, as he has made clear when outlining 'several kinds of signs' that form a 'heterogeneity of relation' in texts including *Proust and Signs* (1964), *Difference and Repetition* (1968) and, with Guattari, in *A Thousand Plateaus* (1980).[50] Central to Deleuze's view of literature, therefore, is that it involves more than linguistic signs; this is what distinguishes his work from more familiar poststructuralist and deconstructive approaches which tend to focus on, to borrow John Hughes' phrase, 'the scrupulous delineation of textual aporias'.[51]

To be sure, this is not to say that Deleuze shares no affinities with other poststructuralists.[52] 'Affinity' is precisely the word used by Derrida, for example, in his eulogy for Deleuze (following the latter's death in 1995), where he writes about feeling 'a proximity or a near total affinity' with Deleuze 'concerning an irreducible difference that is in opposition to dialectical opposition, a difference "more profound" than a contradiction (*Difference and Repetition*), a difference in the joyously repeated affirmation ("yes, yes")'.[53] In Chapter 4 I turn to Derrida's later writings on the animal, and read them alongside Deleuze, but an important difference in Deleuze's work that is central to my study throughout is that where Derrida has been characterised as displaying 'a sort of anxiety of influence [. . .] leading to the redoubtable caution and reflexive awareness of his writing', Deleuze's affirmative philosophy is focused on the creation of the new.[54] This affirmative mode of creation is captured by Deleuze in *Nietzsche and Philosophy* (1962):

> To affirm is still to evaluate, but to evaluate from the perspective of a will which enjoys its own difference in life instead of suffering the pains of the

opposition to this life that it has itself inspired. *To affirm is not to take responsibility for, to take on the burden of what is, but to release, to set free what lives.* To affirm is to unburden: not to load life with the weight of higher values, but *to create* new values which are those of life, which make life light and active.[55]

It is a matter of freeing life from an oppositional framework because 'differentiation', Deleuze writes in *Bergsonism* (1966), 'is never a negation but a creation, and that difference is never negative but essentially positive and creative'.[56] It is precisely this nonoppositional, affirmative and creative difference that interests me in Woolf's writing.

The divergences between both Derrida's and Deleuze's understanding of 'difference' are also marked by their key influences. Derrida's *différance*, promoting the free play of signifiers where, as he puts it in *Writing and Difference* (1967), terms are bound up in 'infinite implication, the indefinite referral of signifier to signifier',[57] comes out of his more clearly 'post-phenomenological' philosophy, where the likes of Hegel, Husserl, and Heidegger are engaged with and critiqued in much more detail than they are in Deleuze's 'material and forceful' philosophy of difference.[58] In his interest in how difference 'makes itself', as he puts it in *Difference and Repetition*,[59] Deleuze turns more to Spinoza, Nietzsche, and Bergson, all of whom are linked by 'their critique of negativity, their cultivation of joy, the hatred of interiority, the externality of forces and relations, the denunciation of power'.[60] Difference for Deleuze is a vital, generative, ontologically primary force. Derrida's philosophy of difference may not be wholly consigned to language, but it is, as Grosz demonstrates, concerned with 'a difference constrained to the functioning of representation, a difference that resides in and infiltrates from the sign or text', whereas Deleuze is more interested in the 'shimmering self-variations' of difference which creates the material entanglements of human and nonhuman becomings, 'the force that enacts materiality' rather than simply being about its representation.[61] Where literature's relationship with life, becoming and difference is therefore concerned, Deleuze himself distances his own approach to texts from Derrida's deconstruction:

> As for the method of deconstruction of texts, I see clearly what it is, I admire it a lot, but it has nothing to do with my own method [. . .] For me, a text is merely a cog in an extra-textual practice. It is not a question of commenting on a text by a method of deconstruction, or by a method of textual practice, or by other methods; it is a question of seeing what *use* it has in the extra-textual practice that prolongs the text.[62]

In Chapter 1 I draw both an inter-textual and extra-textual mapping of Woolf's famous 'granite and rainbow' term as an example of the difference embodied and generated by the terms she uses in her own theorising, and the chapters that follow go on to discuss other materials for theory Woolf provides us with through her texts which continue to live and act on questions of sexual difference and sexuality, animality, and posthuman life, and that extend beyond the concern with writing itself. Accounting for Woolf's own emphasis on the creation of new differences and of the extra-textual and extra-linguistic alongside Deleuzian theory offers new possibilities for our reading of Woolf and of modernism.

Where Deleuze has hitherto been read in a modernist context, he has been considered much more widely alongside the likes of Franz Kafka, Antonin Artaud, Samuel Beckett, and Marcel Proust than Woolf, reflecting the fact that these are the authors Deleuze wrote about most fully. In a collection of essays on *Deleuze and Literature* (2000), for example, Woolf is mentioned only once in passing when one of the essays lists some Anglo-American writers who influenced Deleuze – a list that includes D. H. Lawrence, Henry Miller, and Herman Melville, among others.[63] But although the relationship between Deleuze's philosophy and Woolf's aesthetics has not yet been systematically addressed, there have been an increasing number of attempts by critics to bring them together.[64] The first consideration of Woolf and Deleuze was in 1997 (and thus after the height of theory's power in modernist literary studies) in John Hughes' *Lines of Flight*, which focuses on Deleuze's empiricism and provides readings of Thomas Hardy, George Gissing, and Joseph Conrad along with a chapter on *The Voyage Out* (1915) that involves a discussion of Bergson's 'duration' in an exploration of 'movement'.[65] Whilst focused solely on Woolf's first novel, Hughes' reading is important in opening the dialogue between Woolf and Deleuze at the same time as pointing to the links with Bergson, a key influence on Deleuze and someone who, as noted above, has received critical attention from Woolf scholars. Following Hughes' study, Jean-Jacques Lecercle's *Deleuze and Language* (2002) contains an acute analysis of Woolf's 'Kew Gardens', paying close attention to the textuality of Woolf's short story; Jessica Berman considers Woolf's (ethical) writing alongside Mieke Bal's reconceptualisation of the Deleuzian 'fold' for feminist studies;[66] and Beatrice Monaco's *Machinic Modernism* (2008) aligns Deleuze with what she views as metaphysical aspects of modernist literature. Alongside analyses of Lawrence and Joyce, Monaco offers two chapters on Woolf, providing a reading of immanence and transcendence in *To the Lighthouse*, and form and rhythm in *The Waves* and *Orlando*. In addition to this scholarship, in the time since I began writing this book several further essays have pointed to connections between the writings of Woolf and Deleuze: Jason Skeet has provided a Deleuzian reading of *The Waves* and Woolf's essay 'The Cinema' (1926);[67] Caroline Pollentier has drawn on Deleuze and Guattari's 'becoming-animal' in her discussion of the role of tortoises in Woolf's aesthetics of flânerie;[68] Laci Mattison has offered an elegant reading of *To the Lighthouse* through Deleuze's conceptualisation of 'the fold', and of confluences between Deleuzian 'worlding' and Woolfian moments of being;[69] Gina Potts has used Deleuze to outline Woolf's 'nomadic, anti-authoritarian politics' in *Three Guineas*;[70] Carrie Rohman has integrated Deleuze's conceptualisation of 'the refrain' into her analysis of inhuman elements of *The Waves*;[71] Claire Colebrook has considered new possibilities Deleuze offers for our readings of Woolf and of modernist literature more generally;[72] and Judith Allen has made insightful reference to Deleuze and Guattari's 'rhizome' in her discussion of 'wildness' in Woolf's writing,[73] as well as to Deleuze's notion of 'repetition' in the context of Woolf's repeated use of words such as the conjunction 'but'.[74]

Deleuze then has emerged in recent years as someone who demands serious consideration in dialogue with Woolf's writings. Woolf's influence on Deleuze should not be overlooked, as he refers to her writing, and life, as an important consideration for his philosophical thought in texts spanning from the 1970s to the end of his life in 1995 – including his *Dialogues* (1977) with Claire Parnet and *A Thousand Plateaus* and *What is Philosophy?* (1991) with Félix Guattari – where her texts including *A Room of One's Own*, *Mrs Dalloway* (1925), *Orlando*, and *The Waves* are variously cited as exemplary of concepts I explore in this book such as 'becoming' and 'haecceity'. Woolf also provides rare examples of Deleuze's references to a female author,[75] with implications for how we think of his writing in relation to feminist philosophy, something I address in Chapter 2. Building on the growing interest in the relationship between Woolf and Deleuze, in this book I situate my reading in the wider context of critical debates in Woolf studies alongside those ongoing debates in contemporary theory that engage with Deleuze's thought (and Deleuze studies is itself a growing discipline), including a focus on those aforementioned theorists/philosophers who have yet to be read alongside Woolf. That is, I do not intend to simply impose Deleuzian concepts on Woolf's texts, but to show how her writing is already engaging with similar issues, something borne out in the fact that, as I will demonstrate in the following chapters, recent debates in Woolf studies and in contemporary theory already share many concerns, even if these concerns are articulated in different ways. In the particular theoretical context in which I read Woolf I do not wish to foreclose the significance of Woolf's texts as 'Deleuzian' or any other such term, but rather to open up new perspectives and conceptual paradigms that might provoke new conversations or affect divergent 'lines of flight' in our consideration of Woolf in theory and theory in Woolf. *Virginia Woolf and the Materiality of Theory* aims to revitalise theoretical readings of Woolf, showing that they are as much a part of contextualising her writing as historical or archival perspectives are. Theorising materiality, and materialising theory, through Woolf need not be seen as a violent or naïve act of de-contextualisation at odds with historical and cultural approaches to her writing, but an affirmative acknowledgement that any reading of Woolf today comes from our own materially situated moment, more than seventy years after the 'curtain rose' and Woolf's last novel, *Between the Acts* (1941), was published (*BA* 197).

* * *

The five chapters of this book are concerned with Woolf's theorising of materiality in distinct but interrelated fields of debate, focusing on the natural world, sexual difference, sexuality and desire, human and nonhuman animals, and posthumanist concepts of life, respectively. Throughout I engage with a range of Woolf's novels, short stories, essays, diaries, letters, and autobiographical pieces, but especially texts from her highly productive period of writing between the late 1920s and early 1930s, including *To the Lighthouse*, *Orlando*, *The Waves*, *Flush*, and her modernist feminist manifesto *A Room of One's Own*. My study begins by focusing in Chapter 1 on Woolf's key figuration of 'granite and rainbow' in 'The New Biography' (1927), and opens onto an analysis of how these terms are complicated and extended throughout Woolf's writing, offering a model of theorising that is itself embedded in the material world at the same time as it conceptualises that materiality. In doing so, this chapter provides an exhaustive mapping of Woolf's use of 'granite' and 'rainbow', together and apart, in texts spanning her writing life, from early diary entries and her first novels *The Voyage Out* and *Night and Day* (1919), to various essays and letters and her 'Sketch of the Past'. It also demonstrates that 'digging' granite and 'chasing' rainbows – as the materials for Woolf's theory – entails a consideration of modern scientific developments in geology and physics, as well as art and mythology. The final section considers the ways in which Woolf's multiple granites and rainbows recast the relationship between nature and culture, and I introduce Deleuze's 'repetition' and Braidotti's 'transposition' as theories that offer a fresh perspective on how critics might think about and use Woolf's 'granite and rainbow' in the future. By starting with Woolf's own theory of granite and rainbow, and only later in the chapter introducing Deleuze and Braidotti, I emphasise that my consideration of the materials for theory, and theories of materiality, found in Woolf's writing begins first of all with her own texts, and not the imposing of theoretical frameworks onto her work. Rather than simply representing two opposing sides of reality (the material, factual world and the intangible sphere of personality), Woolf's multiple granites and rainbows are always already pointing beyond binary models of theorising and historicising, of language and materiality, and reveal Woolf's challenge to totalising meanings through her exploration of the material world.

Chapters 2 and 3 focus on long-standing issues in Woolf studies concerning feminism, sexual difference and sexuality. The second chapter approaches the question of materiality by focusing on sexual difference in *A Room of One's Own* and *To the Lighthouse*. The first half of the chapter stages a dialogue between Woolf's much-discussed theory of 'androgyny', Braidotti's 'nomadic subject' (which she distances from the notion of androgyny), and Deleuze and Guattari's 'becoming-woman' (which they themselves find evidence of in *A Room of One's Own*) – three concepts with distinct relationships to the materiality of sexual difference but with shared concerns. Starting with a brief overview of the conflicting responses to Woolf's androgyny, I go on to draw out some of the continuities and dissonances between these theories, emphasising the importance of each to contemporary feminist debates which seek to move beyond the constructivist/essentialist impasse. Influenced by my discussion of androgyny and sexual difference, in the second half of this chapter I analyse Woolf's handling of subjects and objects, bodies and environments, in *To the Lighthouse* in light of striking connections between this novel and Deleuzian concepts of the 'rhizome', 'smooth' and 'striated' spaces, and 'becoming'. I frame this reading by introducing my neologism 'tri-subjectivities' or 'tri-s' as a way of formulating the nonoppositional but also nonoedipal triangular relations found in this novel. In particular, I go on to consider the importance in *To the Lighthouse* of the sea, trees, grass, and paint in Woolf's attempt to articulate an inclusive model of sexual politics which views men and women 'not always in their relation to each other but in relation to reality' (*RO* 149). Moving to issues of sexuality and desire, Chapter 3 presents a queer reading, or rather 'queering', of *Orlando* which reassesses these themes in Woolf's mock-biography. It begins with a section on Woolf and Vita Sackville-West, focusing in particular on the new perspective offered by Braidotti's recent discussion of their relationship in *Transpositions* (2006). It then goes on to consider the ways in which Woolf's theorising of love and desire in *Orlando* involves an array of material objects including wedding rings and a motor-car, and includes a consideration of how Orlando's bedrooms become the site for a reconceptualisation of history. Throughout this chapter I argue that in the relationship that most influenced its composition and the relations formed within the text itself, *Orlando* not only challenges notions of sexuality pertaining to identity categories and of desire founded on lack, but offers an affirmative reconceptualisation of desire as *de*personalised and shared among human and nonhuman forces. *Orlando* finally rejects even the notion of a plural self measured by quantity in favour of a multiplicitous subjectivity engaged in qualitative creation – precisely because of this, Woolf's fictional biography is all the more entangled in the material realities involved in a love story.

In Chapters 4 and 5 I turn to the more recent, growing areas of interest among both literary critics and theorists in the relationship between human and nonhuman animals, and in posthumanist conceptualisations of life. Chapter 4 explores the complex and contested spaces shared by human and nonhuman animals in *Flush: A Biography*. Rather than reading Woolf's fictional biography allegorically as critics have tended to, I focus on its canine protagonist in order to open onto a wider discussion of the question of the animal, and of human-animal relations. This entails a reading of *Flush* in light of contemporary theories of animality, including Derrida's feline-inspired treatise, Haraway's 'companion species' and 'becoming with', and Deleuze's 'becoming-animal'. Considering issues of nudity, mirrors, and gaze, all of which are usually seen as dividing human from nonhuman animals, the chapter instead argues that they are central to Woolf's challenging of our preconceived notions of boundaries between species. My reading takes into account the potential pitfalls of anthropomorphism, but nonetheless demonstrates that *Flush* offers a distinctly nonanthropocentric, symbiotic, and sympathetic vision of human-animal relations; Woolf therefore creates what I term an 'An*i*malous Society', in contrast to the exclusive and hierarchical organisation of The Spaniel Club described in the opening pages of her novel. The chapter concludes with a discussion of vulnerability, flesh and cows. Finally, Chapter 5 turns to the ways in which Woolf, primarily in *The Waves*, engages with the materiality of life itself. The first half of the chapter addresses 'matter' by focusing on how *The Waves* engages with many of the philosophical issues concerning materiality arising out of the new physics in the first decades of the twentieth century, before turning to the ways in which the novel anticipates more recent debates which include Karen Barad's work on Niels Bohr's 'philosophy-physics' and her theory of 'agential realism' and 'intra-action' in *Meeting the Universe Halfway* (2007). The second half of this chapter considers the conceptualisation of 'life' in Woolf's novel, drawing especially on Eugene Thacker's consideration of Aristotelian *psukhē* and the distinction between 'Life' and 'the living', Jane Bennett's 'vital materialism' and 'thing-power', and Deleuze's 'assemblage', 'haecceity', and 'pure immanence'. Through its exploration of the material entanglements of human bodies and nonhuman objects, things, and environments, I read *The Waves* as presenting an immanent, posthuman ontology of life.

In *Transpositions*, Braidotti, following Deleuze, demonstrates that 'the axes of classical "difference" [. . .] are currently being transposed into lines of "becoming". Sexualization, racialization and naturalization transpose into becoming-woman/other/animal/earth, under the impact of the emergence of "Life" as a subject of political and ethical concern.'[76] By arranging my chapters around theoretical debates relevant to our own materially situated moment whilst at the same time being specifically concerned with Woolf's conceptualisation of materiality in relation to issues concerning 'sex', 'animal', and 'life', I am eager to create a cartography of these lines of becoming. Far from attempting to finally resolve contemporary theoretical debates and Woolf's own theorising into a settled consensus, this involves working through the blurring of disciplinary and conceptual boundaries so as to form alliances and affinities, to affirm the differences required to fuel a necessarily ongoing, heterogeneous, 'common project'.[77]

Notes

1. Hussey, 'Virginia Woolf: After Lives'.
2. Sim, 'Virginia Woolf Tracing Patterns', p. 43.
3. Hinnov, 'The Nature of Time', p. 218.
4. Randall, *Modernism*, pp. 157–8.
5. Goldman, *Feminist Aesthetics*, pp. 46–8.
6. 'Theory' is of course a contested term, and I primarily use it here as an umbrella term to include theorists/philosophers from the latter half of the twentieth century to the present day, rather than to make any claims about what does or does not qualify as 'theory' as distinct from, say, 'critical theory' or 'contemporary philosophy'. My use of theory might therefore be a form of 'transdisciplinary philosophizing', to borrow Peter Osborne's recent phrase. See 'Philosophy After Theory', pp. 19–33. For a summary of some of the multiple brands of 'theory' in use today, see Friedman, 'Theory', pp. 237–45.
7. Critics have pointed to the Bergsonian resonance in Woolf's use of 'intuition' here. See Randall, *Modernism*, p. 158 and Mattison, 'Metaphysics of Flowers'.

8. Goldman, *Feminist Aesthetics*, p. 47.
9. Minow-Pinkney, *Virginia Woolf*, p. 162.
10. Ross, 'Introduction', pp. 1–2.
11. Ibid., p. 2.
12. Grubar, *Virginia Woolf*, p. 109 (originally published as *Virginia Woolf: A Study* in 1935). For more on Woolf and Bergson see Hafley, *The Glass Roof*; Kumar, *Bergson*; Gillies, *Henri Bergson*, pp. 107–31. For an excellent recent discussion of Bergson's relationship to modernism, including to Woolf, see Ardoin, Gontarski, and Mattison (eds), *Understanding Bergson*.
13. See for example Beer, *Virginia Woolf*, pp. 29–47; Froula, *Virginia Woolf*; Banfield, *The Phantom Table*; Spiropolou, *Virginia Woolf*; Henke, 'Virginia Woolf's *The Waves*'; and Hussey, *Virginia Woolf and the Singing*. There has been much important scholarship in Woolf studies since the mid-1990s that has been less overtly focused on philosophy but which has opened up Woolf's writing to new theoretical contexts. For some illuminating examples see: readings of Woolf in the context of race and Empire in Marcus, 'Britannia Rules *The Waves*' and Phillips, *Virginia Woolf Against Empire*, which sparked interest in Woolf and postcolonial theory; Barrett and Cramer (eds), *Virginia Woolf: Lesbian Readings*, which opened up fresh discussion on Woolf and theories of sexuality; the focus on questions of cosmopolitanism and community in Berman, *Modernist Fiction*; important feminist readings of Woolf's politics and aesthetics in Goldman, *Feminist Aesthetics* and Black, *Virginia Woolf*; insightful accounts of Woolf and theories of the everyday in Randall, *Modernism* and Sim, *Virginia Woolf*; and readings of Woolf and eco-criticism in Czarnecki and Rohman (eds), *Virginia Woolf and the Natural World*, and, very recently, Scott, *In the Hollow of the Wave*.
14. I am borrowing this phrase from the title of a recent international conference on Woolf held in Paris: 'Virginia Woolf Among the Philosophers' included papers on Woolf and Nietzsche, Benjamin, and Bloomsbury philosophy, as well as more recent thinkers including Derrida, Deleuze, and Rancière (who was also a keynote speaker at the event). The conference therefore demonstrated the productive ways in which we might combine a focus on Woolf and philosophers working prior to or contemporaneous with the period in which she herself was writing, alongside a focus on Woolf and contemporary philosophy. See <http://malaisedanslaculture.files.wordpress.com/2012/02/flyer-woolf-en.pdf> (accessed 1 October 2012).
15. Lackey, 'Modernist Anti-Philosophicalism', p. 95. Lackey's provocative analysis does, however, provide an interesting general discussion of the changing role of philosophy in the twentieth century.
16. Goldman, 'Avant-garde', p. 227. For a thorough exploration of the various ways in which both historicising and theorising continue to be important in contextualising Woolf see Randall and Goldman (eds), *Virginia Woolf in Context*.
17. Ross, 'Introduction', p. 2.
18. Jameson, 'Afterword', p. 248.
19. Ross, 'Introduction', p. 15.

20. See Spivak, 'Unmaking'; Meisel, *The Absent Father*; Kamuf, 'Penelope at Work'.
21. See Caughie, *Virginia Woolf and Postmodernism*, p. 1. The opening line of Caughie's study emphasises the importance of Moi's intervention by claiming that 'In or about December 1985, Virginia Woolf criticism changed.'
22. Moi, *Sexual/Textual*, p. 16.
23. Minow-Pinkney, *Virginia Woolf*, p. x. As evidence of this book's continued influence, it was republished in 2011 with Edinburgh University Press.
24. Bowlby, *Feminist Destinations*, pp. 14–15. Although originally published in 1988, it is the second edition, which included a range of essays subsequently written by Bowlby, that I refer to throughout this book.
25. Caughie, *Virginia Woolf and Postmodernism*, p. 5.
26. Moi, '"I Am Not a Feminist, But . . ."', p. 1735; p. 1740.
27. Caughie, 'Time's Exception', p. 108. See also Caughie, 'Poststructuralist and Postmodernist Approaches'.
28. Colebrook, 'Extinct Theory', p. 63.
29. Caughie herself worries over, and defends, her use of this phrase in the book's conclusion. See Caughie, *Virginia Woolf and Postmodernism*, pp. 194–210.
30. Elliott and Attridge, 'Introduction', pp. 1–2.
31. Barrett, 'Introduction', p. 2.
32. Ibid., p. 5.
33. See Marcus, 'Thinking Back', pp. 1–30, 'Storming the Toolshed', pp. 263–78, 'Quentin's Bogey', pp. 486–97.
34. Barrett, 'Introduction', p. 23.
35. Barrett, *Imagination*, pp. 19–20. Barrett also reflects here on the ways that she herself becomes increasingly critical of Marxist feminism in texts including *Women's Oppression Today* (1980) and *The Politics of Truth* (1992).
36. Barrett, *Imagination*, pp. 62–7.
37. Ibid., p. 196; see also p. 6.
38. See Braidotti, 'The Politics of "Life Itself"', p. 203.
39. Coole and Frost, 'Introducing the New Materialisms', pp. 2–3.
40. See Edwards, 'Historical Materialism', p. 296.
41. Bennett, *Vibrant Matter*, p. xvi.
42. Coole and Frost, 'Introducing the New Materialisms', pp. 8–9.
43. Ibid., p. 7.
44. New materialisms may have gained prominence in contemporary theory over the past decade or so, but their roots go back much further. Indeed, in *Expressionism in Philosophy: Spinoza*, Deleuze outlined how the concept of expression is part of an anti-Cartesian reaction which, led by Spinoza, presented 'a new "materialism"'. Deleuze, *Expressionism in Philosophy*, p. 321. This book focuses primarily on Deleuzian philosophy and the most recent attempts to articulate new materialisms in contemporary theory, but underpinning much of this thought are Spinoza, Nietzsche, and Bergson among others. Whilst it is beyond the scope of this study to provide a systematic treatment of their thought, I do touch on these influences in later chapters.
45. Grosz, *Becoming Undone*, p. 43.

46. Deleuze and Guattari, *A Thousand Plateaus*, p. 454.
47. Deleuze, *Critical and Clinical*, p. 5.
48. This also applies to Deleuze's reception in Anglophone continental philosophy, highlighted by the fact that for the most part there is also a longer delay before translations of Deleuze's texts in comparison with Derrida's. For further details see Patton and Protevi, 'Introduction', p. 9.
49. Minow-Pinkney, *Virginia Woolf*, p. 20.
50. Deleuze, *Proust and Signs*, p. 12, p. 15. See also Deleuze, *Difference and Repetition*, p. 25 and Deleuze and Guattari, *A Thousand Plateaus*, p. 93.
51. Hughes, *Lines of Flight*, p. 16. For a thorough discussion of Deleuze's complex conceptualisation of signs see Colombat, 'Deleuze and Signs'. Where modernism is specifically concerned, Claire Colebrook has recently argued that instead of viewing modernism as a 'default aesthetic' for theories concerned with disclosing 'signs *as signs*', Deleuze makes it possible for us 'to consider modernism not as reflection or interpretation of signs, but as positively creative of new differences, new styles and new signs'. Colebrook, 'Woolf and "Theory"'.
52. For insightful discussion on the relationship between Deleuze and Foucault see Wolfe, *Critical Environments*, pp. 87–128; on Deleuze and Lacan see Smith, 'The Inverse Side', pp. 635–50; on Deleuze and Derrida see Patton and Protevi, *Between Deleuze and Derrida* and Cheah, 'Non-Dialectical Materialism'; on Deleuze and Kristeva see Driscoll, 'The Woman in Process'. Driscoll's article also discusses Woolf's feminism, and I discuss it in Chapter 2's section on 'Becoming-woman'.
53. Derrida, 'I'll have to wander all alone'.
54. Patton and Protevi, 'Introduction', p. 6.
55. Deleuze, *Nietzsche and Philosophy*, p. 174.
56. Deleuze, *Bergsonism*, p. 103.
57. Derrida, *Writing and Difference*, p. 29.
58. Patton and Protevi, 'Introduction', p. 5.
59. Deleuze, *Difference and Repetition*, p. 36.
60. Deleuze, *Negotiations*, p. 6.
61. Grosz, *Becoming Undone*, pp. 91–3.
62. Quoted in Smith, 'Introduction', p. xv. Deleuze was responding here to a question during a 1972 colloquium on Nietzsche. For a thorough analysis of the differences between Deleuze's concept of difference and Derrida's *différance* see Baugh, 'Making the Difference'.
63. See Crawford, 'The Paterson Plateau', p. 57.
64. In addition to the exploration of Woolf and Deleuze in this book, and the other examples noted here that have brought some of their writings together, there will be a special issue of the journal *Deleuze Studies* in 2013 themed on the relationship between Deleuze, Woolf, and Modernism (co-edited by myself and Laci Mattison). This forthcoming issue will include new essays by several of the critics mentioned in the above paragraph.
65. Hughes, *Lines of Flight*.
66. Berman, 'Ethical Folds'. See also Berman, *Modernist Commitments*, pp. 48–62.
67. Skeet, 'Woolf plus Deleuze'.
68. Pollentier, 'Imagining Flânerie'.

69. Mattison, 'Woolf's Un/Folding(s)' and Mattison, 'Woolf's *Heart of Darkness*'.
70. Potts, 'Woolf and the War Machine'.
71. Rohman, '"We Make Life"'.
72. Colebrook, 'Woolf and "Theory"'.
73. Allen, *Virginia Woolf*, pp. 71–3.
74. Allen, '"But . . ."'.
75. Mary Bryden notes, however, the irony in the fact that Deleuze refers to Woolf in part because of her refusal to be thought of as a 'woman writer'. See Bryden, *Gilles Deleuze*, p. 155.
76. Braidotti, *Transpositions*, p. 42.
77. Ibid., p. 139.

Chapter 1

Materials for Theory: Digging Granite and Chasing Rainbows

> If we think of truth as something of granite-like solidity and of personality as something of rainbow-like intangibility and reflect that the aim of biography is to weld these two into one seamless whole, we shall admit that the problem is a stiff one. (*E4* 473)

Perhaps her most famous figuration taken from the natural world, Virginia Woolf's 'granite and rainbow' (*E4* 478) is the centrepiece of a theory which appears to capture both halves of a 'neatly split up' question concerning the aims of biography. Her 1927 essay 'The New Biography' assimilates granite with the 'hard facts' of reality: it is 'truth in its hardest, most obdurate form; it is truth as truth is to be found in the British Museum' (*E4* 473). In Woolf's view this is characteristic of Sir Sidney Lee's *A Life of William Shakespeare* (1898) and *King Edward VII: A Biography* (1925), books which are 'dull' and 'unreadable' respectively, and which, typical of Victorian biographies, are 'stuffed with truth' but not 'those truths which transmit personality'. In contrast, the rainbow is assimilated with the 'artful or highly coloured' which 'consists in personality', and Woolf provides the earlier example of James Boswell's *The Life of Samuel Johnson LL.D* (1791), arguing that upon reading it 'we are aware that there is an incalculable presence among us which will go on ringing and reverberating in widening circles however times may change and ourselves'. This ability to bring the personality of the biographical subject to life tells us that we 'can no longer maintain that life consists in action only or in works. [...] Something has been liberated beside which all else seems odd and colourless' (*E4* 473–4).[1] The successful mixing of both granite and rainbow, fact and personality, has yet to be found, however. Harold Nicolson's *Some People* (1927) is an example of the new twentieth century biography which 'is not fiction because it has the substance, the reality of truth' and 'is not biography because it has the freedom, the artistry of fiction' (*E4*

476), but the combination of granite-like fact and rainbow-like personality ultimately jars – the author takes centre stage and the biographical figures are 'below life size' – even if Nicolson 'waves his hand airily in a possible direction' (*E4* 477–8).

Granite and rainbow are then, as Kathryn Miles summarises, the constituent elements of 'a theory of biography that seeks to reconcile the binaries of truth and fiction, or put another way, action and thought'.[2] Miles uses Woolf's theory of granite and rainbow as a way of reading her mock-biography *Orlando*, published almost exactly one year after 'The New Biography', a move which she claims 'returns *Orlando* to [. . .] its original theoretical rubric: Woolf's own essays'. In dealing with 'each binary' as they 'exist at opposite ends of the spectrum of biography', she interprets the starting point as opposition, and understands the end goal to be the achievement of a 'seamless whole'.[3] Miles concludes that *Orlando* is the 'fictional praxis to underscore [Woolf's] theory',[4] where the successful recognition by the 'modern biographer' of 'his own subjective positioning'[5] allows him to adopt this ironic tone in which he evokes both the historical changes in the facts of Orlando's various environments (granite) at the same time as retaining that elusive quality in Orlando (rainbow) where there is always the possibility of letting the character slip 'out of one's grasp altogether' (*O* 175). But where Miles uses 'The New Biography' to illustrate the success of *Orlando*, Mitchell Leaska has used Woolf's essay to explain the 'failure' of *The Pargiters*.[6] In his 1978 introduction to Woolf's abandoned project, Leaska adopts the theory of granite and rainbow to explain Woolf's initial intention to have essay segments interspersed with fiction and argues that she 'gradually realised that all the factual matter which would constitute the essay portions was weighty substance that somehow collided with the artistic design she originally planned', therefore meaning that 'the truth of fact and the truth of fiction could not meet in felicitous alliance'.[7] Confining Woolf's terms to an oppositional framework, Leaska asserts that she had to abandon *The Pargiters* 'in despair'[8] because she felt 'the pressure of granite against rainbow'.[9]

Specific readings of *Orlando* and *The Pargiters* are not my primary concern here, but as examples of the ways in which Woolf's essay has been utilised by critics, they are important for two main reasons. Firstly, both Miles' and Leaska's appropriations of Woolf's 'granite and rainbow' illustrate that it can be extended and applied to her other writings rather than exclusively being read in relation to academic literature on biography[10] – something that is also emphasised by the fact that Leonard Woolf chose *Granite and Rainbow* (1958) as the title for a posthumously published collection of Woolf's essays; secondly, although using it to different ends, they both employ Woolf's apparently oppositional theory without ever challenging the stability of the terms 'granite' and 'rainbow' themselves.[11] That is, this natural metaphor may be more or less amalgamated but remains, from the start, as two distinct elements working within a binary framework. Rather than understanding this dual term as a fixed and stable metaphor, I would like to argue that the complexity and usefulness of Woolf's theory of granite and rainbow has yet to be fully realised. Little critical attention has been paid to the appearance of the first conditional in the quotation from 'The New Biography' with which I opened this chapter (signalled by Woolf's use of 'if' and 'shall'), but, dealing in likelihood and conditionality rather than certainty, this tense allows Woolf to commit to her theory whilst also maintaining a level of ambiguity and doubt – features Mark Hussey sees as crucial to her writing: 'Beyond doubt, as far as Woolf is concerned, lies not certainty but more doubt [. . .] It is *acting* in the state of radical doubt that characterises Woolf's work.'[12] In this chapter I am interested in asking if, and in what ways specifically, Woolf's 'granite and rainbow' enacts this kind of radical doubt, as well as exploring the role these terms play in affirming various meanings that rely on the entangled relationship between language and the material world. I attempt, therefore, to extend Woolf's theory not by simply applying its dual premise, but by analysing her use of the terms 'granite' and 'rainbow', both coupled and uncoupled, throughout her writings, and then considering how we might reorient our understanding of Woolf's figuration in light of recent attempts to reconceptualise the relationship between nature and culture in meaning-making. Digging granite and chasing rainbows in Woolf's texts will also lead me to consider the significance of these terms in relation to the natural sciences of geology and physics (where the rainbow is concerned I will also touch on its place in mythology, and in art), drawing further links between materiality and theory.

'Nature, who has played so many queer tricks upon us'

Returning briefly to Leaska's reading of *The Years* (1937) as a kind of unwanted offspring of *The Pargiters*, it seems that he fails to take account of the self-reflexive qualities of Woolf's theory of 'granite and rainbow' by refusing to see beyond the granite-like fact of this opposition. As Pamela Caughie has noted, 'Leaska relies on distinctions between fact and fiction, essay and novel, "didactic discourse" and dramatic discourse.'[13] She insists that 'it is not a *form* Woolf abandons but a *motive*', and this failure of motive rather than form is because granite and rainbow in *The Pargiters* is a 'given distinction', rather than an 'operational distinction'.[14] For Caughie, *The Pargiters* was not finished because the premise of the book relied on 'generalised polarities' that Woolf herself was suspicious of, and as this distrust grows we see that 'the essays begin to sound more and more like the novel chapters', evidence that Woolf could not maintain such straightforward distinctions 'between essays and scenes that were meant to reveal the deep ideas beneath the surface forms. Nor could she persist in the dichotomy of genuine feelings and false conventions that inspired the essay-novel divisions.'[15] Where Leaska sees *The Pargiters* as 'a new experiment in form' which creates 'an imaginary audience', concentrates on 'the restrictions imposed upon a woman who chooses writing as a profession', and is interspersed with segments 'explaining how the woman novelist deals with certain principal controlling ideas from factual life and transforms them into fiction',[16] Caughie rightly questions how *new* this really was (could it not describe *A Room Of One's Own*, for example?).[17] Following Caughie's reading, we might view Woolf's unfinished project of *The Pargiters* as a positive disavowal of the static distinction between granite and rainbow, fiction and fact. But more than that, it becomes an affirmative recognition of the difficulties one is bound to encounter when attempting to subvert a binary framework without challenging the stability, or exploring the complexities, of the particular oppositional terms in play. Taking notice of Woolf's use of the first conditional to frame her theory in 'The New Biography' opens up potentiality and flexibility as fundamental elements of the 'granite and rainbow' figuration, and not as proof of its failure. Moreover, Caughie's reading of this essay is in line with her wider argument that Woolf's theorising should be viewed as experimentation: 'She does not start with a theory to be expressed and then discover the appropriate form; rather, she articulates theories as they evolve from her fictional experiments.'[18] Yet while Caughie's emphasis is on 'testing out the possibilities of literature'[19] she misses an opportunity to read this experimentation back into 'granite and rainbow', instead leaving Woolf's essay tantalisingly behind having pointed to what its most important phrase may be: that there is 'no fixed scheme of the universe, no standard of courage or morality' (*E4* 476).

From the second paragraph of 'The New Biography' Woolf is already blurring the distinctions between granite and rainbow, and unsettling our conventional understandings of what these words signify. We learn that even granite-like scientific fact has 'an almost mystic power. Like radium, it seems able to give off forever and ever grains of energy, atoms of light.' And the rainbow-like intangibility of 'that inner life of thought and emotion' in fact 'meanders darkly and obscurely through the hidden channels of the soul' (*E4* 473). The inversion of dark and light properties appears to confuse the opposing granite and rainbow; the bland and dark shades of granite become mystic and filled with light, and the luminous colours of the rainbow become dark and obscure. Furthermore, when Woolf concludes that we cannot yet 'name the biographer whose art is subtle and bold enough to present that queer amalgamation of dream and reality, that perpetual marriage of granite and rainbow' (*E4* 478), self-reflexivity is again displayed; even in this very sentence she undermines the expected parallel by aligning 'dream' with 'granite', 'reality' with 'rainbow'. It is perhaps telling that the only other occurrence of Woolf deploying granite and rainbow in the same sentence also complicates the expected parallel, when in *Orlando* we are told: 'Nature, who has played so many queer tricks upon us, making us so unequally of clay and diamonds, of rainbow and granite' (*O* 46). In one sense, granite's pairing with diamonds is no surprise – being hard, obdurate rocks – and, to a lesser extent, the symmetry of rainbow and clay works in the sense of clay's transformative, non-fixed form. But delighting in 'the muddle and mystery', Woolf is playing with the overlapping possibilities for these 'queer' couples whereby an argument could just as convincingly be made for the rainbow/diamonds symmetry (mysticism, beauty, rarity), and the clay/granite symmetry (as naturally occurring materials). Already we become vigilant to Caughie's warning that 'we cannot count on any one element meaning the same thing from one text to another'.[20] Instead, we must open up the 'case' into which granite and rainbow have been 'stuffed' (*O* 46). Woolf provides us with the tools to perform our own 'queer tricks', uncovering her suitably twisted, unexpected challenges to conventional couples in her figurations where words, as she writes in 'Craftsmanship',[21] combine 'variously and strangely, much as human beings live, by ranging hither and thither, by falling in love, and mating together'. But words 'are much less bound by ceremony and convention than we are' (*E6* 96) and so there are no conventional marriages between them; rather, there are many 'swift marriages' because words have a profound 'need of change': 'It is because the truth they try to catch is many-sided and they convey it by being themselves many-sided, flashing this way, then that. Thus they mean one thing to one person, another thing to another person [. . .] it is because of this complexity that they survive' (*E6* 97).

Free to mate with many other words, Woolf's granites and rainbows often appear uncoupled in her writings, and sometimes within the same text. By turning to Woolf's posthumously published autobiographical 'Sketch of the Past' as well as passages from *Night and Day* and a range of Woolf's essays including '"This is the House of Commons"'

(1932), 'The Novels of E. M. Forster' (1927), and 'The Sun and the Fish' (1928), it becomes clear that the various ways in which Woolf's multiple granites and rainbows 'hang together' (*E4* 96) with different words in different contexts demonstrates that we find solidity and intangibility, truth and fiction, are always already intermingled in the vast majority of occasions when Woolf deploys these terms.[22] Whilst Woolf's 'granite and rainbow' is often seen as having a dualistic, symbolic or emblematic quality, her various usage of these terms instead exposes the limitations of binary, and totalising, models of language and thought that are often upheld by symbolic understandings.[23] Indeed, as Gillian Beer has shown in relation to *To the Lighthouse*, Woolf brings symbolism into question even as she deploys it. By creating a 'post-symbolist' novel, Woolf unsettles symbolism which, Beer argues, 'is the means by which we make *things* serve the human. Symbol gives primacy to the human because it places the human at the centre, if not of concern, yet of signifying. [...] By its means concepts and objects are loaded with human references.'[24] Woolf's often-cited comment about the symbolic significance of the lighthouse is therefore also relevant: 'I meant nothing by The Lighthouse [...] trusted that people would make it the deposit for their own emotions – which they have done, one thinking it means one thing another another. [...] directly I'm told what a thing means, it becomes hateful to me'.[25] *To the Lighthouse* is discussed in the following chapter, including the ways in which it offers a critique of totalisation in a different guise, namely that of uprooting 'arborescence', but digging and chasing Woolf's multiple granites and rainbows also illustrates her attempts to undermine totalising, and human-centred, signification. This chapter aims to demonstrate this by providing details of each instance in which 'granite' or 'rainbow' appears across the span of Woolf's writings,[26] as well as some of the extra-textual dimensions to these terms. The following sections therefore present an account firstly of Woolf's granites, and then of her rainbows, as a creative cartography rather than a straightforward chronology of their appearances in her work.

Obduracy and memorialisation

It would be misleading to claim that there are no examples at all of Woolf offering conventional associations of granite in keeping with the 'hard facts' and 'solidity' it initially appears to represent when set against the rainbow in 'The New Biography' (*E4* 473). Indeed, there are a few instances when granite is used as a figuration for unattractiveness and obduracy, or where it is linked to memorialisation. There are examples of the former in the published manuscript version of *A Room of One's Own* when Woolf uses the simile 'dour as a granite wall' amongst a list of various descriptions of rooms (*WF* 127),[27] and in a letter to Vanessa Bell on 28th June 1938 when Woolf describes 'bathing sheds of granite' in Oban (where she is writing from) as 'grim' (*L6* 249). The obduracy of granite is drawn on for Woolf's description of Peter's interruption of the kiss shared between Clarissa and Sally in *Mrs Dalloway*. This kiss is 'the most exquisite moment of [Clarissa's] whole life [. . .] she felt she had been given a present, wrapped up [. . .] a diamond, something infinitely precious', but when the 'revelation' is disturbed by Peter 'it was like running one's face against a granite wall in the darkness! It was shocking; it was horrible!' (*MD* 30). In addition: in a diary entry in 1937 Woolf likens Julian Bell's 'set & rather self centred' manner to the 'grinding of an iron upon a Granite slab' (*D5* 69); in a letter in 1904 to Violet Dickinson she writes that 'this paper is like granite slabs to write upon' (*L1* 131); in a 1924 letter to Jacques Raverat she describes his wife as 'that granite monolithic Gwen' (*L3* 136); in her diary in 1921 she writes that the 'pertinacity' of Mark Gertler 'would bore holes in granite' (*D2* 150); and writing in 1931 to Ethyl Smyth, with her comments on an article Smyth was writing on music criticism, Woolf uses the image of a 'granite pillar' in a self-deprecating manner, and to humorous effect:

> If I were you I'd train typists and street singers rather than go on whipping these gentrys hard and horny behinds. You will say however that I know nothing, feel nothing and understand less than nothing. So be it. I realise why I am so essential to you – precisely my quality of scratching post, what the granite pillar in the Cornish field gives the rough-haired, burr-tangled Cornish pig – thats you. An uncastrated pig into the bargain; a wild boar, a savage sow, and my fate in life is to stand there, a granite pillar, and be scraped by Ethel's hoary hide. Yes, because not another soul in Woking but lies under you like sweet lavender; there you roll and trample and bellow. I'm the only friend you have who is thoroughly and disgustingly upright and blind and deaf and dumb. (*L4* 348–9)

On a few occasions Woolf records a further conventional use of granite, which points to its links with memorialisation and war: in a diary entry on 10th February 1923 she writes that she 'prowled' among 'several tons of granite crucifix' used to commemorate Belgian soldiers (*D2* 233); in a letter to Julian Bell in 1936 she notes seeing some of the 'granite crosses' situated in and around Falmouth;[28] in *Between the Acts* a line from the village pageant speaks of 'granite and cobble/ From Windsor to Oxford/ Loud Laughter, low laughter/ Of warrior and lover/ The fighter, the singer' (*BA* 77); and in her 1925 essay 'On Not Knowing Greek', Woolf uses granite to contrast the originality and vividness of characters in Greek as opposed to English literature, where in the plays of ancient Greece, 'a fragment of [. . .] speech broken off would, we feel, colour oceans and oceans of the respectable drama [. . .] we meet them before their emotions have been worn into uniformity', whereas we think about the famous figures of Renaissance literature 'posed gracefully on granite plinths in the pale corridors of the British Museum' (*CR1* 27–8). Similarly, in '"This is the House of Commons"', first published in 1932, Woolf imagines that if statues are to be erected one day in the honour of MPs they will be 'like granite plinths set on the tops of moors to mark battles' (*E5* 327). Of the above examples, it is in this essay that Woolf most clearly begins to undermine the value of such memorialising. Notwithstanding the future possibility of becoming granite plinths, these men are already 'featureless, anonymous': 'as [the Secretary of Foreign Affairs] spoke so directly, so firmly, a block of rough stone seemed to erect itself there on the Government benches'. The 'secret' of the House of Commons, the 'code' that unlocks these 'matters of great moment' (*E5* 326), is in the hands of 'plain, featureless, impersonal' men. Woolf is clearly not in any mood to celebrate the granitic substance of patriarchy here.

Granite obelisks: *The Voyage Out* and *Night and Day*

But rather than simply criticising the memorialising function of granite, Woolf subtly twists the conventional symbolic associations of granite monuments erected in the name of patriarchy, war, and empire. In *The Voyage Out* the word 'granite' actually appears only once, in a description of 'massive granite rocks' by the sea in Chapter XVI (*VO* 218), yet as David Bradshaw has recently pointed out, granite is present in the opening pages of the novel in the form of Cleopatra's Needle, a granite obelisk situated on the Victoria Embankment in London and standing at eighteen metres high and weighing 185 tonnes. Made in Egypt in 1460 BC, it was brought to England from Alexandria in a specially designed container and 'set in place on the Victoria Embankment "in a fit of imperial bravura" on 12 September 1878' to commemorate Britain's victory sixty-three years earlier over Napoleon.[29] Bradshaw draws particular attention to the passage when we learn that Helen Ambrose, walking on the Embankment,

> knew how to read the people who were passing her; there were the rich who were running to and from each others' houses at this hour; there were

the bigoted workers driving in a straight line to their offices; there were the poor who were unhappy and rightly malignant. Already, though there was sunlight in the haze, tattered old men and women were nodding off to sleep upon the seats. When one gave up seeing the beauty that clothed things, this was the skeleton beneath. (*VO* 4)

On the one hand the granite obelisk looming over Helen here as she walks is an enduring emblem of imperialist bombast – a symbol of totalisation – but on the other hand it is linked to the meeting and passing of a wide range of society: 'Almost from the outset [. . .] the Victoria Embankment became a space not just where London's genteel and governing classes could disport themselves but, especially at night, an infinitely more abject environment where her myriad dispossessed congregated.' It is therefore significant that 'Helen's distress becomes un-containable in the vicinity of Cleopatra's Needle, where, twice a day, queues of destitute men and women had food doled out to them.'[30] As the historian Raphael Samuel describes:

> The Thames Embankment, the most spectacular of mid-Victorian 'improvements' in inner London, very soon became a by-word for the number of its tramps, some of whom filled the seats beneath the plane trees [. . .] and others of whom used it as an all-night promenade. Its character was reinforced by the Shelters built at either end [. . . and] by charitable distributors of food (such as the Eustace Miles Food Barrow at Cleopatra's Needle) [. . .] by 1910 [the police were] treating the Embankment as a 'kind of corral' where large numbers of tramps were conveniently assembled under the direct observation of law and order.[31]

Focusing on Cleopatra's Needle helps us to uncover the socio-political import of Woolf's novel, demonstrating that here, as with her depiction of London spaces elsewhere, Woolf's writing is immersed in the material world in which she lived.[32] Rather than celebrating its solidity and endurance (it is, after all, almost 3,500 years old), or taking part in imperial bravura, Woolf's focus is firmly on the mixture of social classes and sexes that passed by the monument. She is less interested in basking in the masculine grandeur of what this phallic granite obelisk commemorates and symbolises, and more concerned with how it becomes entangled with the everyday, multiple and diverse lives of Londoners. Woolf denudes the pompous symbolism and reveals the 'skeleton beneath'; the material realities associated with this granite monument – both invisible and present, solid and intangible to the reader – are multiple and changing. Ultimately, Woolf is more concerned with mobilisation than commemoration.

In Chapter XVIII of Woolf's following novel, *Night and Day*, a different granite obelisk becomes the focal point for the very questioning of truth and reality. Before reaching the obelisk, the certainties of granite-like truth are undermined from the beginning of the chapter when both Mary Datchet and Ralph Denham, walking together in Lincoln, have moments of doubt concerning the object of love and of happiness. For Mary it 'seemed a mere toss-up whether she said, "I love you", or whether she said, "I love the beech-trees", or only "I love – I love"' (*ND* 208). And for Ralph: '"Unhappiness is a state of mind [...] it is not necessarily the result of any particular cause"' (*ND* 210). As Bowlby puts it, '*Night and Day* represents being in love as a state which may not have an object, may not be reciprocated and may not know a definite source of its feeling.'[33] Indeed, even as Ralph apparently reconciles this with the realisation that 'his unhappiness had been directly caused by Katharine', he goes on to reveal that the whole matter of such emotion is so often a balancing of illusions and delusions: 'Like most people, I suppose, I've lived almost entirely among delusions, and now I'm at the awkward stage of finding it out. I want another delusion to go on with. That's what my unhappiness amounts to' (*ND* 210). Moreover, when Ralph later sees Katharine he realises that she was 'quite different, in some strange way, from his memory'; the fleshly reality of Katharine, and therefore the object of his unhappiness, had in fact eluded Ralph's mind and 'he had to dismiss his old view in order to accept the new one'. But Katharine's embodied presence is itself characterised by its non-fixity: 'everything about her seemed rapid, fragmentary, and full of a kind of racing speed' (*ND* 222). Ralph's perception of the material world is attuned to minuscule, molecular movements more than pre-determined subjects and objects: 'The people in the street seemed to him only a dissolving and combining pattern of black particles' (*ND* 218). When he does decide to 'examine the objects in the shop windows, and then to focus his eyes exactly upon a little group of women looking in at the great windows of a large draper's shop' in an attempt to find 'order', it is acknowledged that this provides him with only a 'superficial control' (*ND* 219).

Later, when the narrative viewpoint turns to William Rodney and Katharine Hilbery as they decide to disembark the carriage taking everyone home, the elusive 'light of truth' (*ND* 220) comes to focus on 'a lonely spot marked by an obelisk of granite' (*ND* 224). Around two miles short of their return to Lampsher from Lincoln they are let out at the obelisk, and in the scene that follows this granite monument oversees the uncertainties of truth and love. In the first instance granite is linked here to 'the gratitude of some great lady of the eighteenth century who had been set upon by highwaymen at this spot and delivered from death just as hope seemed lost' (*ND* 224), but it soon sparks a narrative shift to a general seasonal description which seems to belong to neither the particular story of this woman nor to any precisely fixed historical moment:

> In summer it was a pleasant place, for the deep woods on either side murmured, and the heather, which grew thick round the granite pedestal, made the light breeze taste sweetly; in winter the sighing of the trees was deepened to a hollow sound, and the heath was as grey and almost as solitary as the empty sweep of the clouds above it. (*ND* 225)

'Here' it is that 'Rodney stopped the carriage and helped Katharine to alight', and the association of granite with the uncertainty of 'Here' is reiterated with a further mention of 'the couple standing by the obelisk'. Far from fitting with a view of *Night and Day* where, as Caughie puts it, the past is 'stationary', 'standard', or 'absolute',[34] the past, the present, and the unknown collide as Katharine 'read the writing on the obelisk [. . .] She was murmuring a word or two of the pious lady's thanks' (*ND* 225). After this episode, when she looks into her own past and asks herself why she had agreed to marry Rodney when she did not wish to, Katharine thinks of it as 'a desperate attempt to reconcile herself with facts – she could only recall a moment, as if waking from a dream, which now seemed to her a moment of surrender'. In other words, the truth of her feelings now betrays the 'fact' that she had tried to acknowledge as an 'illusion' (*ND* 229–30).

The uncertainty surrounding this granite obelisk is accentuated by the fact that, as Michael Whitworth has recently noted, Woolf's chosen topography here 'is that of classic realism, mingling actual places (Lincoln) with imaginary ones (Lampsher), and at this point on the road between the two we may not know whether we are in the actual or the imaginary'.[35] This is reflected in the fact that there is a great deal of uncertainty over whether this obelisk alludes to a particular obelisk Woolf herself knew of in the same way she clearly knew Cleopatra's Needle. Julia Briggs, for example, has suggested that Woolf's source is the Dunstan Pillar, built by Sir Francis Dashwood in 1751, and located a few miles to the south of Lincoln.[36] But as Whitworth points out, 'the Pillar fails to match Woolf's obelisk in several respects: it is not a memorial to a specific incident of robbery; it is not an obelisk in form, and it is far taller than anything we might call an obelisk'.[37] Whitworth offers a second possibility of the Robbers' Stone in Wiltshire, built in 1840 to record the attack and robbery of a Mr Dean of Imber by four highwaymen[38] (a further stone marks the spot where one of the highwaymen died whilst being pursued), but concedes that the narrative fails to exactly match Woolf's obelisk, as do the proportions and location of this stone. 'Both might be *sources*,' Whitworth notes, 'but Woolf isn't *alluding* to them in the conventional sense.'[39] We might say, indeed, that instead of alluding to any particular granite monument – in *The Voyage Out*, *Night and Day* or elsewhere – Woolf is challenging the very notion that allusion can ever be a granite-like fact; that both words and sources will always be productively twisted and transformed, materialised and theorised in different ways, whether by author or reader.

The granite county: Cornwall

Written more than twenty years after *The Voyage Out* and *Night and Day*, doubts about solidity and intangibility, fact and fiction, are nowhere more closely associated with granite than in Woolf's autobiographical 'Sketch of the Past'. Here, Woolf remembers childhood days in the granite county of Cornwall, recalling 'old men and women' who 'danced round Knills Monument – a granite steeple in a clearing' (*MB* 136). She describes everywhere seeing 'walls [that] were thick blocks of granite built to stand the sea storms' and supposes that the 'town was then much as it must have been in the sixteenth century, unknown, unvisited, a scramble of granite houses' (*MB* 133). Importantly, the endurance of granite does not solidify the town's meaning, instead adding to the sense of the 'unknown, unvisited', to a somewhat mysterious existence. It is granite that evades a straightforward entry into linear temporality: 'The eighteenth century had left no mark upon St Ives, as it has so definitely upon every southern village. It might have been built yesterday; or in the time of the Conqueror.' The Church, 'like the houses', was 'built of granite' and therefore 'ageless' (*MB* 133). Indeed, it is the simultaneous endurance and intangibility of Cornish granite that also appears to be captured by another modernist associated with the granite county, D. H. Lawrence, when in 'The Nightmare' chapter of *Kangaroo* (1923) he describes the mysterious materiality of Cornwall's 'huge granite boulders bulging out of the earth like presences' as 'the mystery of the powerful, pre-human earth, showing its might'.[40]

Woolf's reflections of Cornish granite are in fact clear from the earliest to latest of her autobiographical writings. On the 11th of August 1905, during a summer holiday in Carbis Bay, near St Ives, Woolf wrote in her journal of the 'granite blocks in the earth' as one element 'which had impressed itself minutely upon our childish minds' (*PA* 281–2). Three days later Woolf starts a longer diary entry which she continues for many days (without keeping note of the exact date), and where she again returns to the 'granite hills', noting that although they 'loved the conflict' of 'a storm', on 'sunny days', such as the one she is writing on, they contain a 'curious creamy richness' (*PA* 286). Later, she further complicates the notion of granitic solidity by describing how the arrangement of granite walls 'keeps the land fluid':

> The Cornish substitute for a gate is simple; in building a wall of granite blocks they let two or three jut out at convenient intervals so as to form steps; you often find these arranged beside a gate which is heavily padlocked, as though the farmer winked one eye at the trespasser. The system of course has its advantages for the native, or for one well acquainted with the lie of the country; it keeps the land fluid, as it were, so that the feet may trace new paths in it at their will. (*PA* 290)

In her letters, too, Woolf makes reference to Cornish granite. In 1909 she writes to Clive Bell from Cornwall, this time deep in winter on the 26th December, about how she 'staggered up Tren Crom in the mist this afternoon, and sat on a granite tomb on the top, and surveyed the land'. What she sees are 'rocks comparable to couchant camels, and granite gate posts, with a smooth turf road between them' (*L1* 416). And in early spring 1921, whilst in Ponion, near Zennor, Woolf writes of 'granite rocks' and hills that 'lie graceful' and are 'so subtly tinted; greys, all various with gleams in them; getting transparent at dusk' (*D2* 105). The gleaming transparency in these granite hills was also emphasised by Woolf in a letter to Saxon Sydney-Turner two days previously, when she describes them as 'half transparent', elusive entities provoking the imagination and memories, reminding her of childhood. There is little doubt what she sees as the real attraction of Cornwall:

> I'm not sure though that the beauty of the country isn't its granite hills, and walls, and houses, and not its sea. What do you say? Of course its [*sic*] very pleasant to come upon the sea spread out at the bottom, blue, with purple stains on it, and here a sailing ship, there a red steamer. But last night walking through Zennor the granite was – amazing, is the only thing to say I suppose, half transparent, with the green hill behind it, and the granite road curving up and up. (*L2* 462)

The aesthetic appeal and happiness provoked by these hills directly disrupts Woolf's metaphor making in a 1928 letter to Vita Sackville-West, when her use of granite slides into a memory of childhood in Cornwall: 'my happiness is wedged like (but I am using too many metaphors) in between these granite blocks (and now that they are granite blocks I can compare my happiness to samphire, a small pink plant I picked as a child in Cornwall)' (*L3* 521).

In 'Sketch of the Past' Woolf elaborates on the mystery of these hills, 'scattered with blocks of granite; some said of them to be old tombs and altars; in some, holes were driven, as if for gate posts' (*MB* 138). Virginia Stephen and her siblings found great adventure in them, and Woolf alludes to the legend of the Logan Rock – an 80-ton rocking stone, finely balanced at the top of a cliff (so finely balanced that in April 1824 it had been tipped over by a disgraced Lieutenant Goldsmith before the locals demanded it be replaced!).[41] Woolf expresses the childhood wonderment it evoked: 'The Loggan [sic] rock was on top of Tren Crom; we would set it rocking; and be told that perhaps the hollow in the rough lichened surface was for the victim's blood' (*MB* 138). This description is strikingly similar to a passage in *Jacob's Room* (1922):

> These white Cornish cottages are built on the edge of the cliff; the garden grows gorse more readily than cabbages; and for hedge, some primeval man has piled granite boulders. In one of these, to hold, an historian conjectures, the victim's blood, a basin has been hollowed, but in our time it serves more tamely to seat those tourists who wish for an uninterrupted view. (*JR* 47)

Far from these hills always and already signifying their obdurate actuality, it was only her father's 'severe love of truth', Woolf writes in 'Sketch of the Past', that attempted to reduce an already mysterious granite: he 'disbelieved it; he said, in his opinion, this was no genuine Loggan [sic] rock, but the natural disposition of ordinary rocks' (*MB* 138). It is precisely this notion of 'natural disposition', of a fixed and ready-made materiality, that Woolf challenges by sharing her memory of this childhood event. The massive and yet tentative position of this granite rock is recalled and re-appropriated in the fight against patriarchy, and foregrounded are the pervading tensions between fact and fiction, and indeed between materiality and theory – 'whether I mean anything real, whether I make up or tell the truth' (*MB* 138). For Woolf these granite rocks are 'at once real and imaginary' (*E4* 475) – they do not signify one totalising meaning. As she notes plainly in a letter to Katherine Arnold-Forster in June 1923: 'I don't like symbolical granite' (*L3* 49)![42]

Granite origins

The stability of granite is, in fact, already challenged by modern advances in natural science. We do not need to dig too deep into our geological world to discover that whilst granite may be a hard, durable, and dense material, studies since the Enlightenment have led to a less than straightforward understanding of it. The epigraph of Wallace Pitcher's book *The Nature and Origin of Granite* (1993) cites acclaimed geologist Joseph Beete Jukes speaking in 1863: 'Granite is not a rock which was simple in its origin but might be produced in more ways than one.'[43] The extent to which Woolf would have been aware of modern advances in geology, and in particular the controversy involved in accounting for the origin of granite, is unclear, but she did have a copy in her library of the second edition of Charles Darwin's *Journal of Researches into the Natural History and Geology of the Countries Visited during the Voyage of H.M.S. 'Beagle' Round the World* (1845).[44] In this book Darwin writes of the granitic coastal rocks in Brazil, and reflects on the uncertainty over the formation of this granite:

> Was this effect produced beneath the depths of a profound ocean? or did a covering of strata formerly extend over it, which has since been removed? Can we believe that any power, acting for a time short of infinity, could have denuded the granite over so many thousand square leagues?'[45]

Darwin also writes of the granite mountains in Tres Montes, Chile:

> After breakfast the next morning a party ascended one of these mountains, which was 2400 feet high. The scenery was remarkable. The chief part of the range was composed of grand, solid, abrupt masses of granite, which appeared as if they had been coeval with the beginning of the world. [. . .] I took much delight in examining the structure of these mountains. [. . .] Granite to the geologist is classic ground: from its widespread limits, and its beautiful and compact texture, few rocks have been more anciently recognised. Granite has given rise, perhaps, to more discussion concerning its origin than any other formation. We generally see it constituting the fundamental rock, and, however formed, we know it is the deepest layer in the crust of this globe to which man has penetrated. The limit of man's knowledge in any subject possesses a high interest, which is perhaps increased by its close neighbourhood to the realms of imagination.[46]

Woolf's understanding of granite might be closely associated with her personal experience in Cornwall, but it seems at least possible that in reading this text by Darwin, the uncertainty surrounding theories of the origin of this deeply embedded material would have fed her imagination, perhaps partly accounting for some of the more complicated and conflicting uses of 'granite' across the span of her writing.

There is even less excuse for us to fall into stable understandings of granite today, as Pitcher informs us of a resurgence of interest in the twentieth century 'stimulated by the thesis that granites image their source rocks in the inaccessible deep crust, and that their diversity is the result of varying global tectonic context'.[47] With its truth both diverse and context-dependent, it is somewhat appropriate that granite should be formed from magma and contain potential metamorphic properties. As Guo-Neng Chen and Rodney Grapes outline in *Granite Genesis* (2007):

> the overwhelming opinion of most earth scientists is that granite is derived by partial melting of crustal rocks of various compositions. This idea essentially brings together the earlier competing explanations of granite genesis; magmatic (granites are igneous rocks resulting from the crystallization of magma) and metamorphic (granites are the result of a dry or wet granitisation process that transformed sialic sedimentary rocks into granite), because granites are the result of ultra-metamorphism involving melting (anatexis) of crustal rocks.[48]

Due to the complexity of its formation, Pitcher highlights the intense difficulties in attempting to classify granites: 'any attempt to categorize the granite family on a natural basis is doomed to failure given the virtually infinite number of different types which might be generated in response to a variety of generative processes and possible source rock compositions'.[49] Indeed, as Chen and Grapes point out, 'the number of "granite types" has proliferated from at least 20 schemes that have been proposed to classify them'.[50] Although Pitcher concedes that 'a proper order is obviously required for description and comparison', he stresses that 'the resulting arrangements are wholly static, often artificial, and lead nowhere along the path of understanding'.[51] This sounds remarkably close to poststructuralist readings of Woolf which argue, as Caughie puts it, that categorisations 'are not necessarily discrete [...] Rather, they are *constructed* to solve certain problems'.[52] Like Caughie then, Pitcher emphasises what he calls 'process based, dynamic classification'.[53] More than that, Woolf's granite shows that language and the natural world, meaning and matter, theory and materiality, are always already co-involved in their complexity.

Vibrant rainbows

As with her use of 'granite', there are some instances in Woolf's writing where the term 'rainbow' is conventionally employed, associated with beauty and vibrancy, and also several occasions when Woolf's use of this term appears in citations of another author's work. The more conventional or expected figurations of rainbows are evident in two letters Woolf writes to Vanessa Bell, twenty years apart: on 17th January 1918, Woolf speaks of plans 'for establishing [Alix Sargant-Florence] in Ormond Street above Saxon [Sydney-Turner]', in the hope that 'his gloom and her despair meeting may build a rainbow' (*L2* 210), and on 9th June 1938 Woolf writes that one of Bell's paintings is 'complete and entire, firm as marble and ravishing as a rainbow', a phrase which evokes Woolf's 'granite and rainbow' figuration (*L6* 235). But many years previously Vanessa Bell had herself disrupted the luminous resonance of the rainbow – in a letter Woolf writes to Sydney Waterlow on 3rd May 1921 she refers to a party hosted by Clive Bell 'to which all his ladies went in different colours of the rainbow' and yet they were 'utterly outshone by Vanessa in old lace' (*L2* 467). Indeed, the colours of the rainbow are dimmed further by Woolf in a letter to Vita Sackville-West on 2nd March 1926, when she writes of her mongrel fox terrier, Grizzle, who is at the vet (and as it turns out she is put down later that year) 'with eczema, and a cough' (*L3* 249) – the eczema described as 'rainbow stripes across her back' (they are, nevertheless, 'sanguine on the whole') (*L3* 246). Associated here with illness, in a diary entry dated 6th April 1940 Woolf links the rainbow with the type of war memorialisation more often associated with granite: 'Whom did we meet in London this week? Bonamy Dobrée the very moment we arrived. Spick & span, clipped, grey, with a rainbow of medal ribbons across his breast' (*D5* 277).

As well as citing Lawrence's *The Rainbow* (1915) in a letter to Lytton Strachey in February 1916 concerning a 'private indecency press called the Rainbow, for the production of that and other works' (*L2* 82), appearances of the word 'rainbow' occur as quotations in a range of Woolf's essays. In 'The Duchess of Newcastle' (1925), for example, Woolf quotes 'the hangings of a Rainbow made that's thin' from the revised version of Margaret Cavendish's 'The Palace of the Fairy Queen' (1664), a poem which showed the 'fresh and delicate fancy' of her early writings (*CR1* 74–5). In 'Life and the Novelist' (1926), the rainbow has a different import, when Woolf quotes Gladys Bronwyn Stern's description in *A Deputy Was King* (1926) of a Chinese coat as an example of her technique which is too focused on detail to allow character to emerge – we might say too much 'fact' and not enough 'personality' (*E4* 473): 'Quality is added to quality, fact to fact, until we cease to discriminate and our interest is suffocated under a plethora of words' (*E4* 404). Notably, in this instance the rainbow is quite literally embedded in materiality, as we read that this coat has 'a rainbow' embroidered on it behind the 'outstretched wings' of a 'silvery heron' (*E2* 134). Both of these essays pre-date 'The New Biography' by a matter of just a couple of years, but in a citation from *A Room of One's Own*, published two years after her 'granite and rainbow' figuration is presented in that essay, the rainbow becomes both embedded and encased in solidity, when Woolf quotes Christina Rossetti's 'A Birthday' (1857): 'My heart is like a rainbow shell' (*RO* 16).

In the 'Novels of E. M Forster', Woolf quotes her contemporary and friend in his use of the term 'rainbow bridge' in *Howards End* (1910):

> [Forster's] concern is with the private life; his message is addressed to the soul. 'It is the private life that holds out the mirror to infinity; personal intercourse, and that alone, that ever hints at a personality beyond our daily vision.' Our business is not to build in brick and mortar, but to draw together the seen and the unseen. We must learn to build the 'rainbow bridge that should connect the prose in us with the passion.' (*E4* 495)[54]

Indeed, earlier in the paragraph in which she quotes from *Howards End*, Woolf uses the word 'rainbow' herself when outlining Forster's tendency towards both 'the preachers and teachers' and the 'pure artists' of literature (*E4* 494). At first she predictably aligns the rainbow with aesthetics, the light surface which covers the true depth of the 'message': 'Behind the rainbow of wit and sensibility there is a vision which he is determined that we shall see.' But she immediately turns this on its head, and it is Forster's grander 'vision' which is most evasive, for it 'is of a peculiar kind and his message of an elusive nature'. And yet, Woolf writes, the 'soul' which is Forster's concern is actually found to have a quite tangible home: 'The omnibus, the villa, the suburban residence, are an essential part of his design'; 'the soul [. . .] is caged in a solid villa of red bricks somewhere in the suburbs of London' (*E4* 494–5). According to Woolf, however, neither Forster's treatment of the truths of materiality nor the truths of the soul are fully successful:

> if his books are to succeed in their mission his reality must at certain points become irradiated; his brick must be lit up; we must see the whole building saturated with light. We have at once to believe in the complete reality of the suburb and in the complete reality of the soul. (*E4* 495)

Forster's desired 'combination of realism and mysticism' certainly evokes Woolf's 'granite and rainbow' figuration, but Woolf's emphasis on bricks becoming 'lit up' – an image which is the inverse of Rossetti's 'rainbow shell' – suggests that we cannot conceive of two separate and distinct elements coming together and creating a settled whole; rather it would seem to require more intense, even if less fixed, combinations. Citing Henrik Ibsen as the perfect example, Woolf observes that 'the paraphernalia of reality have at certain moments to become a veil through which we see infinity', a material reality that becomes 'luminously transparent'. Ibsen 'gives us it by choosing a very few facts and those of a highly relevant kind. Thus, when the moment of illumination comes we accept it implicitly [...] It has not ceased to be itself by becoming something else.' Forster fails because he cannot capture this; it is always a choice between one and the other within a dichotomous arrangement, 'the change from realism to symbolism' (*E4* 495–6).

'the world tinged with all the colours of the rainbow'

Woolf points towards a reality that necessarily emanates an element of elusiveness, where the intangibility of the rainbow is assimilated with materiality. In the end it is not a question of dimming the rainbow, but of realising that the vibrancy of the rainbow is embedded in the material world. Returning to Woolf's 'Sketch of the Past', this is seen in relation to the formation of subjectivity when, recalling the 'bright colours' and 'many distinct sounds' (*MB* 91) of childhood, Woolf emphasises an embodied 'movement and change', a complicated material 'actual' (*MB* 92) that involves an equally evasive sense of self, 'the little creature':

> One must get the feeling of everything approaching and then disappearing, getting large, getting small, passing at different rates of speed past the little creature [...] driven on as she was by the growth of her legs and arms, driven without her being able to stop it, or to change it, driven as a plant is driven up out of the earth, up until the stalk grows, the leaf grows, buds swell. That is what is indescribable, that is what makes all images too static. (*MB* 91)

Following this, Woolf then appears to associate rainbows straightforwardly with the imagination; describing her first memory of her mother she recalls how 'she told me to think of all the lovely things I could imagine. Rainbows and bells . . .' (*MB* 93). But rather than the intangibility of her memory and imagination being an escape from reality, 'these minute separate details' are very much a part of the material life of the young Virginia Stephen (*MB* 93). For example, as Woolf remembers the elusiveness of her mother's personality, Julia Stephen becomes not so much a 'particular person' as 'generalised; dispersed; omnipresent [. . .] the creator of that crowded merry world'. She was:

> living so completely in her [mother's] atmosphere that one never got far enough away from her to see her as a person [...] She was the whole thing; Talland House was full of her; Hyde Park Gate was full of her [...] She was keeping what I call in my shorthand the panoply of life – that which we all lived in common – in being. (*MB* 94)

Crucially, Woolf is eager to avoid the notion of her mother as a totalising symbolical figure by adding: 'I enclosed that world in another made by my own temperament; it is true that from the beginning I had many adventures outside that world; and often went far from it; and kept much back from it' (*MB* 96).⁵⁵

Exploring the granite/rainbow dynamic in 'Sketch of the Past' illuminates, to borrow a phrase from Woolf's earlier memoir piece 'Old Bloomsbury' (1976), 'the world tinged with all the colours of the rainbow' (*MB* 55). A similar phrase can also be found in *Orlando*:

> What is love? What friendship? What truth? but directly he came to think about them, his whole past, which seemed to him of extreme length and variety, rushed into the falling second, swelled it a dozen times its natural size, coloured it all the tints of the rainbow and filled it with all the odds and ends in the universe. (*O* 60)

What is interesting here is that whilst the rainbow is linked to variety and colour, it is also infused with history ('his whole past') and even a cosmic materiality ('all the odds and ends of the universe'). In 'The Sun and the Fish',⁵⁶ published the same year as *Orlando*, Woolf again uses the image of the rainbow to draw this material world. In this essay she describes witnessing the total eclipse of 1927, and we see the world becoming filled in by colour as the sun slowly appears from behind the moon:

> at first, so pale and frail and strange the light was sprinkled rainbow-like in a hoop of colour, that it seemed as if the earth could never live decked out in such frail tints [. . .] But steadily and surely our relief broadened and our confidence established itself as the great paint brush washed in woods, dark on the valley, and massed the hills blue above them. The world became more and more solid. (*E4* 522)⁵⁷

The connection here between the rainbow and materiality is pronouncedly non-transcendent. The earth soon becomes the familiar and populous place of 'farm-houses', 'villages', and 'railway lines', as the 'rainbow-like' sprinkles of light 'modelled and moulded' the 'whole fabric of civilisation', before Woolf tells us of the true revelation: 'But still the memory endured that the earth we stand on is made of colour; colour can be blown out' (*E4* 522).⁵⁸ It is both the earth as rainbow, and the earth as 'ephemeral as a rainbow' (*TL* 20).

Rainbows in mythology and art

A comparison could be made here between Woolf's 'The Sun and the Fish' and Lawrence's *The Rainbow*, where at the end of his novel 'a faint, vast rainbow' appears to Ursula 'mysteriously' and is described as 'great architecture of light and colour' that 'stood on the earth'[59] – a re-writing of Genesis, where the rainbow is presented to Noah as God's covenant: 'And the bow shall be in the cloud; and I will look upon it, that I may remember the everlasting covenant between God and every living creature of all flesh that [is] upon the earth.'[60] But while Lawrence's rainbow is more earthly, it does not entirely turn away from transcendental symbolism: '[Ursula] saw in the rainbow the earth's new architecture, the old, brittle corruption of houses and factories swept away, the world built up in a living fabric of Truth, fitting to the overarching heaven.'[61] We can not be sure whether or not Woolf had Lawrence's novel or indeed Genesis in mind when writing 'The Sun and the Fish', but they do point to potential wider mythological and artistic resonances – much of which she would surely have been familiar with – to Woolf's rainbows, which themselves complicate a strict opposition between on the one hand materiality or earthliness and on the other intangibility and transcendence. Given her knowledge of Greek mythology, for example, Woolf would likely have known that the rainbow goddess and also messenger of the gods, Iris, is, in some genealogies, the granddaughter of Gaea, Mother Earth.[62] Furthermore, while Woolf initially links the rainbow to personality in 'The New Biography' in line with most Greek philosophers, Xenophanes was one of those who resisted anthropomorphising the rainbow, instead offering naturalistic explanations: 'And she whom they call Iris, this too is by nature a cloud, purple, red and greenish-yellow to behold.'[63] Anaxagoras put it in similar terms: 'we call the reflection of the sun in the clouds a rainbow', and Aristotle's thoughts on the rainbow built from these insights.[64] It is worth noting here that in her own writing Woolf never refers to Iris in the sense of the rainbow, but she does use it to refer to the iris plant, which takes its name from the Greek for rainbow on account of the colours of its flowers and aptly emphasises the vibrantly material import this term has taken on (as does the other surviving usage – the iris of the eye). The most well-known example of this is found in *Orlando*, when suitably enough the sight of 'the red hyacinth, the purple iris wrought [Orlando] to cry out in ecstasy at the goodness, the beauty of nature' (O 91).[65] In addition to the Iris-rainbow, Raymond Lee and Alistair Fraser's *The Rainbow Bridge* (2001) helpfully outlines various understandings of the rainbow in Babylonian times, Judeo-Christian culture, ancient Greece and Egypt, and non-Western and Near Eastern antiquity cultures, highlighting both the emphasis that has been placed on it as a bridge to God, as well as the more materialist readings of the rainbow.[66]

In their discussion of the rainbow in visual art, Lee and Fraser draw attention to the importance of Albrecht Dürer in offering a more solid rendering of the rainbow. In his 1511 painting, *Adoration of the Trinity*, Dürer includes a double rainbow – one on which God sits and rests his robes over, and one which is 'solid enough' to act as a stool for his feet. Whilst the two rainbows are far from naturalistic and still in a heavenly sphere, Lee and Fraser note that there is a curious mixture of materiality and unreality to them based on a 'combination of unnatural rainbow solidity and coloring': 'Compared to the vividly colored clothes of the heavenly and earthly elect, the rainbows [. . .] are wan indeed. Despite their ghostly coloration, though, they retain [. . .] solidity.'[67] Whilst Woolf emphasises the luminosity of the non-transcendent rainbow in her writing, at the beginning of the sixteenth century it was subversive enough to dim the rainbow in order to subtly undermine its godly, transcendent status. There are of course rainbows elsewhere in Dürer's work, and Lee and Fraser note that in his later, enigmatic engraving *Melencolia I* (1514) he 'makes the outside of his [. . .] rainbow darker than the inside – a subtle bit of realism that is superfluous to any purely symbolic reading'. But where the rainbow in *Adoration of the Trinity* is particularly important is the way that Dürer 'relegates it to the status of a minor prop', so that 'within a generation of Dürer's death, artists' use of the rainbow as a support for Father or Son declined rapidly'. Such a decline was 'partly due to the increasing artistic energy devoted to pagan and secular images, yet it also reflects the passing from fashion of a powerful, centuries-old pairing of Christ and the rainbow'.[68] Could *Adoration of the Trinity* have influenced the iconography of the rainbow in Woolf's mind? Although Woolf mentions Dürer in an early essay 'Impressions at Bayreuth' (1909), comparing 'a gigantic old woman, with a blue cotton bonnet on her head' with 'a figure like one of Dürer's' (*E1* 290), and notes in a 1933 letter to Ethyl Smyth that the journalist Kingsley Martin has 'autotypes from Albert Durer [*sic*]' on his wall (*L5* 242), she never refers specifically to this particular painting, nor to Dürer's rainbows. Woolf did, however, have a copy in her library of Thomas Moore's *Albert Dürer* (1905) where *Adoration of the Trinity* is reproduced, along with *Melencolia I*.[69]

Woolf's 'double rainbow' and the art of science

The unweaving of the rainbow as solely signifying intangibility as opposed to the hard facts of our material reality has, of course, also been emphasised by centuries of scientific discovery, most famously by

Descartes in *Discourse on Method* (1637) as well as by Newton.[70] We know today that rainbows are multiplicities of colour as well as type: everyone is familiar with the reds and yellows, greens and blues, but there are also variations which include reflected and refracted rainbows, the supernumerary rainbow, and the double rainbow, as discussed above in Dürer's *Adoration of the Trinity*. Indeed, Virginia and Leonard Woolf themselves witnessed a 'double rainbow' from their terrace in September 1930 – a spectacle that Woolf notes as interrupting her letter writing to Ethel Smyth:

> but look, I have written so much and at such a pace that the words scarcely cover the ideas – these are horrid splits, – and the writing is only an attempt to encircle a few signs. Do you ever show my letters? Do you ever quote them? Do what you like, but I rather hope not, because I am never able to write at leisure; (I'm trying to finish a good many things) and then I cannot be expressive (these interruptions are because of a double rainbow on the terrace – L. has dashed in from the rain to show me). (*L4* 217)[71]

In *Unweaving the Rainbow* (1998) Richard Dawkins describes this relatively rare phenomenon of seeing a double rainbow as a 'delightful complication' where, instead of light from the sun entering a raindrop 'through the upper quadrant of the surface facing the sun, and leav[ing] through the lower quadrant', it enters through the lower quadrant and so 'under the right conditions, it can then be reflected *twice* round the inside of the sphere, leaving the lower quadrant of the drop in such a way as to enter the observer's eye, also refracted, to produce a second rainbow' which has the colours reversed and is around eight degrees higher.[72] We are therefore reminded that the multiplicitous nature of rainbows is not solely due to their colours or types: 'why do you see a complete rainbow? Because there are lots of different raindrops. A band of thousands of raindrops is giving you green light (and simultaneously giving blue light to anybody who might be placed above you, and simultaneously giving red light to somebody else below you.)'[73] *Ad infinitum*, so that there is never only one rainbow that we all see; Virginia and Leonard were not in fact seeing the same 'double rainbow'.

Dawkins' wider argument is that 'Science is, or ought to be, the inspiration for great poetry', and he takes issue with Keats' famous disappointment in his 1819 poem 'Lamia' – a poem which Woolf of course knew (*D2* 130) – that Newton had reduced rainbows to fully understood 'common things':

> [. . .] Do not all charms fly
> At the mere touch of cold philosophy?

> There was an awful rainbow once in heaven:
> We know her woof, her texture; she is given
> In the dull catalogue of common things.
> Philosophy will clip an Angel's wings,
> Conquer all mysteries by rule and line,
> Empty the haunted air, and gnomed mine –
> Unweave a rainbow, as it erewhile made
> The tender-person'd Lamia melt into a shade.[74]

Instead of rendering our material existence mundane and predictable, science has multiplied the rainbow's beauty and mystery:

> far from being rooted at a particular 'place' where fairies might deposit a crock of gold, there are as many rainbows as there are eyes looking at the storm. Different observers, looking at the same shower from different places, will piece together their own separate rainbows using light from different collections of raindrops. Strictly speaking, even your two eyes are seeing two different rainbows [...] A further complication is that the raindrops themselves are falling, or blowing about. So any particular raindrop might pass through the band that is delivering, say, red light to you then move into the yellow region. But you can continue to see the red band, as if nothing had moved, because new raindrops come to take the places of the departed ones.[75]

Nor are rainbows, it should be added, always so evasively distant from us, and can even be seen 'as a complete circle only a few feet in diameter, racing along the near side of a hedge as you drive by'.[76] There is then a kind of solid intangibility, a granite-like illusion. As Dawkins states: 'The illusion of the rainbow itself remains rock steady.'[77]

Against totalisation: transposing language and nature

Having created an inter-textual mapping of Woolf's multiple usage of 'granite' and 'rainbow', as well as considering some of their extra-textual resonances, we might think about these various granites and rainbows as performing a kind of lexical and extra-lexical polygamy. The many 'swift marriages' these terms create with other words and worlds (as well as each other) are part of a critique of totalisation – whether of language or of matter, of culture or nature, of theory or materiality – that runs through Woolf's texts, and which I explore in the following chapters in relation to sexual difference, sexuality, animality, and life itself. In her recent work on Woolf and realism, Pam Morris has argued that Woolf's rejection of totalisation is linked to her wariness 'of aspects of subjective interiority and of the metaphorisation of language, even though these are often regarded as defining features of modernist writing'.[78] Although not working with the 'granite and rainbow' figuration in her reading of Woolf, Morris does imply the importance of considering granite-like reality alongside rainbow-like personality: Woolf's 'representations of public world, individual consciousness and interpersonal discourse retain a realist underpinning in conjunction with experimental form'. Drawing on Derrida's critique of metaphor as supporting the idealist tradition in Western metaphysics, and working with Roman Jakobson's definitions of metaphor as centripetal and metonymy as centrifugal, Morris therefore emphasises that where metaphor has a vertical structure, totalising meaning by turning heterogeneity into unity, metonymy (including synecdoche) is marked by horizontal contiguity, producing, as Morris puts it, 'an unending chain moving through a diverse particularity'.[79] In her readings of *Mrs Dalloway* and *The Waves*, she emphasises Woolf's writing as characterised by an 'inclusive metonymic syntax' that reveals an 'epistemological open-endedness and materiality',[80] and she therefore favours a 'metonymic realism' that is symptomatic of a contiguous materialism, rather than metaphoric or symbolic, where 'symbolism and metaphoric idealisation function to impose totality and universality upon diversity, to deny a troublesome material heterogeneity by merging' together. Keen to move away from an inflated and dominant subjectivity, Morris insists that Woolf seeks 'outwardness as much as inwardness'.[81]

It is precisely because of Woolf's attentiveness to external environments and materiality that it is too easy to assume a unified and ideal order underlying her 'granite' and 'rainbow' terms. But at the same time Woolf's granites and rainbows pose problems for the form of metonymic realism advocated by Morris, as well as for metaphor. If 'granite' and 'rainbow' are the materials for Woolf's theory of 'The New Biography', then these materials expand and become more complicated throughout her writings to form an inter-textual and extra-textual map that appears to end with neither the metaphorical nor metonymical; neither centripetal nor centrifugal; neither a flight into 'idealisation' nor a settling into a simply agreed 'actual non-fictional world'.[82] The limitation of emphasising either metaphorical or metonymic significances onto Woolf's granites and rainbows is that this reinforces a (human) linguistic construction of the natural world without revealing anything about the ways in which, through these terms, Woolf explores the very materiality of that world, how she reconceptualises 'Nature, who has played so many queer tricks upon us'. Indeed, we might recast Woolf's theory of 'granite and rainbow' in terms of recent theoretical debates which seek to move beyond postmodernist constructivism and towards a new understanding of the relationship between meaning and matter, language and materiality. In *Quantum Anthropologies* (2011) Vicki Kirby offers a sophisticated critique of the generalised postmodernist view of language (and culture) as constructing a kind of 'unnatural' nature, creating the solipsistic view of the human subject as 'interpretive architect of the world and origin of language' rather than exploring the ways in which our understandings of language might help us to explore nature's complexity.[83] As Kirby puts it, 'Nature is, already, all of those mutating, complex plasticities that Culture's corrective would animate it with.'[84] Concerned with language as well as matter, the textual as well as the extra-textual, we might say that Woolf's granites and rainbows articulate 'the complexity that Culture seems to bring to Nature' precisely in order to 'radically reconceptualize Nature'.[85] Kirby emphasises that this concerns

> a fault line that runs throughout all of human nature. It articulates the nonlocal within the local, Nature within Culture, and human within nonhuman. [. . .] This is a comprehensive process, a process of comprehension, a material reality.
>
> What happens if Nature is neither lacking nor primordial, but rather, a plentitude of possibilities, a cacophony of convers(at)ion? Indeed, what if it is that same force field of articulation, reinvention, and frisson that we are used to calling – 'Culture'?[86]

Woolf's granites and rainbows are not tracing any overarching meaning in her texts, but are forming a map where lines cannot easily be drawn to separate culture (language, the human) and nature (materiality, the nonhuman) into a hierarchical relation. Woolf shows us that the textual and extra-textual, language and materiality, are co-involved in their productive variations; it is 'the question of language not as loss of the referent, Nature, the world, but as their playful affirmation'.[87]

Far from becoming an abstract, transcendent figuration, Woolf's 'granite' and 'rainbow' terms embody her theorising of materiality, and the materiality of her theorising. As these terms are repeated in Woolf's writing, coupled and uncoupled, they return in new ways, producing as well as further complicating their inter- and extra-textual mapping. We might say that they repeat in a Deleuzian sense of that word, where 'repetition', he explains in *Difference and Repetition*, has little to do with resemblance and everything to do with the creation of difference, and therefore the creation of the new:

> To repeat is to behave in a certain manner, but in relation to something unique or singular which has no equal or equivalent. And perhaps this repetition at

the level of external conduct echoes, for its own part, a more secret vibration which animates it, a more profound, internal repetition within the singular.[88]

Passing through different texts and contexts, mixing with different words and worlds, the decoupling of Woolf's 'granite and rainbow' onto a mapping of the repetition of each term in her writing shows how 'granite' and 'rainbow' are complex terms that always already differ in themselves; an 'internal repetition' that is 'a condition of action',[89] creating further external repetitions.[90] Woolf's multiple granites and rainbows cannot, therefore, be understood as coherent emblems or symbols, nor as totalising metaphors, because the complex singularity of each element is repeated in its difference each and every time it appears. In other words, if 'granite and rainbow' represents 'the Janus-like qualities' of Woolf's writings as Goldman posits, it is not just that she 'combines' the two. She is 'as committed to fact as to imagination'[91] as tools to wedge open a multiplicity of doors, of gateways simultaneously offering escapes from unity and entrances into the nondualistic affirmation of disjunction and diversity. Although Kirby doesn't refer to Deleuze in her discussion, we could describe this generative, affirmative repetition of difference in Woolf's textual and extra-textual granites and rainbows as creating what she calls the 'Earth's grammar', the mapping of 'virtual geometry'.[92]

If Woolf's granites and rainbows, coupled and uncoupled, reverberate different relations between culture and nature, language and materiality, that evade metaphoric (with its tendency towards totalisation) or even metonymic (where the part stands for the whole) capture, then how can we as critics describe Woolf's 'granite and rainbow' phrase? A term that might be useful here is 'transposition', which is conceptualised by Rosi Braidotti in *Transpositions* as an alternative to metaphor and metonymy: 'Transposing is a gesture neither of metaphorical assimilation nor of metonymic association. It is a style, in the sense of a form of conceptual creativity, like a sliding door, a choreographed slippage.'[93] In this chapter I have referred at various points to 'assimilation' and 'association' in describing Woolf's granites and rainbows, but 'transposition' provides a more useful and accurate description of the non-linear leaps, mobility and cross-referencing of Woolf's terms. Reoriented through transpositions, Woolf's 'granite' and 'rainbow' are 'notions that drift nomadically among different texts', producing creative combinations where the 'visible and hidden complexities' of phenomena are revealed.[94] In all of this, Braidotti emphasises that transposing 'is no mere rhetorical device';[95] instead, it is 'connecting philosophy to [science and] social realities; theoretical speculations to concrete plans' – transpositions are 'discursive and also materially embedded'.[96] It is by emphasising the multiplicitous and complex mixing of meaning-making and materiality – starting in the next chapter in relation to sexual difference – that we can discover 'the positivity of difference as a specific theme of its own'.[97] Braidotti combines music and genetics, herself crossing disciplines concerned with culture and nature, as the 'double source of inspiration' for transpositions, where both are exemplars of non-linear transfer, working as 'dissociative shifts or leaps'. Transposing Woolf's multiple granites and rainbows onto this model, could they become 'the double source of inspiration'[98] for the complex inter- and extra-textual map created by her writings, where these terms are freed from the assignment of unification and from *a priori* associations, and where their heterogeneity is celebrated? As transpositions that are sustained and enduring precisely because of their fluidity, uncertainty and adaptability, granites and rainbows would, then, be considered as the 'perpetual marriage' becoming many 'swift marriages'; a polygamy of synchronisations; or, to use Braidotti's own words, 'a joyful kind of dissonance'.[99] Perhaps it is transpositions that help explain why when we are digging granite and chasing rainbows we are at the same time unearthing rainbows and – as Woolf writes in *Jacob's Room* – 'piercing the sky [. . .] like granite cliffs' (*JR* 61).

Notes

1. For an in-depth discussion of the earlier development in Woolf's interest in biography, see Briggs, *Reading Virginia Woolf*, pp. 25–41. Briggs argues that long before writing 'The New Biography' Woolf 'was committed to extending [biography's] range and increasing its flexibility, to writing against it as well as within it' (25).
2. Miles, '"That perpetual marriage"', p. 212.
3. Ibid., p. 212.
4. Ibid., p. 213.
5. Ibid., p. 217.
6. Leaska, 'Introduction', p. xviii. For more on his reading of *The Years*, see Leaska, 'Virginia Woolf, the Pargeter', pp. 172–210. For the significance of the verb 'to parget', meaning 'to whitewash, patch over, suppress', see Goldman, *Cambridge Introduction*, p. 79. Leaska's 1998 biography of Woolf also, of course, took the title *Granite and Rainbow*.
7. Leaska, 'Introduction', p. xiv.
8. Ibid., p. xiv.
9. Ibid., p. vii.
10. In a recent article, Ray Monk laments that Woolf's essay is probably the most cited in this field. He claims that Woolf's theory of biography is very

closely tied to her thoughts on fiction, but rather than recognising the potential for using 'The New Biography' to explore both biography and fiction alike, he argues that the essay shows Woolf's 'fundamentally flawed' thoughts. He maintains that her writing is characterised by an unwillingness to blur boundaries at all – her 'determination to keep the two ("truth of fiction" and "truth of fact") separate' – and indeed he labels any readings which suggest that Woolf felt positive potential in the confusion of fact and fiction to be 'strained' and 'perverse'. See Monk, 'This Fictitious Life', pp. 1–40. Focusing on Woolf's later 'The Art of Biography' (1939) has led other critics to conclude that Woolf rejects the idea that fact and fiction can intermix. Again a frustration with the incompatibility of oppositions as necessarily negative and a failure of unity is seen in the comments of Thomas Lewis: 'There is a note of resignation here; granite and rainbow are not to be.' See Lewis, 'Combining', p. 396. In any case, Elizabeth Cooley reminds us that Woolf's own frustrations whilst writing *Roger Fry* may have clouded her argument in the later essay. See Cooley, 'Revolutionizing Biography', pp. 398–407.
11. This also applies to Ann Banfield's *The Phantom Table*, which aligns Woolf's 'granite and rainbow' at various points to further dichotomies of being and existence, mysticism and logic, vibrant sexuality and sexlessness, and impersonality and personality. See Banfield, *The Phantom Table*, p. 153; pp. 191–8; p. 201; p. 382.
12. Hussey, '"Hiding Behind the Curtain"', pp. 13–14.
13. Caughie, *Virginia Woolf and Postmodernism*, p. 95.
14. Ibid., p. 96.
15. Ibid., pp. 98–9.
16. Leaska, 'Introduction', p. xvi.
17. Caughie, *Virginia Woolf and Postmodernism*, p. 96.
18. Ibid., p. 20.
19. Ibid., p. 23.
20. Ibid., p. 101.
21. 'Craftsmanship' is based on Woolf's talk broadcast on BBC radio on 29th April 1937 as part of their 'Words Fail Me' series.
22. Methodologically, my search for granite and rainbow in Woolf's writings recalls the different but complementary approaches of Rachel Bowlby and Jane Goldman, to take two insightful examples. Bowlby, for example, draws attention to the inverted (comma) occurrences of being 'in love' throughout Woolf's novels by emphasising that 'the line of "in love" is not a straight one, smoothly declining itself downhill all the way from ineffability at the beginning to commonplace at the end'. Not wishing to fall for a conclusive and overarching meaning of love in Woolf's texts, she posits multiple possible and changing significances: speeches of love as 'eerie insistent ghosts' in *The Voyage Out*; 'a state which may not have an object' in *Night and Day*; and finally 'in love' as cliché in *Between the Acts*. See Bowlby, *Feminist Destinations*, p. 174; p. 175; p. 183; p. 190. Goldman follows Woolf's canine tropes, emphasising that her signifying dog does not lead us towards any final meaning: 'Woolf's signifying dog is a constructed, monstrous, multivalent figure whose "referent" is certainly not just a dog.' As 'marked and marking', the dog for Goldman is associated with the non-

fixed narrator of *A Room of One's Own*, with slave, with woman, and – as she demonstrates through careful reading of the 'fine negress' passage (and responding to Jane Marcus' reading in '"A Very Fine Negress"') of Woolf's manifesto – with men. In Chapter 1 I demonstrate that the 'canine business' of 'digging' and 'chasing' need not necessarily be tied to the collar of dogs. See Goldman, '"Ce chien est à moi"', p. 50; p. 54; p. 51 ; p. 81.
23. Some critics have fallen into the trap of claiming final meanings for terms that recur in Woolf's texts. An early example can be found in Jean Love's tracing of Woolf's 'lighthouse' throughout her novels, where Love traces a strikingly linear development of the symbolic meaning of the lighthouse. See *Worlds in Consciousness*, p. 194.
24. Beer, *Virginia Woolf*, p. 41.
25. Bell, *Virginia Woolf*, p. 129.
26. In my efforts to verify these instances I am extremely grateful, like many other Woolf scholars, to Mark Hussey for his careful archival work in compiling the Woolf CD-ROM (1997). It is, I think, the perfect example of the ways in which important (digital) archival material can enable the type of theoretical approach I have taken in this chapter. As such, my digging and chasing of Woolf's granites and rainbows provides in its very methodology an example of refusing the opposition between archive/theory and granite/rainbow.
27. Woolf, *Women and Fiction*, 1992.
28. Woolf, 'Nineteen Letters', p. 186.
29. Bradshaw, '"Great Avenues"', p. 192. For a brief summary of Cleopatra's Needle, including its treacherous journey from Alexandria, Egypt, see <http://www.historic-uk.com/HistoryUK/England-History/CleopatrasNeedle.htm> (accessed 3 October 2012).
30. Bradshaw, '"Great Avenues"', p. 192; p. 195.
31. Cited in ibid., p. 192.
32. See Snaith and Whitworth (eds), *Locating Woolf*.
33. Bowlby, *Feminist Destinations*, p. 183.
34. Caughie, *Virginia Woolf and Postmodernism*, p. 102.
35. Whitworth, 'Woolf, Context, and Contradiction', p. 13.
36. Briggs, *Night and Day*, p. 446.
37. Whitworth, 'Woolf, Context, and Contradiction', p. 13.
38. See <http://www.geograph.org.uk/photo/535208> (accessed 3 October 2012).
39. Whitworth, 'Woolf, Context, and Contradiction', p. 13.
40. Lawrence, *Kangaroo*, p. 225.
41. 'Myths and Legends of Cornwall', *Cornwall in Focus*, 2010, <http://www.cornwallinfocus.co.uk/history/legends.php> (accessed 3 October 2012).
42. This statement comes as a response to a question asked in a previous letter sent by Katherine Arnold-Forster to Woolf, but I have been unable to trace what this precise question was.
43. Pitcher, *The Nature and Origin of Granite*, p. vii.
44. See <http://www.wsulibs.wsu.edu/masc/onlinebooks/woolflibrary/woolflibraryonline.htm> (accessed 3 October 2012).
45. Darwin, *Journal of Researches*, p. 12.
46. Ibid., p. 284.

47. Pitcher, *The Nature and Origin of Granite*, p. v.
48. Chen and Grapes, *Granite Genesis*, p. 4. For more on the controversy over the origin of granite, see Young, *Mind Over Magma*, pp. 81–103.
49. Pitcher, *The Nature and Origin of Granite*, p. 19.
50. Chen and Grapes, *Granite Genesis*, p. 4.
51. Pitcher, *The Nature and Origin of Granite*, pp. 19–20.
52. Caughie, *Virginia Woolf and Postmodernism*, p. 20.
53. Pitcher, *The Nature and Origin of Granite*, p. 19.
54. See Forster, *Howards End*, p. 69; p. 158.
55. This can be regarded as a cautionary note to those who would argue that because Woolf is writing autobiography then somehow we are perceiving the real 'I' that constituted her childhood. Alex Zwerdling, for example, has written of 'Sketch of the Past' as though it takes away a pretence that is evident in fiction and moves us nearer to 'truth': 'Woolf allows herself to write about her childhood more personally than she had ever done, without pretending that "I" could easily be translated into "we"' (Zwerdling, *Virginia Woolf*, p. 269). De-linking 'granite and rainbow' from a compulsory relationship with biography frees it from its often restricted use, but the fact that the complexity of these terms, and the relationship between them, is then further illuminated by returning to autobiographical writing (in this instance Woolf's 'Sketch'), reminds us that readings of auto/biography do not simply represent material realities as opposed to fictional writing which deals in theories; rather, Woolf's letters, diaries, and memoir pieces can encourage us to reconceptualise the very notions of fact and fiction, materiality and theory.
56. 'Rainbow' is also, of course, a kind of fish. In her essay 'Herman Melville' (1919) Woolf uses the phrase 'rainbow fish sparking in the water' (*E3* 81).
57. For an in-depth analysis on Woolf and the 1927 eclipse (including 'The Sun and the Fish') see Goldman, *Feminist Aesthetics*.
58. A description of the eclipse is also found in Woolf's diary entry on 30th June 1927, although there is no mention there of a rainbow (*D3* 143–44).
59. Lawrence, *The Rainbow*, p. 493.
60. Gen:16, <http://www.kingjamesbibleonline.org/Genesis-Chapter-9> (accessed 3 October 2012).
61. Lawrence, *The Rainbow*, p. 494. For an insightful discussion of *The Rainbow* and Genesis see Wright, *D. H. Lawrence and the Bible*, pp. 84–109.
62. Lee and Fraser, *The Rainbow Bridge*, p. 18.
63. Xenophanes, *Xenophanes of Colophon*, p. 89. For further commentary see pp. 139–48.
64. Anaxagoras, *Anaxagoras of Clazomenae*, p. 74.
65. For passing references to iris flowers see *L3* 312 and *JR* 85. For an extensive account of the iris and other flowers in Woolf's writing see Sparks, '"Everything tended". Woolf's other references to 'iris' are to the character of that name in *Between the Acts*, and in her letters and diaries to Marchesa Iris Origo.
66. See Lee and Fraser, *The Rainbow Bridge*, pp. 2–33. One example of a more tangible mythic rainbow that Woolf would likely not have been as familiar

with is that the Siberian Yakuts and Buryats 'identify it as a graceful, colourful arc of urine', produced by 'the she-fox'! Ibid., p. 31.
67. Ibid., p. 52.
68. Ibid., p. 55.
69. Jane Goldman has recently made illuminating links between Woolf and Dürer's *Melencolia I* in relation to their respective figurations of dogs. See Goldman, '"When Dogs Will Become Men" and Goldman, 'The Dogs That Therefore'.
70. For a summary of their respective studies of the rainbow see Lee and Fraser, *The Rainbow Bridge*, pp. 168–205.
71. A much rarer 'quadruple rainbow' was recently captured on film for the first time. See <http://www.bbc.co.uk/news/science-environment-15197774> (accessed 3 October 2012).
72. Dawkins, *Unweaving the Rainbow*, p. 48.
73. Ibid., p. 46.
74. Keats, 'Lamia', p. 188.
75. Dawkins, *Unweaving the Rainbow*, p. 47.
76. Ibid., p. 48.
77. Ibid., p. 47.
78. Morris, 'Woolf and Realism'.
79. Morris, 'Virginia Woolf's Metonymic Realism'.
80. Morris, 'Woolf and Realism'.
81. Morris, 'Virginia Woolf's Metonymic Realism'.
82. Ibid.
83. Kirby, *Quantum Anthropologies*, p. 15. Kirby is especially seeking to reclaim Derrida from those postmodernist interpretations of his work as advocating the dominance of language over matter.
84. Ibid., p. 84.
85. Ibid., p. 88.
86. Ibid.
87. Ibid., p. 20.
88. Deleuze, *Difference and Repetition*, p. 1.
89. Ibid., p. 113.
90. This means that in Woolf's writings 'granite' and 'rainbow' can be said to embody and affirm difference in a similar fashion to her use of the conjunction 'but', which can also, as Judith Allen has recently shown, be understood through Deleuze's 'repetition' where 'with each repetition, an incremental change takes place, altering the meaning in some substantial way – creating difference'. Allen, '"But...", p. 8.
91. Goldman, 'Avant-Garde', p. 227.
92. Kirby, *Quantum Anthropologies*, p. 39.
93. Braidotti, *Transpositions*, p. 9.
94. Ibid., pp. 6–7.
95. Ibid., p. 146.
96. Ibid., p. 7.
97. Ibid., p. 5.
98. Ibid., pp. 5–6.
99. Ibid., p. 93.

Chapter 2

Sexual Difference in Becoming: *A Room of One's Own* and *To the Lighthouse*

Combining the Greek roots andro (male) and gyn (female), the term 'androgyny' has historical ties to a wide range of myths and religions, as well as philosophy, psychology, and literature. Critics have explored its links to the Yin and Yang of Taoism, the Upanishads and Puranas of Hinduism, various aspects of the Judeo-Christian tradition, and noted that versions of androgyny can be found in Plato's philosophy, Freud's psychoanalytic theory, and Jung's psychology.[1] In her own famous passage on androgyny in *A Room of One's Own*, Woolf points to Samuel Taylor Coleridge:

> the sight of the two people getting into the taxi and the satisfaction it gave me made me also ask whether there are two sexes in the mind corresponding to the two sexes in the body, and whether they also require to be united in order to get complete satisfaction and happiness. And I went on amateurishly to sketch a plan of the soul so that in each of us two powers preside, one male, one female; and in the man's brain, the man predominates over the woman, and in the woman's brain, the woman predominates over the man. [. . .] If one is a man, still the woman part of the brain must have effect; and a woman also must have intercourse with the man in her. Coleridge perhaps meant this when he said that a great mind is androgynous. It is when this fusion takes place that the mind is fully fertilised and uses all its faculties. (*RO* 127–8)[2]

Woolf appears to see intrigue and subversive potential in the notion of an androgynous mind that is 'resonant and porous', 'transmits emotions without impediment' and is 'naturally creative, incandescent and undivided'. But if she is clearly influenced by Coleridge, Woolf is quick to point out that his thinking does not much concern women: 'Coleridge certainly did not mean, when he said that a great mind is androgynous, that it is a mind that has any special sympathy with women; a mind that takes up their cause or devotes itself to their interpretation' (*RO* 128). Woolf herself, as Bowlby notes, seems to betray an asymmetry in the way in which this model of androgyny comes about, where the man would simply have a 'woman part' to his brain whereas the woman 'must have intercourse with the man in her' (*RO* 128): 'the masculine dominates as whole to part, and we have returned to another version of the patriarchal structure'.³ The tension that is therefore created – between androgyny as promising creative potential beyond sexual divisiveness and Woolf's appropriation of it in a context in which she is concerned with the material restrictions facing women writers – has led critics to view her theory as 'contradictory',⁴ echoing Woolf's narrator who in the British Museum scene contrasts her 'contradictory jottings' with 'the reader next door who was making the neatest abstracts, headed often with an A or a B or a C' (*RO* 38). Indeed, at several points of *A Room of One's Own* contradiction is evident: Jane Austen and Emily Brontë are praised by writing 'as women write, not as men write' (*RO* 97) at the same time as stressing 'the fully developed mind [. . .] does not think specially or separately of sex' (*RO* 129); Woolf's narrator simultaneously claims that Proust, as a man, 'is terribly hampered and partial in his knowledge of women' (*RO* 108) and that he is 'wholly androgynous, if not perhaps a little too much of a woman' (*RO* 135); and Charles Lamb is listed as a writer who 'never helped a woman yet' (*RO* 99) and who is androgynous (*RO* 135).

These contradictions are mirrored in the numerous critical responses to androgyny in terms of both its general relevance to feminism and its specific treatment by Woolf in the above 'principal offending or inspiring passage'.⁵ These responses are well known to Woolf scholars, but it is worth briefly recounting two main phases. The first concerns the range of views in the 1970s, when the term gained traction in feminist debates, and includes celebratory readings of androgyny as a liberating concept in classic studies by Carolyn Heilbrun and Nancy Topping Bazin.⁶ More pessimistic responses to these accounts include assessments by Cynthia Secor, who dismisses the term as 'essentially a male word' that fails to dispose of gender/sexual dualisms,⁷ and by Daniel Harris, who notes that androgyny has always been aligned with sexism and heterosexism, including in its Greek and Roman usage.⁸ Where Woolf is concerned, Harris therefore sees the passages on androgyny as 'a compromise, a retreat from the more radically feminist fury Woolf feared to express',⁹ a comment echoed by Elaine Showalter's notorious accusation that 'Androgyny was the myth that helped [Woolf] evade confrontation with her own painful femaleness and enabled her to choke and repress her anger and ambition.'¹⁰ Nonetheless, in the poststructuralist readings which followed this wave of interest androgyny is judged as valuable in its destabilising of binary constructions of identity. Focusing on the combining forces of Woolf's aesthetic and feminist vision, Mary Jacobus finds that Woolf's androgyny concerns 'a mind paradoxically conceived of not as one, but as heterogeneous, open to the play of difference',[11] Minow-Pinkney sees androgyny as the 'rejection of sameness' which 'aims to cultivate difference on an individual level',[12] and for Caughie it is a 'refusal to choose', where Woolf is 'testing out the consequences of different concepts of language and identity' without settling on any position.[13] In the most well-known poststructuralist approach to Woolf's androgyny, Toril Moi criticises not only Showalter for writing off the 'abstract merits' of androgyny and for claiming that Woolf was guilty of 'the separation of politics and art';[14] Moi is also critical of Heilbrun for distinguishing Woolf's androgyny from her feminism and of Bazin for positing a simple union of dualities of masculinity and femininity 'that retain their full essential charge of meaning'. She instead argues that Woolf's feminist politics and modernist aesthetics are closely bound,[15] and suggests that Woolf anticipates Kristeva's third 'attitude' of feminism, as outlined in her hugely influential essay 'Women's Time', which involves challenging 'the very notion of identity' and de-massifying difference so as to resist the oppositional struggle 'between rival groups and thus between the sexes'.[16] It is therefore distinguished from – although not an erasure of – the first stage characterised by the demand for '*insertion* into history' and for 'equal footing with men', and the second by the demand for 'recognition of an irreducible identity, without equal in the opposite sex'.[17]

In *A Room of One's Own*, Mary Carmichael's writing certainly appears indicative of this 'third attitude', and of poststructuralist readings more generally, where 'Men were no longer to her "the opposing faction"; she need not climb on to the roof and ruin her peace of mind longing for travel, experience and a knowledge of the world and character that were denied her. Fear and hatred were almost gone' (*RO* 120). And later, just after the narrative shifts from Mary Beton, Woolf more directly addresses this viewpoint: 'All this pitting of sex against sex, of quality against quality; all this claiming of superiority and imputing of inferiority, belong to the private-school stage of human existence where there are "sides", and it is necessary for one side to beat another side [. . .] Praise and blame alike mean nothing' (*RO* 138). But given that Moi herself now claims that for feminism and theory alike 'the poststructuralist paradigm' is 'exhausted',[18] the question becomes whether the subversive potential signalled by poststructuralist readings of Woolf's androgyny has been fully realised. Indeed, Brenda Helt has recently argued that not only is androgyny not a useful term for feminists but Woolf herself was always resistant to this 'male-promoting concept', with her comments on Coleridge providing evidence that she 'engaged in encouraging women to write history, psychology, even science from a woman's perspective, not an androgynous one'.[19] Yet whilst recent criticism has met with suspicion any attempt to return to the subversive potential of androgyny, in the first half of this chapter I want to reconsider Woolf's use of it as a theoretically agile term which still has something to add to feminist considerations of sexual difference.[20] Where the previous chapter explored the ways in which an extended understanding of Woolf's theory of 'granite and rainbow' reconceptualises the relation between fact and fiction, nature and culture, materiality and language, here I am interested in reassessing Woolf's 'androgyny' in order to demonstrate that in her wider exploration of sexual difference Woolf is not simply concerned with the play of language or the (de)construction of identity, nor about the transcendence of mind over body. Before going on to explore how the sexual politics of *To the Lighthouse* are intertwined with human bodies and nonhuman objects, materials, and environments, I will therefore look closely at the context in which androgyny is introduced in *A Room of One's Own*, as well as at some of the ways in which Woolf's use of the term extends into contemporary feminist debates, especially concerning Braidotti's nomadic model of sexual difference which pays attention to the lived realities of female embodied subjectivity (a model which she distances from the notion of androgyny), and Deleuze and Guattari's controversial 'becoming-woman' concept (which they themselves find evidence of in *A Room of One's Own*) – three concepts with distinct relationships to the materiality of sexual difference but with shared interests, and all concerned with the materiality of theory. Ultimately, I want to suggest that Woolf's reasons for writing about the material necessity of having 'five hundred a year and a room with a lock on the door' (*RO* 137) at the same time as theorising a move beyond sex-consciousness and becoming androgynous might be thought of as complementary rather than contradictory aspects of *A Room of One's Own*.[21]

Androgyny and nomadism

If there was one sense in which Showalter was right in her reading of Woolf, it was in warning against the notion of a utopian androgynous mind as somehow an escape from material realities. As a leading figure of contemporary feminist debates on sexual difference, Braidotti too associates the concept of androgyny with a type of fleeing from material realities. In *Transpositions* she warns against 'blurring the boundaries of sexual difference, in the sense of a generalized androgynous drive',[22] and in her earlier *Nomadic Subjects* (1994) she specifically opposes androgyny to the embodied female feminist subject: 'we come to opposing claims: the argument that one needs to redefine the female feminist subject' versus the argument that 'the feminine is a morass of metaphysical nonsense and that one is better off rejecting it altogether, in favour of a new androgyny'.[23] Braidotti does not refer directly to Woolf in her invocations of androgyny here, but given Woolf's association with the term and Braidotti's references to her on various other occasions, for example in her theorising of sexuality and desire discussed in the following chapter, it seems reasonable to suggest that Woolf may not be far from her mind. In addition, the dichotomous choice Braidotti presents recalls the aforementioned disagreements critics have had about Woolf's own notion of androgyny, on issues relating to both materiality and theory. But despite Braidotti distancing her nomadic feminism from androgyny, a consideration of Woolf's particular theorising of the term in the context of Braidotti's project of nomadic feminism – and in particular her model of a non-unitary subjectivity which is nonetheless founded on a materially embodied sexual difference – is important in at least two ways: firstly, Woolf's androgyny shares some valuable features with the figuration of the 'nomadic subject', helping us to think about it as both materially embedded and theoretically useful; secondly, far from limiting or misleading us in our understanding of Woolf's feminism, androgyny can be a valuable concept in thinking through some potential limitations in Braidotti's model of sexual difference, raising issues crucial to contemporary debates.

Braidotti's affirmation of sexual difference as a subversive and necessary 'fact' permeates her work, evident in her first book *Patterns of Dissonance* (1991), and throughout her trilogy consisting of *Nomadic Subjects*, *Metamorphoses* (2002), and *Transpositions*. Her philosophical and political project rests on the attempt to negotiate a future for feminism, and for what she calls the 'female feminist subject',[24] that 'offers a way out of the essentialism–constructivism impasse'[25] and therefore also moves beyond the opposition between nature and culture, materiality and theory. It is possible to see Braidotti's aim as that of bringing together aspects of second- and third-wave feminisms in an attempt to move beyond this impasse, and her own rhetoric, especially in *Nomadic Subjects*, learns a lot from their respective militant and postmodern vocabularies: on the one hand her argument is founded on 'the recognition of a band of commonality among women'[26] or 'the common world of women',[27] but on the other is the emphasis that women 'are not, in any way, the same', we must acknowledge 'the importance of rejecting global statements about all women'.[28] Defining her project of nomadic feminism, and strongly influenced by Luce Irigaray, Braidotti posits 'sexual difference as providing shifting locations for multiple female feminist embodied voices'[29] – a paradoxical, pragmatic, and politically charged foregrounding of sexual difference that is the foundational element of a non-unitary subject as a 'nomadic, dispersed, fragmented vision, which is nonetheless functional, coherent and accountable, mostly because it is embedded and embodied'.[30] At the heart of Braidotti's materially embedded theory of nomadism is her three-level 'diagram' or 'methodological map'[31] of sexual difference outlined in *Nomadic Subjects*, consisting of: 1) 'Difference Between Men and Women', 2) 'Differences Among Women', 3) 'Differences Within Each Woman'.[32] Level 1 is the 'will to assert the specificity of the lived, female bodily experience; the refusal to disembody sexual difference [. . .] the will to reconnect the whole debate on difference to the bodily existence and experience of women'.[33] Wishing to avoid the pitfalls of essentialism, Braidotti's second level focuses on heterogeneity between women, their different lived experiences, and level 3 attempts to hone in on each woman's 'multiplicity in herself: split, fractured' which entails 'an imaginary relationship to variables like class, race, age, sexual choices'.[34] As she states in *Metamorphoses*, 'internal or other contradictions and idiosyncrasies are indeed constituent elements of the subject'.[35] Along similar lines to other contemporary materialist feminists such as Elizabeth Grosz, we are presented with a model which therefore proposes a sexed female body as the ground of subjectivity but which also refuses the notion of fixed foundations and locations; a subjectivity that is irrevocably feminine and female, but where this feminine or female must be determined in specific cases. On several occasions Braidotti cites Jinny's statement in Woolf's *The Waves* – 'I am rooted, but I flow' (W 83)[36] – as exemplary of a nomadism which is 'not fluidity without borders, but rather an acute awareness of the nonfixity of boundaries'.[37]

Considering Woolf's own use of androgyny alongside this shifting, non-unitary, but also situated and materialist, model of sexual difference, the question I am posing is whether and to what extent the subject created by Woolf's theory of androgyny (primarily of course the writing subject, although her discussion has implications beyond this) fits the mould of nomadism. On the evidence of the many contradictory readings of androgyny, and readings of androgyny as contradictory, it is certainly a term which does not sit easily under one definition for long. But more than that, Woolf's formulation of androgyny appears to anticipate the three levels of sexual difference that Braidotti lays out. If we recall Mary Beton's vision of the 'the girl and the young man' getting into a taxi in *A Room of One's Own* (*RO* 125) we might well view this as the bringing together of the sexes, where Woolf's narrator goes on to extend an offer of 'collaboration' between woman and man 'before the art of creation can be accomplished' (*RO* 136). But throughout Woolf's text there are also instances where differences between men and women are emphasised, and therefore where the first level of Braidotti's paradigm is evident: in the aforementioned remarks by Woolf's narrator that Coleridge did not have women much in mind in his formulation of the androgynous mind; in the discussion of the way in which 'the values of women differ very often from the values which have been made by the other sex' (where 'it is the masculine values that prevail') (*RO* 95–6); where the 'mind' (*RO* 99), the 'shape' of a 'man's sentence' (*RO* 100), and the 'nerves that feed the brain would seem to differ in men and women'– and note the very bodily, materialist descriptions of writing and the mind here (*RO* 101); and in the context in which *A Room of One's Own* itself is written, during such a 'stridently sex-conscious' (*RO* 129) age created largely because in writing 'virility has now become self-conscious – men, that is to say, are now writing only with the male side of their brain' (*RO* 132). More important than these differences, however, is the desire, exemplified in the famous 'Chloe liked Olivia' scene, to write 'relationships between women' rather than depicting women always 'in their relation to men' (*RO* 107), and therefore to provide 'more complicated' explorations of women, including the differences *between* women and *within* each woman – levels 2 and 3 of Braidotti's model.

Rather than setting women's writing against men's in a fixed and essential way, *A Room of One's Own* continually explores differences between women writers. The 'four famous names' that are foregrounded in Chapter IV – Jane Austen, Charlotte Brontë, Emily Brontë, and George Eliot – represent 'incongruous characters': 'what had George Eliot in common with Emily Brontë? Did not Charlotte Brontë fail entirely to understand Jane Austen?' (*RO* 85–6) When the narrator then outlines the differences between *Jane Eyre* (1847) and *Pride and Prejudice* (1813), the differences between women are described precisely by focusing on the moment in Brontë's novel when she emphasises similarities between men and women both in the content of what she is writing ('but women feel just as men feel') and through her tone of 'indignation' (*RO* 90). Therefore, as Woolf's narrator puts it earlier when realising the limitations of her own anger, she was 'angry because he was angry' (*RO* 44).[38] Woolf, then, does not stop at writing the differences between women and men; rather she concurrently begins to de-emphasise such categorical differences based in identity. When Woolf praises the 'genius' and 'integrity' of Austen and Emily Brontë writing 'as women write, not as men write', she is clearly not defining or prescribing a feminine or female sentence, an *écriture féminine* or an essentialist form of writing necessarily shared by all women – after all, these are only two 'of all the thousand women who wrote novels then' – but a writing that does not define itself either for or against the 'perpetual admonitions' of patriarchy to 'write this, think that' (*RO* 97). Writing 'as women write' is itself historically and artistically variable, seen later when Mary Carmichael had 'broken up Jane Austen's sentence' so that 'there was no likeness between them'. Here too, by breaking 'the sequence – the expected order', Mary Carmichael wrote not 'as a woman' but 'as a woman would, if she wrote like a woman' (*RO* 119). This somewhat odd phrasing raises the question of who precisely 'she' refers to. Yet whether the 'she' is Mary Carmichael or 'woman', it is a 'she' separated from writing 'like a woman', the term 'woman' being thrown into confusion.

The emphasis Woolf places on differences between women, then, is also apparent in her reluctance to offer a fixed definition of 'feminine' or 'woman'. Indeed, in her essay 'Women Novelists' written ten years before in 1918, Woolf touches on this issue in her remarks upon Brimley Johnson's critique of women's writing: 'As Mr Brimley Johnson again and again remarks, a woman's writing is always feminine; it cannot help being feminine; at its best it is most feminine: the only difficulty lies in defining what we mean by feminine' (*E2* 316). Similarly, towards the end of *A Room of One's Own* Woolf bemoans the view in 'newspapers and novels and biographies that when a woman speaks to women she should have something very unpleasant up her sleeve. Women are hard on Women. Women dislike women. Women – but are you not sick to death of the word? I can assure you that I am' (*RO* 145). Woolf's assertion here should not be mistaken for a rejection of the material concerns of women (and in the following paragraph she notes what she likes about women and turns on men) but rather a criticism of the ways in which 'women' – as with Brimley Johnson's 'feminine' – are discussed and appropriated by patriarchal culture. In both of these examples the serious point underlying the arch tone is a suspicion that terms such as 'women' and 'feminine' are of limited subversive potential because they are always defined in relation to 'men' and the 'masculine' (and indeed often defined and discussed by men). Whilst continuing to use these words throughout her writing – after all they are signifiers that need to be re-appropriated and worked through rather than rejected out of hand – Woolf is keen to look beyond the traditional categorisations they have hitherto created. Pointing to the heterogeneity within the category 'woman', Woolf therefore does not present a common room of one's own:

> One goes into the room – but the resources of the English language would be much put to the stretch, and whole flights of words would need to wing their way illegitimately into existence before a woman could say what happens when she goes into a room. The rooms differ so completely [. . .] one has only to go into any room in any street for the whole of that extremely complex force of femininity to fly in one's face. How should it be otherwise? (*RO* 113–14)

As Peggy Kamuf comments in her reading of this passage, the dash in the opening sentence signifies a 'punctuated hesitation' creating doubt as to the identity of the 'one'. The entry of women into a language from which they were previously excluded 'will not simply substitute a "feminine" one for a masculine. Indeed, it cannot for a multiplicity already inhabits the site of this writing. [. . .] In effect, Woolf displaces the issue of the "one" who enters the room by figuring in rapid succession a series of rooms to be entered, surveyed, plotted, described.'[39] In her later, posthumously published essay 'Professions for Women' (1942), Woolf also emphasises that whilst gaining 'rooms of your own in the house hitherto exclusively owned by men' is of the utmost importance for women, these rooms, and the women inside them, will differ: 'But this freedom is only a beginning; the room is your own, but it is still bare. It has to be furnished; it has to be decorated; it has to be shared. How are you going to furnish it, how are you going to decorate it? With whom are you going to share it, and upon what terms?' (*E6* 483–4).

As well as differences within the category 'women' there are moments when emphasis is placed on differences within each woman in Woolf's text. The inadequacy of language to express such non-unitary subjects is evident in the well-known discussion of the one-letter pronoun 'I', where its 'dominance' (*RO* 131) is linked to the patriarchal subject and male writer: 'after reading a chapter or two a shadow seemed to lie across the page. It was a straight dark bar, a shadow shaped something like the letter "I" [. . .] the worst of it is that in the shadow of the letter "I" all is shapeless as mist' (*RO* 130). This often-cited passage places women in the shadow of this dominating 'I' and shares similarities with the use Braidotti makes of it for her nomadic feminist subject: 'According to this vision of a subject that is both historically anchored and split, or multiple, the power of synthesis of the "I" is a grammatical necessity, a theoretical fiction that holds together the collection of differing layers.'[40] As Goldman points out in her lucid reading of the above passage, the fact that 'Phoebe' (meaning 'the bright one') then enters as the woman who is in the shadow illuminates precisely such differing layers: 'In describing woman both as a source of light and as imprisoned in shadow, this passage shows how women's place historically has been conceptually marked out (or inscribed) as shadow by the discourse of masculine enlightenment, and how women's emancipation yet lies with the very illumination of this shadow.'[41] Always interested in bringing women out of the shadow, Woolf's use of 'I' throughout a book that has multiple narrators (although the narrative does at times shift to 'we' and 'one') creates not an 'I' that is an internalised fragmentation, collapsing in on itself, but a multiplicity open to new attachments, where 'the experience of the mass is behind the single voice' (*RO* 85). There is something playful in Woolf's 'I', where she uses this one letter word 'just for kicks', to borrow a phrase from Deleuze and Guattari, re-appropriating it in each and every use, bringing out the multiplicity within the singular, injecting a lightness of touch to the 'dark bar' (*RO* 130) and showing that it does not have to remain a symbol of patriarchal dominance: 'it is relatively easy to stop saying "I," but that does not mean that you have gotten away from the regime of subjectification; conversely, you can keep on saying "I," just for kicks, and already be in another regime in which personal pronouns function only as fictions'.[42] It is this lighter, more flexibile and fictionalised, less self-conscious – that is to say more androgynous – use of the letter 'I' that holds potential for Woolf in *A Room of One's Own*. After all, '"I" is only a convenient term for somebody who has no real being' (*RO* 5). That Woolf's discussion of this 'I' immediately follows her most famous passage on androgyny serves as a reminder that becoming man-womanly or woman-manly – and also bearing in mind the unfixed nature of these sexed nouns – is not to cement a unitary 'I', but to reveal the multiplicity already within the androgynous subject.

Woolf's theory of androgyny, and her concerns for the marginalisation of women in writing and in their materially situated position 'in the shadow' of men, both aim their criticism at a misplaced over-consciousness of a rigid division between two sexes. This is emphasised when after sketching the theory of androgyny the first words to actually be written (in the sixth and final chapter of the text) on the piece of paper entitled 'Women and Fiction' are:

> it is fatal for anyone who writes to think of their sex. It is fatal to be a man or woman pure and simple; one must be woman-manly or man-womanly. It is fatal for a woman to lay the least stress on any grievance; to plead even with justice any cause; in any way to speak consciously as a woman. And fatal is

no figure of speech; for anything written with that conscious bias is doomed to death [. . .] it cannot grow in the minds of others. (*RO* 136)

Whilst there is a further asymmetry in that the fatality of speaking as a woman has historically been dictated by patriarchy (it has clearly not been fatal in the same way for men to speak as men), Woolf is aware that maintaining this asymmetry is both pragmatically and theoretically limiting in that it reasserts the binary framework that keeps men and women apart. Her theory of androgyny is not, then, an unproblematic celebration of a subjectivity which dispenses with differences between men and women, but one which multiplies difference to create a subject that is more complicated and that is not defined by an oppositional relation. The androgynous subject is an emergent one with the potential to redraw the lines of asymmetry through collaboration. That is, the difference between Woolf's androgyny and Braidotti's nomadism is that where Braidotti maintains level 1 of her model – differences between men and women – as a category seemingly undisturbed by the multiple differences between women (level 2) and within women (level 3), Woolf's androgyny points the way to more complex levels and combinations which challenge models that privilege differences of women against men.

The very last words we read from Mary Beton are perhaps most revealing of all: 'the taxi took the man and the woman, I thought, seeing them come together across the street, and the current swept them away, I thought, hearing far off the roar of London traffic, into that tremendous stream' (*RO* 137). The enduring image is not of the man and woman getting into the taxi but of the taxi cruising through the London traffic, and our attention is drawn to the material context in which this image first appeared. For Mary Beton did not simply observe the man and the woman standing together at the taxi; she saw them walking towards each other from the streets of London where 'no two people are ever alike' (*RO* 124), and she watched as 'the cab glided off' back into those streets. It is this movement towards and away from a partial, momentary connection that is the model in which androgyny is rooted, I would argue, where the further connections that these figures will make and have made before is brought into view, challenging the notion that this 'girl in patent leather boots' and this 'young man in a maroon overcoat' are emblems or symbols that stand in for all men and all women. If there is a 'collaboration' or a 'marriage of opposites' here – where 'the mind celebrates its nuptials' (*RO* 136) – then we are presented with a model similar to my description of Woolf's granites and rainbows in Chapter 1. That is, I think of 'marriage' here as the many 'swift marriages' Woolf describes in 'Craftsmanship', of becoming man-womanly or woman-manly as I did transposing granites and rainbows, where the coming together, or consummation, of these terms (in this instance 'woman' and 'man') does not represent two discrete entities creating one whole; rather we have the committed – but partial and fleeting – attraction of two non-fixed terms which create their own distinct meanings in their own distinct textual frameworks and material contexts.

Moreover, by including men in these nomadic 'marriages', Woolf's androgynous feminist vision demonstrates a complex model of subjectivity that shares features of Braidotti's nomadic subject, but ultimately goes further. Where Braidotti's nomadic model of sexual difference often only has women in mind (where men are discussed they are invariably defined in opposition to women, as with level 1 of her model), Woolf considers, however ironically at times, differences between men and within each man. Therefore, one of the implications of considering Woolf's theory of androgyny alongside Braidotti's theory of nomadism is that we might extend Braidotti's three-levelled model of sexual difference to include a fourth level of 'differences among men' and a fifth level of 'differences within each man'. This fourth level can be seen from near the beginning of *A Room of One's Own* when Woolf's narrator cites 'a direct contradiction' between Pope and La Bruyère in their writings on women, and between such contrary figures as Napoleon and Dr Johnson, Goethe and Mussolini (*RO* 38). Where androgyny is concerned, certain male writers such as Shakespeare, Keats, and Sterne are judged to have been man-womanly whilst many, epitomised by Mr A but also including Milton, Wordsworth, and Tolstoy who had 'a dash too much of the male in them', were not (*RO* 135). The fifth level is evident in the very fact that Woolf's theory of androgyny is an inclusive one, therefore the 'I' that is multiple is also an 'I' that is open to those men who become androgynous. Adding these levels of male difference to Braidotti's levels of female difference only further unsettles the first level of her model, where differences between men and women are always already in place. It is in this sense that we might consequently think of Woolf's feminism and her theory of androgyny as providing a positive model of complex, nomadic, and non-unitary subjectivity – not just on a theoretical level, but also a strategic one – which points beyond the binary apparatus of sexual difference.

In *Undoing Gender* (2004) Judith Butler considers both the subversive potential and limitations of Braidotti's nomadism. In the first place, Butler does endorse Braidotti's 'relentless search for what is mobile and generative'[43] and her emphasis on multiplicity as 'a way of understanding the play of forces that work upon one another and that generate new possibilities of life. Multiplicity is not the death of agency, but its very condition [. . .] the very dynamism of life.'[44] For Butler, however, sexual difference is something more elusive than Braidotti allows, a space from which to create questions rather than provide the firm basis for definitions, however mobile they may appear to be:

> sexual difference is the site where a question concerning the relation of the biological to the cultural is posed and reposed, where it must and can be posed, but where it cannot, strictly speaking, be answered. Understood as a border concept, sexual difference has psychic, somatic, and social dimensions that are never quite collapsible into one another but are not for that reason ultimately distinct. Does sexual difference vacillate there, as a vacillating border, demanding a rearticulation of those terms without any sense of finality? Is it, therefore, not a thing, not a fact, not a presupposition but rather a demand for rearticulation that never quite vanishes – but also never quite appears?[45]

Of course, it is precisely this elusiveness which Braidotti finds problematic, and which she dismisses as 'theoretical illusions of an infinitely malleable, free-floating gender'.[46] But a question that Butler posed to Braidotti in an earlier interview on the subject remains pertinent to theorists of sexual difference:

> what does it mean to establish that asymmetry [between men and women] as irreducible and irreversible, and then to claim that it ought to serve as a foundation for feminist politics? Doesn't that simply reify a social asymmetry as an eternal necessity, thus installing the pathos of exclusion as the 'ground' of feminism?[47]

Or as Butler challenges in *Undoing Gender*, 'must the framework for thinking about sexual difference be binary for this feminine multiplicity to emerge? Why can't the framework for sexual difference itself move beyond binarity into multiplicity?'[48] The paradox in Braidotti's vision of sexual difference as 'fact' is that she is, of the two, the most firmly opposed to the anthropocentric landscape, the most fervent proponent of the positivity of difference, and the most committed to a theorisation of non-unitary subjectivity that takes into account the material, ontological co-involvements with animals, the environment, and with technology.[49] Emphasising the entanglements of agencies, and pointing beyond the limitations of Braidotti's model, Woolf's theory of androgyny in *A Room of One's Own* captures multiplicity as the very condition of writing sexual difference.

Becoming-woman and minoritarian writing

In *Kafka: Toward a Minor Literature* (1975), Deleuze and Guattari outline three interrelated characteristics of a 'minoritarian' writing or 'minor' literature. Firstly, rather than 'reterritorialising' language within a dominant discourse, upholding its conventional utterances, minor literature involves writing with 'a high co-efficient of deterritorialization' so that a major language speaks in new ways.[50] Secondly, minoritarian writing is intensely political. Where major literature is focused on the private concerns of the individual and the relegation of the social, political, environmental context to mere background, minor literature's 'cramped space forces each individual intrigue to connect immediately to politics. The individual concern thus becomes all the more necessary, indispensible, magnified, because a whole other story is vibrating within it.' This leads to a story thus escaping a concern only with the familiar and familial, for 'in this way, the family triangle connects to other triangles – commercial, economic, bureaucratic, juridical – that determine its values'.[51] Thirdly, minor literature is always concerned with collectives, 'everything takes on a collective value'.[52] With its deterritorialisation of the patriarchal 'I', its emphasis on the material, social, artistic, and political struggles facing women, and its continued concern with collective relations between men and women 'in relation to reality' (*RO* 149), we might think of *A Room of One's Own* as an example of such 'minor' – and therefore all the more subversive – literature. Moreover, Woolf's theory of androgyny, with its deterritorialisation of terms such as 'male' and 'female', could be understood as an example of a specific form of minoritarian writing, what Deleuze and Guattari describe as the 'becoming-woman' of writing.

Deleuze and Guattari make reference to Woolf when discussing minoritarian writing and their concept of 'becoming-woman', to be understood not as being about representation of the woman as 'molar entity [...] defined by her form, endowed with organs and functions and assigned as a subject', but as involving a deterritorialisation of subjectivity and the creation of 'molecular', multiplicitous, non-hierarchical attachments.[53] In *Dialogues*, Deleuze suggests that Woolf forms such connections because she 'forbade herself "to speak like a woman"' and 'harnessed the becoming-woman of writing all the more for this'.[54] And, in *A Thousand Plateaus*, Deleuze and Guattari allude to Mary Carmichael's writing 'as a woman, but as a woman who has forgotten that she is a woman, so that her pages were full of that curious sexual quality which comes only when sex is unconscious of itself' (*RO* 121), by insisting that '[Woolf] was appalled at the idea of writing "as a woman." Rather, writing should produce a becoming-woman as atoms of womanhood capable of crossing and impregnating an entire social field, and of contaminating men, of sweeping them up in that becoming.'[55] Becoming-woman is therefore open to all, women and men, who form connections which are not based on models of opposition and ownership:

> the majoritarian as a constant and homogeneous system; minorities as subsystems; and the minoritarian as a potential, creative and created, becoming. The problem is never to acquire the majority, even in order to install a new constant. There is no becoming-majoritarian; majority is never becoming. All becoming is minoritarian. Women, regardless of their numbers, are a minority, definable as a state or subset; but they create only by making possible a becoming over which they do not have ownership, into which they themselves must enter; this is a becoming-woman affecting all of humankind, men and women both.[56]

If Woolf's androgyny is as an attempt to overcome sex-consciousness founded on binary oppositions and instead to present a more complex model of sexual differences (where emphasis is on intra-category and intra-subjective difference as much as it is on inter-category difference), then we can understand it in Deleuze and Guattari's terminology as rejecting molar identities. Moreover, we can view her 'man-womanly' and 'woman-manly' formulation as the starting point of an attempt to articulate a becoming-minoritarian of both women and men, allowing for a multiplicity of different combinations, of different sexes where in the figuration of androgyny 'the two sexes imply a multiplicity of molecular combinations bringing into play [. . .] the man in the woman and the woman in the man [. . .] a thousand tiny sexes'.[57] It may be, then, that there are more than 'two sexes in the mind corresponding to two sexes in the body'. As we read later in *A Room of One's Own*, 'two sexes are quite inadequate [. . .] For we have too much likeness as it is, and if an explorer should come back and bring word of other sexes looking through the branches of other trees at other skies, nothing would be of greater service to humanity' (*RO* 114).[58] Considering that androgyny is so much about a rejection of patriarchy and phallogocentric (major) writing, becoming androgynous and becoming-woman form something of an affinity. As Catherine Driscoll notes, androgyny is an example of where 'for Woolf, as for Deleuze [. . .] woman is an infinitive, a process or event, a speaking position perhaps but not an identity'.[59]

Just as some critics view Woolf's androgyny as sitting uneasily with her feminist aims relating to the material conditions of women, however, so there has been criticism of Deleuze's becoming-woman by feminist critics. In a recent article Gillian Howie associates becoming-woman with androgyny (albeit that she is not referring specifically to Woolf's formulation) in her criticism of the term:

> Becoming-woman suggests a radically androgynous transvaluation of values, and it certainly appears to leap over the risk of dimorphic essentialism in an un-gendered becoming. It does so by risking, instead, de-contextualising and appropriating the affective body; interning the same dimorphic values whilst cutting the ground from critical interjection.[60]

Becoming-woman also marks a site of contention for Braidotti, where she describes the 'confrontation between Deleuze's theories of multiplicity and becoming-minority and feminist theories of sexual difference and the becoming subject of women'.[61] She argues that where 'Deleuze proceeds [. . .] as if there was clear equivalence in the speaking positions of the two sexes' it is important from a feminist perspective to remember that 'the identification of points of exit from the phallogocentric mode takes asymmetrical forms in the two sexes'[62] – a point that is familiar to readers of Woolf's theory of androgyny. Braidotti therefore takes issue with what she sees as Deleuze's suggestion that feminists

> should instead draw on the multisexed structure of the subject and claim back all the sexes of which women have been deprived; emphasis on the feminine is restrictive [. . .] Women, in other words, can be revolutionary subjects only to the extent that they develop a consciousness that is not specifically feminine, dissolving 'woman' into the forces that structure her.[63]

These criticisms point to challenging aspects of Deleuze and Guattari's concept of becoming-woman, where it can be seen to dispose of subjectivity at the very moment in history when feminism is beginning to gain a sense of identity, to undermine the lived realities of women and romanticise women's struggles, and to function as another example of appropriation by masculine philosophy.[64] Critics of becoming-woman could even point to Woolf's own warning in *A Room of One's Own* about how 'woman' can be appropriated and exploited by men: 'Imaginatively she is of the highest importance, practically she is completely insignificant' (*RO* 56).

It is not difficult to see some of the concerns about the kind of terminology used by Deleuze and Guattari when they talk about the women not having 'ownership' over their becomings. But rather than seeing becomings as a negative loss of agency, it is important to remember in all this that for Deleuze and Guattari it is molar identities and major categories that are sedentary; becomings are fundamentally about the creation of new events, new modes of life. There is agency here, but, rather than belonging to an individuated subject it is a symbiotic form of agency that is shared with those other human and nonhuman elements that are entangled in a minoritarian becoming-other. Moreover, Deleuze and Guattari already anticipate questions such as those raised by Braidotti on 'becoming-woman', or, as Alice Jardine has put it, 'why then do [Deleuze and Guattari] privilege the word woman?'[65] Deleuze and Guattari form their response to this type of challenge by way of another question: 'why are there so many becomings of man, but no becoming-man?' Their answer is that 'man is majoritarian par excellence, whereas becomings are minoritarian; all becoming is becoming-minoritarian'.[66] They are far from ignorant of the specifically feminist political struggles of women:

> the woman as a molar entity has to become-woman in order that the man also becomes – or can become – woman. It is, of course, indispensable for women to conduct a molar politics, with a view to winning back their own organism, their own history, their own subjectivity: 'we as women . . .' makes its appearance as a subject of enunciation. But it is dangerous to confine oneself to such a subject, which does not function without drying up a spring or stopping a flow.[67]

In other words, becoming-woman, consistent with other becomings, goes beyond a politics of representation. Just as Woolf criticises Charlotte Brontë for 'protesting that she was "as good as a man"' (*RO* 96), 'becoming-woman' is not a question of women or indeed men becoming 'like' an idealised image of woman – it is not a question of identity – an oversight often made in feminist discussions which tend to judge Deleuze and Guattari's concept within a framework of specifically female or feminine subjectivity.

Feminist critics of becoming-woman (and of androgyny) too often *identify* sexual difference with a kind of natural asymmetry between men and women, so that even when certain feminist theorists are influenced by Deleuze there is a tension between the privileged form of 'difference' in 'sexual difference' and the Deleuzian form of 'difference' they advocate elsewhere in their work as taking us back to materiality and ontology, as rejecting cultural forms of understanding nature as purely constructed by language. Along with Braidotti's work, this is evident in Grosz's most recent book, *Becoming Undone*, where she brings Deleuze together with Darwin and Irigaray to argue that

> Nature itself is dynamized, historical, and subject to dramatic change. Sexual difference remains the most creative and powerful means by which this

transformation is brought about. It is the means by which the natural cultivates culture, rather than culture cultivating nature. We do not leave nature behind, we do not surround ourselves with culture in order to protect ourselves against nature, for culture, cultures in their multiplicity, are complex forms of variation of natural forces, both human and nonhuman.[68]

In contrast, by the end of *A Room of One's Own* Woolf does not privilege sexual difference as 'the engine of all lived difference'[69] precisely by pointing towards a material reality that is more than human, by referring to 'the common life which is the real life', by viewing 'human beings not always in their relation to each other but in relation to reality; and the sky, too, and the trees or whatever it may be in themselves; [. . .] our relation is to the world of reality and not only to the world of men and women' (*RO* 149). Beyond concerns with the terminology of 'becoming-woman' there are many important contributions Deleuze can make to our understanding of an embodied, materialist but also nomadic sexual difference which challenges the boundaries between nature and culture, nonhuman and human, and which does not allow the 'difference' of sexual difference to become privileged, to become its own majoritarian term. Becoming-woman calls for us, as Claire Colebrook puts it, to 'think of new modes of relationality: not a world which is synthesised by man as a thinking subject, who then turns back upon his own organising systems, but a world of divergent lines of relationality'.[70] As both nomadic and minoritarian, I would suggest that Woolf's theory of androgyny continues to be a key marker of what Pelagia Goulimari terms 'minoritarian feminism', the becoming-minoritarian of feminism. This therefore involves a double process of deterritorialisation – of the term androgyny from its perceived status as a 'male-promoting concept',[71] and of feminism from the privileging of sexual difference in binary, hierarchical, static oppositions.

It is precisely with this attempt to view men and women in relation to the material world, and the emphasis on androgyny as a powerfully minoritarian and deterritorialising concept – one that offers lines of flight to the creation of new concepts – that I now turn to *To the Lighthouse*. Bearing in mind that Woolf's woman-manly/man-womanly formula for androgyny is put forward by a persona, Mary Beton, rather than Woolf herself, Gayatri Spivak reminds us that we should be wary of reducing her other texts to '*successful* articulations' of her theory.[72] I would also hesitate to claim *To the Lighthouse* (or indeed any of her other texts) as wholly representative of Woolf's theory – and wouldn't want to make the claim, as Heilbrun does, that it is Woolf's 'best novel of androgyny'[73] – but my discussion of androgyny does lead me to my own formulation of 'tri-subjectivities' or 'tri-s' which I introduce to frame my analysis of the ways in which *To the Lighthouse* recasts triangular models of subjectivity at the same time as moving beyond dualistic models of sexual difference. Having focused on 'becoming-woman', in the remainder of this chapter I want to extend the dialogue between Deleuze and Woolf to look at various concepts including 'smooth' and 'striated' spaces, and the 'rhizomatic' image of thought. As Grosz put it in *Volatile Bodies* (1994), whilst acknowledging the difficulties of 'becoming-woman', 'further points of overlap – points feminists may find of value in their projects – remain an open question, dependent on the kinds of work on Deleuze and Guattari's texts that feminists are prepared to undertake.'[74] Where Woolf's exploration of subjectivity and sexual difference in *To the Lighthouse* is concerned, Deleuze and Guattari illuminate their relationship to a materiality that reaches beyond the embodied human subject to include nonhuman objects and environments. Woolf's novel engages with a mode of sexual difference which reimagines materiality precisely to move beyond the privileging of sexual difference.

Lines of becoming: from triangulation to tri-s

> The only way to get outside the dualisms is to be-between, to pass between, the intermezzo – that is what Virginia Woolf lived with all her energies, in all of her work, never ceasing to become.[75]

In their discussion of triangular relations in *Kafka*, Deleuze and Guattari are concerned with moving away from what they see as 'the hierarchy of triangles',[76] a 'triangulation of the subject' which is familial in origin and 'consists in fixing one's position in relation to the two other represented terms (father-mother-child)'.[77] Put simply, where inter-subjective relationships are concerned triangles too often resemble an Oedipal design, and Deleuze and Guattari seek a way out of the insular environment or 'intimate familial theatre' of psychoanalysis.[78] In *Anti-Oedipus*, they heavily criticise the fact that, broadly speaking, psychoanalysis continues to resort to the Oedipal triangle despite the known limitations of this framework within the field itself.[79] Aiming to bring 'production into desire' and 'desire into production',[80] they are interested in 'a nonfigurative and nonsymbolic unconscious',[81] and in a Real that begins with 'the immanent process of desire and seeks to mark both the interruptions of this process (reterritorializations) and its continuations and transformations (becomings, intensities ...)' in contrast to psychoanalysis which 'begins with the symbolic and seeks out the "gaps" that mark the irruption of an "impossible" Real'.[82] Theirs is a Real, as Grosz notes, that learns from Bergson its positivity and dynamism, 'with defining and refining being or reality so that its difference from itself, its fundamental structure of becoming or self-divergence, is impossible to ignore'.[83] As Deleuze and Guattari explain in *A Thousand Plateaus*, where psychoanalysis relies on molar identities that are 'totalizable and organizable', they want to emphasise molecular becomings that are 'intensive' and 'constantly construct and dismantle themselves in the cause of their communications';[84] it is the difference between 'rigid segmentarity' and 'supple segmentation'.[85]

In *To the Lighthouse*, Woolf creates a supple textual framework through the productive entanglements of characters with their environments, the human with the nonhuman. Woolf's novel begins with what critics often claim to be an Oedipal relationship of Mr Ramsay, Mrs Ramsay, and James, and yet from the very first pages these characters actually re-shape this triangular model of inter-subjective relations through their connections with their external environments (extra-subjective) as well as their internal complexities (intra-subjective). Indeed throughout her novel Woolf creates a series of what I am terming 'tri-subjectivities' or 'tri-s', which continually re-draw the lines and re-shape the design of triangular relations. Following the above discussion of the relationship between Woolf's 'androgyny', Braidotti's 'nomadic subject', and Deleuze's 'becoming-woman', my formulation of tri-s has three key components: 1) As a reading strategy, tri-s involve an analysis of characters in groupings of (at least) three, but do so only as a starting point. As I demonstrate in the following section, in *To the Lighthouse*, even when Woolf appears to be directly contrasting one character with another, she continually points outwards to other subjects and objects, bodies and environments, and in the process complicates these distinctions and undermines views of sexual difference as a dualistic construct. Tri-s remind us as readers and critics to *try* different combinations so as not to foreclose the relations between subjects in a fixed textual framework, whether dualistic or triangular. 2) As a theoretical framework, a geometry of tri-s moves beyond Braidotti's three-level model of sexual difference (differences between men and women, differences among women, and differences within each woman) or a simple extension of it as remaining open to the additional levels of differences among men and differences within each man. Tri-s reveal contours of difference that are not rooted in identity or invested in a teleological project of subject formation; rather tri-s account for a process, a movement, an assembling of subjectivities which never resolve into a fixed, (pre)destined subject. 3) As a linguistic construct, the term tri-s is pronounced *tries*, working between its homonymic and synonymic relation to this word. The focus is on the *tri-s* that the characters make, the trajectories they form, their *attempts* to form connections rather than to fix subjectivity.

Where the sexual politics of Woolf's novel are concerned, then, the lines of becoming shared between human and nonhuman are crucial, and the remaining sections of this chapter aim to highlight that tri-s in *To the Lighthouse* transform triangles into multiplicities, setting into motion various creative becomings rather than a settling into categories of being. It is to 'test what one meant by man-womanly, and conversely by woman-manly' (*RO* 128) but to do so by considering 'the world of reality and not only [. . .] the world of men and women' (*RO* 149), to account for men and women as 'part of the nature of things' (*TL* 213).

Mr Ramsay – Mrs Ramsay – James: severity and suppleness

Psychoanalytic critics have focused on the triangular relationship between the Ramsays and their son James as highlighting what Elizabeth Abel calls 'Woolf's Oedipal plot' in *To the Lighthouse*.[86] Laura Marcus notes that James' role in particular is often understood in relation to Freud's Oedipal complex; pointing to a passage in the latter part of Woolf's novel when, stationary on the boat, 'a rope seemed to bind him there and his father had knotted it and he could only escape by taking a knife and plunging it' (*TL* 213), she suggests that 'James is literally becalmed, like the Ancient Mariner, by this narrative, and metaphorically bound, as Oedipus was bound by the chains with which his father sought to secure his death.'[87] Similarly, Bowlby notes that 'the resentment of James [. . .] for Mr Ramsay's prior claims to his mother parallels Freud's Oedipal scenario, where the boy wants nothing less than to put out of the way the father who asserts his rights to the mother.'[88] Indeed, whilst acknowledging Woolf's distrust of Freud,[89] Nicole Ward Jouve aligns Woolf's writing with a psychoanalysis that is 'forever fending off the threat of disintegration, blurred boundaries, insecure identities'.[90] Contrary to these readings, I would like to suggest that the relationship between Mrs Ramsay, Mr Ramsay, and James in *To the Lighthouse* has little to do with an Oedipal triangle. Moreover, whilst acknowledging the autobiographical elements of the novel – for example the clear influence of Woolf's parents on the characters in the text, and Woolf's well-known reflection in 'Sketch of the Past' that writing it exorcised the ghost of her mother (*MB* 92) – I do not wish to foreground Woolf's own familial relations here as psychoanalytic readings have tended to. Rather than understanding Woolf's writing as resisting the 'threat' of 'blurred boundaries', the problem is instead, I would argue, the limitations of reading Woolf's depiction of the Ramsays through an Oedipal lens. Woolf, as Driscoll puts it, explores 'assemblages of subject positions which escape Oedipal frames',[91] and in this section I want to focus on the early part of To the Lighthouse in order to bring out the supple segmentations that create new combinations later in the novel.

To see James' narrative in To the Lighthouse as an Oedipal one risks overshadowing those nonfamilial experiences that are hinted at from the very beginning of Woolf's novel. In only the second paragraph James connects with a range of objects which are irreducible to the figures of his parents, including a 'wheelbarrow', 'lawn-mower', 'poplar trees', 'brooms', and 'dresses': 'all these were so coloured and distinguished in his mind that he had already his private code, his secret language' (TL 5). In addition, the kind of nonparental attachments formed by James are also evident in To the Lighthouse when Mrs Ramsay watches on as her daughter Cam

> dashed past. She was off like a bird, bullet, or arrow, impelled by what desire, shot by whom, at what directed, who could say? What, what? Mrs Ramsay pondered, watching her. It might be a vision – of a shell, or a wheelbarrow, of a fairy kingdom on the far side of the hedge; or it might be the glory of speed; no one knew. (TL 63)

If children not only form connections with parents, but also enter into what Deleuze and Guattari call 'the line of flight of the building, the street, etc.',[92] then here Cam's line of flight takes on a more literal quality as she runs away from the parental framework: 'she would not stop for her father [. . .] nor for her mother' (TL 63). This recalls Woolf's own memories of childhood in 'Sketch of the Past' where she emphasises the importance of such nonparental exploration, how she had 'many adventures outside' her familial world, and 'often went far from it; and kept much back from it' (MB 96). James' 'private code' or 'secret language', Cam's line of flight, and Woolf's own nonfamilial 'adventures', serve as reminders that, as Deleuze and Guattari argue,

> children don't live as our adult memories would have us believe [. . .] Memory yells 'Father! Mother!' but the childhood block is elsewhere, in the highest intensities that the child constructs with his sisters, his pal, his projects and his toys, and all the nonparental figures through which he deterritorializes his parents every chance he gets.[93]

It is not only nonparental childhood connections that Woolf hints at; her depiction of the Ramsays points beyond the molar identities that they are so often seen as representing, whether as stand-ins for Woolf's own parents, or as symbols of Victorian marriage. At the very beginning of the novel Mr Ramsay displays his dominance and severe manner in the patriarchal familial set-up: '"But," said his father, stooping in front of the drawing-room window, "it won't be fine"'; 'What he said was true. It was always true. He was incapable of untruth; never tampered with a fact' (*TL* 6). But 'severity' is precisely, and somewhat ironically, what links Mr Ramsay to his wife and child in these opening exchanges: Mr Ramsay's ruling against the lighthouse trip; Mrs Ramsay's declaration '"Nonsense"' is made with 'great severity' which she then turns against Nancy (*TL* 8); and even the young James outwardly 'appeared the image of stark and uncompromising severity' (*TL* 6). When the narrative later points to Mr Ramsay's own 'compound of severity and humour' (*TL* 37), it is as if Woolf is gently satirising the tendencies we have to polarise into extreme categories, to emphasise severe differences. Thus there is a self-reflexive hint early on of how such severity and extremity will be undermined by a more nuanced vision of these characters' relations. From these opening pages, and as I demonstrate in the following sections by focusing on further relations formed in *To the Lighthouse* – the tri-s that continually re-draw the lines and re-shape the design of triangular relations – Woolf may provide another example of what Deleuze and Guattari discover in Kafka's writing: 'triangles that remain in Kafka's novels show up only at the beginning of the novels; and from the start, they are so vacillating, so supple and transformable, that they are ready to open into a series that break their form and explode their terms'.[94]

Despite what initially seems like a reassertion of difference as rigid and oppositional, a more flexible, supple form of difference begins to appear through Mrs Ramsay when, a few pages after the scene discussed above, the eight Ramsay children make way to their bedrooms 'to debate anything, everything; Tansley's tie; the passing of the Reform Bill; sea-birds and butterflies; people'. We are told of two kinds of 'differences':

> Strife, divisions, difference of opinion, prejudices twisted into the very fibre of being, oh that they should begin so early, Mrs Ramsay deplored. They were so critical, her children [. . .] It seemed to her such nonsense – inventing differences, when people, heaven knows, were different enough without that. The real differences, she thought, standing by the drawing-room window, are enough, quite enough. (*TL* 11)

The 'real differences' for Mrs Ramsay appear to be felt in the molar, binary oppositional categories of 'rich and poor, high and low' (*TL* 11). Similarly, there are many often-cited examples of how Mrs Ramsay props up molar identities of well-defined male and female roles, and by upholding 'the greatness of man's intellect [. . .] the subjection of all wives' (*TL* 14) she has been compared to the idealised patriarchal looking-glass Woolf describes in *A Room of One's Own*, 'possessing the magical and delicious power of reflecting the figure of man at twice its natural size' (*RO* 45). Critics have pointed to instances in the novel where Mrs Ramsay is seen giving her husband sympathy (*TL* 45), her 'mania' for marriage (*TL* 58, 83, 199), her role as mother (*TL* 38, 45) and her short-sightedness (*TL* 14, 36, 83, 182).[95]

But whilst it is tempting to view Mrs Ramsay as stuck within an oppositional framework, there are also moments when she looks beyond this. In the above passage her own relationship to these 'real differences' of rich and poor is somewhat ambiguous, with 'the great in birth receiving from her, half grudging, some respect' due to her own noble blood, and at the same time her concern with poverty, 'the things she saw with her own eyes, weekly, daily, here or in London' (*TL* 12). Mrs Ramsay's engagement with political issues is more pronounced later, with her concern 'about hospitals and drains and the dairy. About things like that she did feel passionately, and would, if she had had the chance, have liked to take people by the scruff of their necks and make them see. No hospital on the whole island. It was a disgrace' (*TL* 67). More gravely, her concern for 'the eternal problems' of 'suffering; death; the poor' are twice repeated: 'there was always a woman dying of cancer even here' (*TL* 70; see also 74). But as well as her contradictory relationship to these class differences, it is intriguing that at the very moment Mrs Ramsay's difference from her children is most pronounced she is 'holding James by the hand' (*TL* 11) – a phrase that is repeated on the following page – hinting at a connection with his more molecular experience of the world. Indeed James in this moment undermines her notion of what real differences are, for he escapes his own molar identity (as one of 'her children') 'since he would not go with the others' (*TL* 11). In relation to sexual difference, it is worth nothing here that the 'molar aggregates' par excellence, men and women, are not actually mentioned in the above quotation.[96] Might Mrs Ramsay be less contented after all by the 'relief of simplicity' that 'men, and women too, letting go the multiplicity of things, had allowed'? Even here, the narrative quickly moves from the 'simplicity' of men and women to Mrs Ramsay's sense of dissatisfaction with the 'vanity' she recognises in her own efforts to please and uphold societal and familial frameworks (*TL* 49). She is not, after all, entirely able or willing to reduce multiplicity to simplicity.

In 'The Window' section of *To the Lighthouse* there are further examples when Mrs Ramsay does not appear to be as rigidly Victorian in her ideals, as unflinchingly supportive of the status quo, or as 'short-sighted' as is initially presented. As Goldman notes, we can see both 'Mrs Ramsay's complicity with patriarchy and her potential to overthrow it',[97] and this more complicated view of Mrs Ramsay plays itself out at moments when she shows a level of awareness as to the ways in which her 'singleness of mind' consists of her ability to find 'truth which delighted, eased, sustained' but did so 'falsely perhaps' (*TL* 34). The fragility of her supposed 'instinct for truth' (*TL* 64) is reflected when 'she made herself look in her glass a little resentful that she had grown old, perhaps, by her own fault. (The bill for the greenhouse and all the rest of it.)' (*TL* 114). This time viewing the looking-glass rather than acting as though she herself is one, its reflection enables Mrs Ramsay's acknowledgement of the transience of life matched by her awareness that things could and perhaps should be different in the future: 'even if it isn't fine tomorrow [. . .] it will be another day' (*TL* 31). It could be argued, then, that Mrs Ramsay is as aware of the fabrication of familial, sexed roles as Lily Briscoe, but is less willing or less able to let go of that illusion:

> she let it uphold her and sustain her, this admirable fabric of the masculine intelligence, which ran up and down, crossed this way and that, like iron girders spanning the swaying fabric, upholding the world, so that she could trust herself to it utterly, even shut her eyes, or flicker them for a moment, as a child staring up from its pillow winks at the myriad layers of the leaves of a tree. Then she woke up. It was still being fabricated. (*TL* 122)

Mrs Ramsay's view that 'windows should be open' (*TL* 33) – and later in 'Time Passes' it is Mrs McNab who is 'directed to open all windows' (*TL* 148) – as well as the fact that herself, her husband and James all stand or sit by the window at various points in the 'The Window' section of the novel, hints at a wish to maintain some connection with the social and material world outside of the familial, perhaps a less polemical portrayal of Deleuze and Guattari's frustration with family-centred psychoanalysts: 'Do these psychoanalysts who are oedipalizing women, children [. . .] know what they are doing? We dream of entering their offices, opening their windows and saying, "It smells stuffy in here – some relation with the outside, if you please"'![98] Or, as we read in a different context in *A Room of One's Own*: 'I thought how unpleasant it is to be locked out; and I thought how it is worse, perhaps, to be locked in' (*RO* 31).

Mrs Ramsay's vision does not always, therefore, focus on the familial: 'She took a look at life, for she had a clear sense of it there, something real, something private, which she shared neither with her children nor with her husband' (*TL* 69). Moreover, whilst their specific concerns may be different, the short-sighted/long-sighted opposition of Mrs Ramsay and Mr Ramsay does not always ring true. As she regrets the lack of 'a model dairy and a hospital up here – those two things she would have liked to do, herself' but is unable to 'with all these children', and then immediately reflects upon the contentment of her position and that 'she never wanted James to grow a day older, or Cam either [. . .] She would have liked always to have a baby [. . .] was happiest carrying one in her arms' (*TL* 68), we are reminded of her husband's own simultaneous regret ('the father of eight children has no choice') and contentment ('he was for the most part happy; he had his wife; he had his children') (*TL* 52; see also 80–1). Indeed, we even see in these early chapters an example of the Ramsay parents and James combined in a vision that goes further than their familial relationship when, despite the fact all three of them are present to Lily's gaze, it is their materially embedded relation to the nonhuman surroundings, the entanglement of embodiment and environment, which is emphasised:

> The sky stuck to them; the birds sang through them. And what was even more exciting, she felt, too, as she saw Mr Ramsay bearing down and retreating, and Mrs Ramsay sitting with James in the window and the cloud moving and the tree bending, how life, from being made up of little separate incidents which one lived one by one, became curled and whole like a wave which bore one up with it and threw one down with it, there, with a dash on the beach. (*TL* 55)

In this passage Mrs Ramsay, Mr Ramsay, and James are contained in parenthetical commas, and it is the way that 'the sky stuck to them' and 'birds sang through them', as well as 'the cloud moving and the tree bending', which takes Lily's thoughts on life away from 'little separate incidents which one lived one by one' (as a sequence of subjective experiences) to life as 'curled and whole like a wave'. Rather than a psychoanalytic family portrait, here Woolf re-frames the Ramsay familial triangle as the image of tri-s.

Mrs Ramsay – Mr Ramsay – Lily: bending trees and becoming grass

In *Dialogues*, Deleuze and Parnet argue that 'trees are planted in our heads: the tree of life, the tree of knowledge'. Their interest lies not in the tree as metaphor, but as the dominant 'image of thought' in Western philosophy:[99]

a whole apparatus that is planted in thought in order to make it go in a straight line and produce the famous correct ideas. There are all kinds of characteristics in the tree: there is a point of origin, seed or centre; it is a binary machine or principle of dichotomy, with its perpetually divided and reproduced branchings, its points of arborescence; [. . .] a hierarchical system or transmission of orders [. . .] The whole world demands roots. Power is always arborescent.[100]

They go on to contrast the tree as image of thought with grass: 'not only does grass grow in the middle of things but it grows itself through the middle [. . .] Grass has its line of flight and does not take root. We have grass in the head and not a tree.'[101] As Deleuze and Guattari clarify in *A Thousand Plateaus*, where the tree grows with arborescent rigidity, is rooted in phallogocentrism and promotes the binary machine, grass is aligned with the horizontal, multiple growths of the subterranean 'rhizome':

The tree imposes the verb 'to be,' but the fabric of the rhizome is the conjunction, 'and . . . and . . . and'. This conjunction carries enough force to shake and uproot the verb 'to be'. Where are you going? Where are you coming from? What are you heading for? These are totally useless questions [. . .] seeking a beginning or a foundation – all imply a false conception of voyage and movement.[102]

What counts most for Deleuze then is always 'the middle and not the beginning or the end, grass which is in the middle and which grows from the middle, and not trees which have a top and roots. Always grass between the paving stones.'[103]

In relation to Woolf, this 'grass between the paving stones' brings to mind the opening episode of *A Room of One's Own*, when the narrator provokes 'horror and indignation' by strolling onto the Oxbridge turf reserved for the male 'Fellows and Scholars' (*RO* 7), and the territory of sexual politics is clearly but also complexly marked. As Judith Allen writes in *Virginia Woolf and the Politics of Language*, this 'gendered landscape [. . .] holds within, in its sedimentary layers, the archaeological remains of its ancient past'. An exploration of this geological and textual site prompts readers to think about the 'ground on which the social, political and economic events of the past have made their marks, developed their cultures and created their so-called "civilisations"'.[104] But as well as prompting us to dig into the past, *A Room of One's Own* looks forward, and contemporary revisitings to this scene suggest that readers continue to 'look carefully' for that elusive 'thought' which was 'laid on the grass' precisely as we are presented with the image of a 'burning tree', and moments before the narrator trespasses (*RO*

6). My focus in this section is not so much on determining what this thought precisely was or is, but on the very association Woolf makes here between thought and grass as one that she has already explored two years previously in *To the Lighthouse*. Whilst Allen's aforementioned book makes reference to *A Thousand Plateaus* in exploring Woolf's rhizomatic 'wild flowing grasses' as a place where women are linked together at the 'exclusion of men',[105] in *To the Lighthouse* grass actually becomes an important site in which Woolf points beyond a politics of exclusion (whether of women or of men); ultimately, her grass becomes an inclusive space in which no one is locked out or locked in. By focusing firstly on the relations between Mrs Ramsay, Mr Ramsay, and trees, and secondly between Lily, Mr Carmichael, and grass, I want to emphasise that the movements of tri-s resist arborescence and are rhizomatic; in other words, the rhizome grows tri-s instead of trees.

The fragility of arborescent foundations in *To the Lighthouse* is hinted at early on when a pear tree in the orchard is shaken by Lily's 'undeniable, everlasting, contradictory' thoughts about Mr Ramsay and 'a flock of starlings' (*TL* 29–30), and also the aforementioned passage when Lily watches Mr and Mrs Ramsay surrounded by a 'tree bending' (*TL* 55). Later, Woolf's exploration of the rhizomatic and arborescent is seen in the final two sections of 'The Window'. In the opening paragraphs here Mrs Ramsay appears to be searching for clearly defined points: 'She felt rather inclined just for a moment to stand still after all that chatter, and pick out one particular thing; the thing that mattered; to detach it; separate it off; clean it of all the emotions and odds and ends of things' (*TL* 129). In contrast to the inseparability of rhizomatic entanglements, Mrs Ramsay even wishes to introduce 'the moment' to patriarchal judgement, to institutionalise it: 'bring it to the tribunal [. . .] the judges she had set up to decide these things. Is it good, is it bad, is it right or wrong? Where are we going to?' Thus rooted to arborescence – exemplified by this last question which echoes Deleuze and Guattari's 'false conception of voyage and movement' above – she 'used the branches of the elm trees outside to stabilise her position'. Her 'sense of movement' is here a restricted one where 'all must be order. She must get that right and that right, she thought, insensibly approving of the dignity of the trees' stillness' (*TL* 130).

What follows, however, is a reminder that the arborescent and rhizomatic are not fixed oppositions creating their own binary framework but always already holding the potential to transpose each other. As Deleuze and Guattari put it: 'there are two kinds of voyage, distinguished by the respective role of the point, line and space [. . .] Tree travel and rhizome travel [. . .] But nothing completely coincides, and everything intermingles, or crosses over.'[106] In *To the Lighthouse* we witness a rhizomatic transformation of the tree itself, the becoming-cosmic of the tree: 'It was windy, so that the leaves now and then brushed open a star, and the stars themselves seemed to be shaking and darting light and trying to flash out between the edges of the leaves' (*TL* 130). In contrast to the ending of the previous section of the novel where Mrs Ramsay seems to abide by an arborescent point-system of time and memory when she comments, following her dinner, that 'it had become, she knew, giving one last look at it over her shoulder, already the past' (*TL* 128), now her rhizomatic becoming refuses a settling into melancholic nostalgia, instead transforming into something affirmative:

> They would, she thought, going on again, however long they lived, come back to this night; this moon; this wind; this house; and her too [. . .] wound about in their hearts, however long they lived she would be woven; and this, and this, and this, she thought, going upstairs, laughing, but affectionately, at the sofa on the landing (her mother's) at the rocking chair (her father's) at the map of the Hebrides. All that would be revived again in the lives of Paul and Minta. (*TL* 130)

As Mrs Ramsay becomes entangled with her surroundings, there is a diffusion of subject, object and time, and a rhizomatic movement prevails in which 'the line frees itself from the point, and renders points indiscernible'[107] and which emphasises the conjunction 'and . . . and . . . and'[108] – 'and this, and this, and this', as Woolf writes in the above passage. This rhizomatic movement brings forth 'that community of feeling with other people which emotion gives as if the walls of partition had become so thin that practically (the feeling was one of relief and happiness) it was all one stream, and chairs, tables, maps, were theirs, it did not matter whose' (*TL* 131).

While Mrs Ramsay's evasion of arborescent thinking in this moment is fleeting, it becomes apparent that some change has endured. For example, even when she is seduced again by the idea of marriage – 'How extraordinarily lucky Minta is! She is marrying a man who has a gold watch in a wash-leather bag!' (*TL* 134) – there is a hint of self-mocking as she is 'tickled by the absurdity of her thought' (*TL* 135). Moreover, it initially appears that Mr Ramsay brings his wife back to arborescence with his presence in the same vein in which he earlier appears to stifle Lily's creativity: 'she grew still like a tree which has been tossing and quivering and now, when the breeze falls, settles, leaf by leaf, into quiet' (*TL* 136). But to Mrs Ramsay this stillness appears to have been reimagined, somehow liberated, perhaps becoming what Deleuze and Guattari refer to as 'motionless voyage'[109] where the question of beginning or ending is superfluous, where we 'voyage in place: that is the name of all intensities [. . .] To think is to voyage.'[110] In her motionless voyage Mrs Ramsay decides that 'it didn't matter, any of it, she thought. A great man, a great book, fame – who could tell?' (*TL* 136) In grasping at something beyond the confines of her familial relationship with her husband, 'dismissing all this', Mrs Ramsay affirms 'there is something I want – something I have come to get' (*TL* 136). As she murmurs of 'trees and changing leaves' from Charles Elton's 'Luriana Lurilee', the description of her then reading lines from William Browne's 'The Siren's Song' – in the book she finds on the table – is a rhizomatic one, and one which signals the becoming-rhizome of the tree itself: 'zigzagging this way and that, from one line to another as from one branch to another' (*TL* 137).[111]

The sound of Mr Ramsay then 'slapping his thighs' would ordinarily signal another interruption and overcoding of the arborescent, but instead sees him swept up in a rhizomatic entanglement: 'Their eyes met for a second; but they did not want to speak to each other. They had nothing to say, but something seemed, nevertheless, to go from him to her [. . .] now, he felt, it didn't matter a damn who reached Z (if thought ran from an alphabet from A to Z). Somebody would reach it – if not he, then another' (*TL* 137–8). This 'if not he, then another' echoes the 'it did not matter whose' from Mrs Ramsay's earlier 'stream'. In addition, the sex-neutral terms the narrator employs here ('somebody', 'another') are important, and the parenthetical use of the second conditional – a tense used for improbable events – indicates a doubting of the arborescent linearity through which he had previously thought of his philosophical endeavours. Again temporarily escaping his familial role, Mr Ramsay reads Walter Scott writing about 'these fishermen, the poor old crazed creature in Mucklebackit's cottage made him feel so vigorous, so relieved of something that he felt roused and triumphant and could not choke back his tears' (*TL* 138). In the mocking tone that follows as he 'forgot himself completely (but not one or two reflections about morality and French novels and English words and Scott's hands being tied but his view perhaps being as true as any other view)', it seems as though this time Mr Ramsay is also in on the joke, which adds to the sense in which the arborescent Mr Ramsay who took himself and his philosophy so seriously is beginning to be uprooted. Feeling 'more secure' in his less rooted state of mind, he 'could not remember the whole shape of the thing'. In what could almost be a direct response to Mrs Ramsay's earlier depiction of her judges, Mr Ramsay realises he must 'keep his judgement in suspense' (*TL* 138). He now resists the temptation to demand sympathy from his wife: 'One ought not to complain, thought

Mr Ramsay, trying to stifle his desire to complain to his wife that young men did not admire him. But he was determined; he would not bother her again' (*TL* 139). Whilst it is important to remember that Woolf does not present us with a utopian vision here – after all, we do still see Mr Ramsay interrupting Mrs Ramsay (*TL* 134) and patronising her when she is reading (*TL* 140) – the fact Mr Ramsay is capable of being swept up (even if momentarily) in this nonarborescent becoming would suggest that the particular form of sexual difference at play in the novel looks further than the male/female binary and towards a politics of inclusion.

As difficult as it may be to let go of old traditions – and sections of 'Time Passes' are certainly an elegy of and for that – the vision Woolf presents us with as the novel continues is one of molecular connections rather than molar categorisations: 'there was scarcely anything left of body or mind by which one could say "This is he" or "This is she"' (*TL* 144). If, as Deleuze and Guattari suggest, 'the tree has implanted itself in our bodies, rigidifying and stratifying even the sexes',[112] then the 'wind and destruction' of 'Time Passes' is therefore necessary to triumph over arborescence. In other words, to bend a tree requires a storm: 'the trees plunge and bend and their leaves fly helter skelter until the lawn is plastered with them and they lie packed in gutters and choke rain pipes and scatter damp paths' (*TL* 146). Crucially, it is here that the focus turns from the plunging and bending trees to the grass lawn on which part of 'The Lighthouse' section of the novel will be set. Amongst the death and ruin of 'Time Passes', this lawn becomes a site of the regeneration of art when Mrs McNab is clearing out the house and realises that the 'mouldy' books have 'to be laid out on the grass in the sun' (*TL* 154).

In 'The Lighthouse' section, the fact that the final lines of both the painting and Woolf's novel occur while Lily is sitting on this lawn is significant in itself as an example of reclaiming the grass and rejecting the arborescent. That Lily shares this lawn with Mr Carmichael, however, points to Woolf's grass as an inclusive space which welcomes an inclusive politics irreducible to dualistic antagonisms between men and women. Silent for almost all of the novel, Mr Carmichael does not adopt the role of the dominating male – to borrow Goldman's description, he 'does not threaten, but seems, muse-like, to assist Lily's progress'.[113] Indeed he shares a thought-connection with Lily: 'A curious notion came to her that he did after all hear the things she could not say' (*TL* 203); he 'seemed (though they had not said a word all this time) to share her thoughts' (*TL* 220). Rather than being a 'blank or absence in the text', as Minow-Pinkney claims,[114] we might say that he partakes with Lily in their becoming-grass together, where sitting on the lawn is 'sitting on the world', a world envisaged beyond arborescent thought and patriarchal exclusion: 'The lawn was the world; they were up here together, on this exalted station' (*TL* 220). Have they achieved the kind of imperceptible, impersonal connection that Deleuze and Guattari claim makes one 'like grass: one has made the world, everybody/everything into a becoming' (*TL* 309)? *To the Lighthouse* would therefore be refusing to steer clear of the grass just as the narrators (and readers) of *A Room of One's Own* are caught 'audaciously trespassing' (*RO* 7) on the turf that patriarchy had tried to keep exclusively for men. It would mean that both Lily and Mr Carmichael, in silent collaboration with each other and perhaps even with the Ramsays, are affirming: 'I refuse to allow you, Beadle though you are, to turn me off the grass'! (*RO* 98)

Mr Ramsay – Cam – James: smoothing the sea

In *A Thousand Plateaus*, Deleuze and Guattari argue that different molar and molecular, rigid and supple, movements are brought into play variously in what they term 'smooth' and 'striated' spaces, where the smooth is 'an intensive rather than extensive space [. . .] not of measures and properties' and the striated where 'one goes from one point to another' (*TL* 528):

> The smooth and the striated are distinguished first of all by an inverse relation between the point and the line (in the case of the striated, the line is between two points, while in the smooth, the point is between two lines); and second, by the nature of the line (smooth-directional, open intervals; dimensional-striated, closed intervals). Finally, there is a third difference, concerning the surface or space. In striated space, one closes off a surface and 'allocates' it according to determinate intervals, assigned breaks; in the smooth, one 'distributes' oneself in an open space, according to frequencies and in the course of one's crossings[.][115]

For Deleuze and Guattari it is the sea that provides the best illustration that the smooth and striated is no fixed opposition, but one that 'gives rise to far more difficult complications, alternations, and superpositions':[116]

> This is where the very special problem of the sea enters in. For the sea is a smooth space par excellence, and yet was the first to encounter the demands of increasingly strict striation [. . .] the striation of the sea was a result of navigation on the open water [. . .] *bearings*, obtained by a set of calculations based on exact observation of the stars and the sun; and *the map*, which intertwines meridians and parallels, longitudes and latitudes, plotting regions known and unknown onto a grid.[117]

The smooth space of the sea is therefore described as having always been there 'before longitude lines had been plotted', where 'there existed a complex and empirical nomadic system of navigation based on the wind and noise, the colours and sounds of the seas'.[118]

In *To the Lighthouse*, smooth and striated spaces are crossed when Mr Ramsay, Cam, and James attempt to row out to the lighthouse in the final part of Woolf's novel. At first it seems as though Mr Ramsay inhabits the sea as a striated space, or turns it into this with his presence, for example when he mocks Cam's ignorance of 'the points of the compass' (*TL* 190).[119] But it would be too simple to depict Mr Ramsay as holding a striated space whilst Cam and James participate in the smoothing of the sea. As Deleuze and Guattari again clarify, this time with the example of the land: 'As simple as this opposition is, it is not easy to place it. We cannot content ourselves with establishing an immediate opposition between the smooth ground of the nomadic animal raiser and the striated land of the sedentary cultivator.'[120] Mr Ramsay may be 'acting instantly his part' (*TL* 189) as sedentary regulator of the sea as well as 'sedentary cultivator' of the land in *To the Lighthouse*, but we cannot reduce him to pure striation. The possibility of a more subversive space occupied by Mr Ramsay is signalled by his becoming engaged with the smoothing of the sea. As Deleuze and Guattari repeatedly state, 'becoming' always happens 'through the middle',[121] and it is worth pausing at the moment in Woolf's novel when we are told that Mr Ramsay 'sat in the middle of the boat' which itself stops still in the 'middle of the bay' (*TL* 206). Abel views this motionless moment as the point where 'the Oedipal structure that dominates James' childhood in "The Window" is completed'. She suggests that 'in the motionless "middle of the bay" – which mirrors the empty middle of the text, in which Mrs Ramsay vanishes – James submits to his father's will and "cease[s] to think" about his mother'.[122] But rather than seeing this as a moment of Oedipal completion where James identifies with his father and becomes separated from his mother, it is partly Mr Ramsay's move away from his dominating role which means James can join him. Instead of representing a site where 'thoughts have ceased, their velocity is no more and they stagnate in familial tensions',[123] what we see is a molecular, 'motionless voyage' similar to Mrs Ramsay's in the previous section, where you 'keep moving even in place'.[124] What we see is, indeed, their shared becoming, for as Deleuze writes in his essay 'What Children Say', 'it is becoming that turns the most negligible of trajectories, or even a fixed mobility, into a voyage'.[125] It is whilst 'the boat made no motion at all' (*TL* 184) that Mr Ramsay is portrayed more affectionately by his children, albeit that their other view of him as 'tyrant' is never quite erased. This is Mr Ramsay's capacity to inhabit smooth as well as striated spaces. For example, whilst Cam continues to feel the pressure of her father's dominance, alongside this we also see her smoothing the way to pass 'a private token of the love she felt' for him: 'no one attracted her more; his hands were beautiful to her and his feet, and his voice, and his words, and his haste, and his temper, and his oddity, and his passion, and his saying straight out before every one, we perished, each alone, and his remoteness' (*TL* 191).

As they are stationed in the middle of the sea, even James realises that it is the system of patriarchy, and not specifically his father, that he detests: 'now, as he grew older, and sat staring at his father in an impotent rage, it was not him, that old man reading, whom he wanted to kill, but it was the thing that descended on him – without his knowing it perhaps' (*TL* 209). Could this be James' becoming-minoritarian or even his becoming-woman?: 'he would track down and stamp out – tyranny, despotism, he called it – making people do what they did not want to do, cutting off their right to speak' (*TL* 209). Importantly, it is at this moment that James goes on to think about the multiple potential actions of his father, showing a sensitivity to molecular creativity rather than molar fixity. Mr Ramsay becomes filled with the subversive potential of supple movement rather than rooted to his more despotic utterances such as 'Come to the lighthouse. Do this. Fetch me that' (*TL* 209):

> then next moment, there he sat reading his book; and he might look up – one never knew – quite reasonably. He might talk to the Macalisters. He might be pressing a sovereign into some frozen old woman's hand in the street, James thought; he might be shouting out at some fisherman's sports; he might be waving his arms in the air with excitement. Or he might sit at the head of the table dead silent from one end of the dinner to the other. Yes, thought James, while the boat slapped and dawdled there in the hot sun; there was a waste of snow and rock very lonely and austere; and there he had come to feel, quite often lately, when his father said something which surprised the others, were two pairs of footprints only; his own and his father's. They alone knew each other. (*TL* 209–10)

'What then was this terror, this hatred?' James' conclusion appears to associate his father with the childhood recollection of 'a wagon crush[ing] ignorantly and innocently, someone's foot'. But if Mr Ramsay is here becoming-wheel, it is important to note that 'the wheel was innocent' (*TL* 210). As James tries to locate in his memory the episode of the wagon and the wheel, he recalls the enunciation: '"It will rain," he remembered his father saying. "You won't be able to go to the Lighthouse"' (*TL* 211). If the wheel is not in full control of the wagon, then the voicing of this utterance, the narrative seems to imply, cannot be forever rooted to, and held against, his father.

As their boat starts to move again, Mr Ramsay in this middle space raises his hand and lowers it 'as if he were conducting some secret symphony' (*TL* 213) – recalling James' 'secret language' (*TL* 5) and Mrs Ramsay's 'secret chambers' (*TL* 60) – in contrast to the more rigid linearity of his other preoccupation with walking 'up and down' (*TL* 18, 140, 168). Later, as they reach the lighthouse, the expectations of Mr Ramsay from Cam and James, and from the reader, are confounded when, instead of declaring once again in his self-indulgent tone 'But I beneath a rougher sea', he finally praises James: '"Well done!" James had steered them like a born sailor' (*TL* 234). Immediately following this, James' reaction is revealed through Cam's thoughts, and the supple movements of tri-s are evident once again through the narrative's shifting (free) indirect discourse,[126] creating what Deleuze often refers to as a 'collective assemblage of enunciation',[127] signalling a connection and collaboration between Cam and James, female and male:

> she knew that this is what James had been wanting, and she knew that now he had got it he was so pleased that he would not look at her or at his father or at any one [. . .] He was so pleased that he was not going to let anybody take a grain of his pleasure. His father had praised him. They must think that he was perfectly indifferent. But you've got it now, Cam thought. (*TL* 234–5)

Mr Ramsay is crucial to this collaboration, and plays his own part in resisting Cam and James' instinct to offer him the chance to reassert his patriarchal rule. Both Cam and James have the urge to ask him 'What do you want?' and they are poised to give him whatever is required. Yet, as with his earlier decision not to demand sympathy from Mrs Ramsay, 'he did not ask them anything'. Patriarchal demands are replaced by potentialities: 'he might be thinking, We perished, each alone, or he might be thinking, I have reached it. I have found it, but he said nothing' (*TL* 236).

Lily – Canvas – Line: becoming paint

Between Lily, her canvas and her final brushstroke, the ending of *To the Lighthouse* is not so much a celebration of the individual achievement of the female artist as it is a collective creation beyond molar divisions. It is the moment in the text when Woolf's theorising of sexual difference is located in the materiality of paint and canvas; it is the becoming-paint of sexual difference, the shaping of molecular intensities rather than molar forms, the latter of which, we know from early on in *To the Lighthouse*, Lily does not attempt to capture. Her first painting, recalling the 'secret' molecular world of James, Mrs Ramsay, and Mr Ramsay, is 'the residue of her thirty-three years, the deposit of each day's living, mixed with something more secret than she had ever spoken or shown in the course of all these days' (*TL* 61). Certainly not myopic, Lily has an ability to keep everything in view at once, the smallest material detail and her larger environs: 'Even when she looked at the mass, at the line, at the colour, at Mrs Ramsay sitting in the window with James, she kept a feeler on her surroundings' (*TL* 22). From its very inception, then, Lily's painting is much more than an attempt to present an image of Mrs Ramsay and James on a blank canvas. Indeed, as Deleuze argues in *Francis Bacon: The Logic of Sensation* (1981),

> it is a mistake to think that the painter works on a white surface [. . .] If the painter were before a white surface, he – or she – could reproduce on it an external object functioning as a model. But such is not the case. The painter has many things in his head, or around him, or in his studio. Now everything he has in his head or around him is already in the canvas, more or less virtually, more or less actually, before he begins his work. [. . .] He does not paint in order to reproduce on the canvas an object functioning as a model; he paints on images that are already there[.][128]

As a result, Deleuze suggests that it is important to 'define [. . .] all these "givens" that are on the canvas before the painter's work begins, and determine, among these givens, which are an obstacle, which are a help'.[129] Entangled in her surroundings, I want to consider the role of Mr Ramsay and the other men in *To the Lighthouse* as a part of Lily's painting, where at the beginning they are seen to impede Lily's creativity, to be an obstacle on the canvas, but where they collaborate more and more throughout the novel.

Like the inclusive sexual politics in *To the Lighthouse* modelled on the rhizomatic grass, Lily's painting, completed sitting on the grass lawn, seems to anticipate the affirmation in *A Room of One's Own* that a writer's pages should be filled with a 'sexual quality' that is 'unconscious of itself' (*RO* 121): 'subduing all her impressions as a woman to something much more general; becoming once more under the power of that vision which she had seen clearly once and must now grope for among hedges and houses and mothers and children – her picture' (*TL* 62). As the picture is dissociated from Lily's own subjectivity – 'it had been seen; it had been taken from her' – we learn that by observing the painting William Bankes 'had shared with her something profoundly intimate'

(*TL* 63). Crucially, Lily does not credit his sex for this intimacy, nor even him as a separated and determined subject: 'thanking Mr Ramsay for it and Mrs Ramsay for it and the hour and the place, crediting the world with a power which she had not suspected, that one could walk away down that long gallery not alone any more but arm-in-arm with somebody' (*TL* 63). As if to emphasise the connection to her painting, even her paint-box is entangled in this 'most exhilarating moment' as we are told that 'she nicked the catch of her paint-box to, more firmly than was necessary, and the nick seemed to surround in a circle for ever the paint-box, the lawn, Mr Bankes, and that wild villain, Cam, dashing past' (*TL* 63). It is important, too, to recognise Mr Ramsay as a part of the becoming-paint of *To the Lighthouse*. In 'The Lighthouse' section of the novel, Lily's vision seems to be initially blocked by Mr Ramsay and his demands, where 'he permeated, he prevailed, he imposed himself. He changed everything. She could not see the colour, she could not see the lines [. . .] That man, she thought, her anger rising in her, never gave; that man took' (*TL* 169–70). For good or for ill, however, we cannot overlook the fact that 'he permeated' and 'changed everything'; any vision we attribute to Lily should not therefore be seen as a complete escape from, or erasure of, Mr Ramsay. That is, Lily's ability to continue with her painting is not achieved by an outright rejection of Mr Ramsay or the men in the novel; there must be some collaboration between them despite their differences because opposition is an inadequate design: 'For whatever reason she could not achieve that razor edge of balance between two opposite forces; Mr Ramsay and the picture; which was necessary. There was something perhaps wrong with the design? Was it, she wondered, that the line of the wall wanted breaking, was it that the mass of the trees was too heavy?' (*TL* 219)

The place of men in Lily's art is noted by Goldman when she argues that 'Lily is no longer painting in the same social and political space [. . .] her picture must come, not from opposition to Ramsay, but from her new sense of collectivity.'[130] As well as her connection with Mr Carmichael on the lawn, there are clear instances elsewhere in the text where Lily connects with men. There is the revelation, for example, that 'one could talk of painting then seriously to a man. Indeed, his friendship had been one of the pleasures of her life. She had loved William Bankes' (*TL* 200). This world that 'seemed to dazzle him' is also a world in which, again recalling my discussion above, the tree is not given precedence, but is just another part of their surroundings: 'they strolled through the courtyards, and admired, summer after summer, the proportions of the flowers [. . .] as they walked, and he would stop to look at a tree, or the view over the lake, and admire a child (it was his great grief – he had no daughter)' (*TL* 201). Domesticated roles are not fixed to any stereotypes: 'he must buy a new carpet for the staircase. Perhaps she would go with him to buy a new carpet for the staircase' (*TL* 201). Lily and William then share their androgynous gaze towards Mrs Ramsay as '[Lily] saw, through William's eyes, the shape of a woman' (*TL* 201). But whilst Goldman concludes that for Lily 'it is a social, multi-subjective view of Mrs Ramsay that she comes to desire', it is not, ultimately, a view that goes beyond the sexed binary: Lily's painting shows Mrs Ramsay as 'the feminine object of the feminine gaze', and her final line, no longer a tree as in her first painting, 'suggests the feminine reclamation of the first person'.[131]

There is certainly an element of this in Lily's final line, but taking into account the rhizomatic connections which involve many characters, male and female, in this novel, I would agree with Beatrice Monaco's claim in *Machinic Modernism* that Lily's painting expresses 'the liberation of the psyche from social and sexual limitations' of a binary nature,[132] and would argue that the 'lines running up and across' suggests the rhizomatic aesthetic, and politics, of the painting – that there is the impossibility of determining the precise angle of the final 'line there, in the centre' (*TL* 237). We are not only left with a line that rejects arborescence, but this line could, conceivably, reach anywhere on the canvas; it takes on a conceptual dimension, resisting what Deleuze and Guattari call the 'submission of the line to the point',[133] at the same time as it exemplifies the kind of modernist brushstroke that Deleuze and Guattari claim is 'without origin', a line that

> begins off the painting, which only holds it by the middle [. . .] it is without localizable connection, because it has lost not only its representative function but any function of outlining a form of any kind [. . .] the line has become abstract, truly abstract and mutant [. . .] The line is between points, in their midst, and no longer goes from one point to another. It does not outline a shape.[134]

Lily's line also coincides with the uncertainty that surrounds the lighthouse at the end of the novel, where this previously monolithic object 'had become almost invisible, had melted away into a blue haze' (*TL* 236); the becoming-paint of *To the Lighthouse*, which is the becoming-imperceptible of the lighthouse.

Lily's 'vision' (*TL* 137) at the end of the novel would therefore paint her as one 'of those with long-distance vision, the far-seers, with all their ambiguities [. . .] They see a whole microsegmentarity, details of details [. . .] tiny movements that have not reached the edge, lines or vibrations that start to form long before there are outlined shapes [. . .] A whole rhizome.'[135] As with the final brushstroke of the painting, this far-sightedness is evident in the use of the present perfect in the final sentence of the novel: 'I have had my vision' (*TL* 137). A tense ambiguous about its place in time, we do not know whether Lily is referring to the very recent past as she finished her painting or indeed to the decade before or before that still; it is in all these potentialities that her vision is perfectly present.

Notes

1. For a thorough discussion of these various links see the special issue of *Women's Studies* (1974).
2. Woolf refers here to Coleridge's statement that 'a great mind must be androgynous' in *The Table Talk and Omniana of Samuel Taylor Coleridge* (1918) which she first wrote about in a review for the TLS in 1918, entitled 'Coleridge as Critic' (*E2* 221–5).
3. Bowlby, *Feminist Destinations*, p. 39.
4. Goldman, *The Cambridge Introduction*, p. 100; Hargreaves, 'Virginia Woolf', p. 52.
5. Bowlby, *Feminist Destinations*, p. 35.
6. Heilbrun, *Toward a Recognition*; Bazin, *Virginia Woolf*.
7. Secor, 'Androgyny', p. 162.
8. Harris, 'Androgyny', p. 174.
9. Ibid., p. 175. Whilst sharing some of these concerns and claiming that Woolf's androgyny is 'an ambivalent and limited concept', Marilyn Farwell argues that Woolf also provides us with 'the tools to go beyond that'. See Farwell, 'Virginia Woolf and Androgyny', p. 451.
10. Showalter, *A Literature*, p. 264. In this respect Showalter precedes critics such as Alex Zwerdling who see Woolf as compromising her artistic integrity to appease men in a short-term strategy of conciliation in order to achieve political goals and Jane Marcus who holds Woolf up as a 'guerrilla fighter in a Victorian skirt'. See Zwerdling, *Virginia Woolf*, p. 259, and Marcus, 'Thinking Back', pp. 1–30.
11. Jacobus, 'The Difference of View', p. 20.
12. Minow-Pinkney, *Virginia Woolf*, p. 9.
13. Caughie, *Virginia Woolf and Postmodernism*, p. 82, p. 80.
14. Showalter, *A Literature*, p. 288.
15. Moi, *Sexual/Textual*, p. 16.
16. Kristeva, 'Women's Time', p. 875.
17. Ibid., pp. 864–5.
18. Moi, '"I Am Not a Feminist, But ..."', p. 1735.
19. Helt, 'Passionate Debates', p. 132; p. 151.
20. I focus primarily, although not uncritically, on 'sexual difference' rather than 'gender' in this chapter, following the preferred term used by materialist feminists such as Braidotti and Grosz, who are interested in the epistemological and ontological workings of sexual differences that do not pertain to the separation of essentialist/constructivist, material/

discursive, sex/gender. In addition, in the other texts I focus on in this chapter, Deleuze and Woolf discuss 'sex' and not 'gender'.
21. By bringing androgyny into the context of our own contemporary debates around sexual difference I am answering Bazin and Freeman's call to 'expand it, alter it, and, above all, render it more concrete by defining it in terms of our own historical situation [. . .] we must go beyond past definitions of androgyny'. Bazin and Freeman, 'The Androgynous Vision', p. 185.
22. Braidotti, *Transpositions*, p. 49.
23. Braidotti, *Nomadic Subjects*, p. 153.
24. Ibid.
25. Braidotti, *Transpositions*, p. 185.
26. Braidotti, *Nomadic Subjects*, p. 163.
27. Ibid., p. 168.
28. Ibid., p. 163.
29. Ibid., p. 172.
30. Braidotti, *Transpositions*, p. 4.
31. Braidotti, *Nomadic Subjects*, 2nd edn, p. 151. Braidotti notes that this model is not intended to provide 'dialectically ordained phases' or 'categorical distinction[s]', though she maintains the urgency of viewing them 'from the perspective of sexual difference'. Braidotti, *Nomadic Subjects*, p. 158
32. Braidotti, *Nomadic Subjects*, pp. 158–65.
33. Ibid., p. 160.
34. Ibid., p. 165.
35. Braidotti, *Metamorphoses*, p. 39.
36. See Braidotti, *Metamorphoses*, p. 1; Braidotti, *Transpositions*, pp. 199–200; Braidotti, *Nomadic Subjects*, 2nd edn, p. 21.
37. Braidotti, *Nomadic Subjects*, p. 36.
38. In contrast, Jane Marcus has strongly argued that anger is 'a primary source of creative energy' for female writers: 'Rage and savage indignation sear the hearts of female poets and female critics.' See 'Art and Anger', pp. 94–5. Brenda Silver also comments that anger is 'the most compelling source of our [feminism's] strength'. See 'The Authority of Anger', pp. 340–70. Lili Hseih has more recently offered a nuanced contribution to the debate on Woolf and anger where she argues the political merits of indifference in *Three Guineas*. See 'The Other Side', pp. 20–54.
39. Kamuf, 'Penelope at Work', pp. 16–17.
40. Braidotti, *Nomadic Subjects*, p. 166.
41. Goldman, *Feminist Aesthetics*, p. 17.
42. Deleuze and Guattari, *A Thousand Plateaus*, p. 152.
43. Butler, *Undoing Gender*, p. 196.
44. Ibid., p. 193.
45. Ibid., p. 186.
46. Braidotti, *Transpositions*, p. 185. Braidotti's problems with the term 'gender' range from what she sees as its politically unfocused project, its Anglo-centric roots, and its academic institutionalisation. See Braidotti, *Nomadic Subjects*, 2nd edn, pp. 141–50.
47. Braidotti and Butler, 'Feminism', pp. 43–4.

48. Butler, *Undoing Gender*, p. 196.
49. Butler admits plainly in *Undoing Gender* that she is 'not a very good materialist. Every time I try to write about the body, the writing ends up beings about language' (198).
50. Deleuze and Guattari, *Kafka*, p. 16.
51. Ibid., p. 17.
52. Ibid.
53. Deleuze and Guattari, *A Thousand Plateaus*, p. 304.
54. Deleuze and Parnet, *Dialogues*, p. 32. This text translates Deleuze's concept as 'woman-becoming' rather than the more common translation of 'becoming-woman'. For consistency, I have changed all citations to 'becoming-woman'.
55. Deleuze and Guattari, *A Thousand Plateaus*, p. 304.
56. Ibid., p. 117.
57. Ibid., p. 235.
58. Some critics have linked this quotation to Edward Carpenter's notion of a 'third-sex' in *The Indeterminate Sex* (1912). For a summary see Hargreaves, 'Virginia Woolf', pp. 10–20.
59. Driscoll, 'The Woman in Process', p. 80. Drawing links between Kristeva's 'subject in process', Braidotti's 'nomadic subject', and Deleuze's becoming, Driscoll places Woolf firmly on the side of Deleuze: 'Woolf's style is not amorphous and fluid, after the style of Kristeva's maternalising vision of the postmodern, nor simply an internalised contradiction of identification after Braidotti's postmodern woman.'
60. Howie, 'Becoming-Woman', p. 103.
61. Braidotti, *Nomadic Subjects*, 2nd edn, p. 251.
62. Ibid., p. 253.
63. Braidotti, *Nomadic Subjects*, p. 78.
64. Colebrook, 'Introduction', p. 10. For a thorough and balanced discussion of both the limitations and subversive potential of Deleuze's 'becoming-woman' for feminism, see Grosz, *Volatile Bodies*, pp. 160–83.
65. Jardine, 'Woman in Limbo', p. 53.
66. Deleuze and Guattari, *A Thousand Plateaus*, p. 320.
67. Ibid., p. 304.
68. Grosz, *Becoming Undone*, p. 168.
69. Ibid., p. 168.
70. Colebrook, 'How Queer', p. 29
71. Helt, 'Passionate Debates', p. 132.
72. Spivak, 'Unmaking', p. 42.
73. Heilbrun, *Toward a Recognition*, p. 156.
74. Grosz, *Volatile Bodies*, p. 182.
75. Deleuze and Guattari, *A Thousand Plateaus*, p. 305.
76. Deleuze and Guattari, *Kafka*, p. 56.
77. Ibid., p. 53
78. Deleuze and Guattari, *Anti-Oedipus*, p. 335
79. Ibid., p. 15.
80. Deleuze, *Negotiations*, pp. 17–18.
81. Deleuze and Guattari, *Anti-Oedipus*, p. 385.
82. Smith, 'The Inverse Side', pp. 645–6.

83. Grosz, *Becoming Undone*, p. 54.
84. Deleuze and Guattari, *A Thousand Plateaus*, p. 36.
85. Ibid., p. 221.
86. Abel, *Virginia Woolf*, p. 50. For a recent survey of psychoanalytic readings of Woolf's work, see Minow-Pinkney, 'Psychoanalytic Approaches'. See also Minow-Pinkney, *Virginia Woolf*, p. 87.
87. Marcus, *Virginia Woolf*, p. 114.
88. Bowlby, *Feminist Destinations*, p. 59.
89. See for example Woolf's 1920 essay 'Freudian Fiction' (*E2* 195–7).
90. Jouve, 'Virginia Woolf and Psychoanalysis', p. 256.
91. Driscoll, 'The Woman in Process', p. 65.
92. Deleuze and Guattari, *A Thousand Plateaus*, p. 15.
93. Deleuze and Guattari, *Kafka*, p. 79.
94. Ibid., p. 54.
95. For an excellent recent survey of the changing critical responses to Mrs Ramsay, see Silver, 'Editing Mrs. Ramsay', pp. 1–10.
96. Deleuze and Guattari, *A Thousand Plateaus*, p. 45.
97. Goldman, *Feminist Aesthetics*, p. 173.
98. Deleuze and Guattari, *Anti-Oedipus*, p. 391.
99. For a discussion of some examples of trees in philosophy, and an alternative reading of trees in Woolf's writing from the one I provide in this section, see Mao, *Solid Objects*, pp. 43–58. In addition to philosophy, Goldman reminds us that the tree is also a symbol of patriarchal patronage in pastoral poetry. See Goldman, *Feminist Aesthetics*, p. 170.
100. Deleuze and Parnet, *Dialogues*, p. 19.
101. Ibid., p. 30.
102. Deleuze and Guattari, *A Thousand Plateaus*, p. 27.
103. Deleuze and Parnet, *Dialogues*, p. 19.
104. Allen, *Virginia Woolf*, p. 66.
105. Ibid., p. 70.
106. Deleuze and Guattari, *A Thousand Plateaus*, p. 531.
107. Ibid., p. 324. Jean Love, in a different context, has argued that we find 'subject-object diffusion' in Woolf's writing, where 'persons do not have fixed and consistent boundaries [. . .] their minds and consciousness and, at times, even themselves as entire beings are confluent with the external world'. Love, *Worlds*, p. 35. Love also discusses space-diffusion, time-diffusion, and object-diffusion (35–62).
108. Deleuze and Guattari, *A Thousand Plateaus*, p. 27.
109. Ibid., p. 177.
110. Ibid., p. 532.
111. In his eight-hour interview with Claire Parnet, Deleuze ends with a discussion of the movement of a 'zigzag' which, he says, 'is perhaps the elementary movement, perhaps the movement that presided at the creation of the world'. See Deleuze and Parnet, *From A to Z*.
112. Deleuze and Guattari, *A Thousand Plateaus*, p. 20.
113. Goldman, *Feminist Aesthetics*, p. 182.
114. Minow-Pinkney, *Virginia Woolf*, p. 115.
115. Deleuze and Guattari, *A Thousand Plateaus*, p. 530.
116. Ibid., p. 531.

117. Ibid., p. 529.
118. Ibid.
119. Landefeld, 'Becoming Light', p. 61.
120. Deleuze and Guttari, *A Thousand Plateaus*, pp. 530–1.
121. Ibid., p. 323.
122. Abel, *Virginia Woolf*, p. 46. See also Minow-Pinkney, *Virginia Woolf*, p. 112.
123. Landefeld, 'Becoming Light', p. 61.
124. Deleuze and Guattari, *A Thousand Plateaus*, p. 177.
125. Deleuze, *Critical and Clinical*, p. 65.
126. Michael Whitworth notes that free indirect discourse allows Woolf to explore 'several distinct consciousnesses' and also 'consciousnesses that were several but indistinct, a "group consciousness"'. Whitworth, *Authors in Context*, p. 95. Though Woolf is so often conflated with 'stream-of-consciousness' writing, Whitworth goes on to outline some key differences between the style in Joyce's *Ulysses* and Woolf's writing. For an early discussion of 'stream of consciousness' and Woolf's novels see Naremore, *The World*, pp. 60–76. See also Doyle, '"These Emotions"'. Influenced by French phenomenologist Maurice Merleau-Ponty, Doyle proposes 'intercorporeal narrative' as a description of Woolf's narrative technique in *To The Lighthouse*. For an insightful discussion of Woolf's free indirect discourse in relation to the public and private realms see Snaith, *Virginia Woolf*, pp. 63–87. Snaith offers the term 'communal free indirect discourse' as a way of understanding Woolf's use (74).
127. Deleuze and Guattari, *A Thousand Plateaus*, p. 93.
128. Deleuze, *Francis Bacon*, p. 61.
129. Ibid.
130. Goldman, *Feminist Aesthetics*, p. 182.
131. Ibid., p. 183; p. 185.
132. Monaco, *Machinic Modernism*, p. 51.
133. Deleuze and Guattari, *A Thousand Plateaus*, p. 323.
134. Ibid., p. 328. Deleuze and Guattari refer to Klee, Kandinsky, and Monet here.
135. Ibid., p. 222.

Chapter 3

Queering *Orlando* and Non/Human Desire

Vita was here; & when she went, I began to feel the quality of the evening – how it was spring coming: a silver light; mixing with the early lamps; the cabs all rushing through the streets; I had a tremendous sense of life beginning; mixed with that emotion, which is the essence of my feeling, but escapes description [. . .] I felt the spring beginning, & Vita's life so full & flush; & all the doors opening. (D3 287)

In *Transpositions*, Rosi Braidotti reads this diary entry by Virginia Woolf – dated 16th February 1930 – as evidence of the 'shimmering intensity' of her love affair with Vita Sackville-West, which had earlier famously inspired the mock-biography *Orlando*.[1] In her groundbreaking study *Vita and Virginia*, Suzanne Raitt uses similar language when describing how Woolf's letters to Sackville-West 'shimmer with the luminosity of shared sexual pleasure',[2] and she emphasises that from its inception Woolf's writing of *Orlando* was 'bound up with her desire for Sackville-West'.[3] Indeed, for some time it has been commonplace for critics to refer to the correspondences and entangled biographies of Woolf and Sackville-West in their readings of Woolf's text and this has helped to uncover a particularly lesbian thematic in the novel (importantly countering Quentin Bell, among others, in his wish to downplay this aspect of Woolf's life):[4] Raitt shows how 'explicit acknowledgement of sexual attraction was a part of their relationship, and a decisive factor in their experiences of one another', an experience as 'married lesbians';[5] Sherron Knopp sees *Orlando* as both 'a public proclamation' and 'a way to heighten intimacy' between Woolf and Sackville-West, 'not as a substitute for physical lovemaking but an extension of it';[6] and for Leslie Hankins *Orlando* 'crafts a lesbian moment for all readers – refreshingly rare in the climate of 1928 [. . .] a radical text that enables readers to experience panic-free lesbian desire [. . . Woolf] makes us all lesbians'.[7] Others such as Elizabeth Meese have been scathing about scholars who do not foreground the lesbian in Woolf's mock-biography, arguing that 'it matters when a critic avoids (a form of suppression) the word *lesbian*; as long as the word matters, makes a social, political, or artistic difference, it matters when *lesbian* is not spoken'.[8]

What is different about Braidotti's 'shimmering intensity', however, is that it moves beyond the limitations of strictly biographical and lesbian readings which often invest in a 'logic of identity' where, as Chris Coffman puts it, 'rhetorical multivalence' and 'polyvocal narrative' are reduced to 'an elaborate screen for lesbian desire'.[9] If *Orlando* is in part Woolf's attempt to answer the question she plainly asks in a 1926 diary entry when considering her feelings for Sackville-West, 'what is this "love"?' (*D3* 85), then Braidotti departs from lesbian approaches in that she uses the biographical evidence of their love affair not to emphasise the particular sexual preferences of either, nor to celebrate same-sex relationships or lesbian identities, but to spark an affirmative reconceptualisation of love and desire as *de*personalised and firmly 'disengaged from the political economy of exchanges regulated by phallocentrism'.[10] In *queering* Woolf's mock-biography, this chapter follows Braidotti in starting with the materials of (auto)biography precisely in order to move beyond a concern with pinning down the 'real' lives of Woolf and Sackville-West, or the importance of a specifically 'lesbian' identity.[11] Having discussed in the previous chapter how Woolf theorises the material entanglements of sexual difference, here I demonstrate – by forging 'queer affiliations'[12] between Woolf's novel and the theories of Braidotti and Deleuze and Guattari, among others – that in the relationship that most influenced *Orlando*'s composition (Vita and Virginia), as well as the relations formed within the text itself (between Orlando and his/her various lovers, but also Orlando and nonhuman objects and environments), we are presented with a 'becoming-queer'[13] of sexuality which does not settle into established, oppositional modes and models of identity and being, and is irreducible to the human subject. After all, whilst the 'biography' in Woolf's full title *Orlando: A Biography* has its etymological roots in the Greek 'bios' meaning one's qualified way of life (as distinct from 'zoē' meaning the simple fact of life shared by all the living, human and nonhuman),[14] the name of the person whose biography most inspired the text's composition, and to whom it was dedicated, Vita, comes from the Latin for 'life', which does not make such distinctions. It is precisely because Woolf's queering of desire engages with 'life so full & flush' that *Orlando* is all the more entangled in the material realities involved in a love story.

Accidental lovers

When considering the relationship between Sackville-West and Woolf, a crucial aspect for Braidotti is that the category 'same sex' does not sufficiently 'account for the complex and multiple affects, generated in the relation between two beings'.[15] As she has argued at length throughout her writings, any ethically and conceptually viable model of sexual difference, including the productive ways in which it impacts on the material world, has to take into account not only the nature of differences between men and women, but the differences that exist within the category 'women' as well as in each individual woman. Therefore,

> the fact that Virginia and Vita meet within this category of sexual 'sameness' encourages them to look beyond the delusional aspects of the identity ('woman'), which they are alleged to share. This proliferation of differences between women and within each one of them is evident in the outcomes and the products of their relationship, be it in the literature which Virginia and Vita produced, or in the many social, cultural and political projects they were engaged in. These included marriages, motherhood and child-rearing, political activism, socializing, campaigning, publishing and working as a publisher, gardening and the pursuit of friendships, of pleasures and of hard work.[16]

For Braidotti, Woolf's relationship with Vita Sackville-West brought about 'a heightening of sensorial perception, the flowing of deep-seated affinity, of immense compassion'; a process of becoming, in other words, which she claims 'goes beyond their psychological, amorous and sexual relationship'.[17] She presents a material-discursive theory of desire and creativity, where bodies and meanings co-evolve in entanglements which are not restricted to the coming together of two human subjects, and which do not privilege language or culture over materiality or nature. Braidotti claims that 'a polymorphous and highly sexual text such as *Orlando* is the perfect manifesto' for this variegated and productive sexuality.[18]

In Woolf's novel, Orlando's multitude of encounters over four centuries provide many well-known examples of the proliferation of differences between and within sexual categories, differences that complicate the notion of 'same-sex' desire. The stability of the male/female binary is, for example, continuously challenged by the narrator/biographer's reiteration that Orlando is only classified as male or female because this is what society – and language – expects. As is often noted by critics, when Orlando undergoes sexual metamorphosis there is no immediate feeling of essential difference in identity:

> Orlando looked himself up and down in a long looking-glass, without showing any signs of discomposure [. . .] The change of sex, though it altered their future, did nothing whatever to alter their identity [. . .] The change seemed to have been accomplished painlessly and completely and in such a way that Orlando herself showed no surprise at it. (O 87)

Before the reader's eyes Orlando has changed from a he to a she, a 'himself' to 'herself', yet we are reminded throughout that this classification is an arbitrary one and only 'for conventions sake' (O 87); after the sex-change, Orlando was still 'in a highly ambiguous condition' (O 108) where 'her sex was still in dispute' (O 153). Moreover, even when the narrator/biographer appears to offer a more stable definition of sexual difference, this very notion is subtly undermined:

> there is much to support the view that it is clothes that wear us and not we them [. . .] That is the view of some philosophers and wise ones, but on the whole, we incline to another. The difference between the sexes is, happily, one of great profundity. Clothes are a symbol of something hid deep beneath. It was a change in Orlando herself that dictated her choice of a woman's dress and of a woman's sex. (O 120–1)

Where the text appears to offer the possibility of essential sexual differences as an alternative to the philosophers' theory, it ironically reinforces their 'wise' argument. For if 'a change in Orlando herself' (Orlando as 'she') can prompt the choice of 'a woman's sex' (also Orlando as 'she') then exactly what type of change has occurred becomes unclear – the change is presented as 'she' becoming 'she', and therefore cannot be linked to a sexual metamorphosis within an oppositional binary framework. As Minow-Pinkney explains, this 'sentence becomes circular, its first and last phrases coinciding with each other. It is the word and fact of "change" itself that loses its obviousness.' Therefore, the 'vacillation from one sex to another' becomes a change between states which themselves are not fixed or clearly defined.[19] According to Christy Burns' Butlerian reading, it 'points only to the essential instability of essence, the reversibility inscribed within the "truth." What is essential here is to be *without* an essence.'[20] Thus when the courts later attempt to impose an official sex upon Orlando it only emphasises the absurdity of society's need to distinguish based on sexual difference; the question of 'truth' doesn't seem to come into it. Orlando's sex becomes what Maria DiBattista terms a 'legal fiction'.[21]

Rather than reinforcing sexuality as a highly personalised aspect of a fixed sexual identity, for Braidotti depersonalisation is key in order to keep multiple potentialities in view; a willingness for a positive kind of self-effacement that is not an escape from embodied, material reality but which, on the contrary, opens up space for various new encounters and entanglements. Beyond the sexual identities we usually think of as being involved in a love affair, the *intensity* of a 'love encounter' produces

> the enlargement of one's fields of perception and capacity to experience. In pleasure as in pain, in a secular, spiritual, erotic mode that combines at once elements from all these, the decentring and opening up of the individual ego coincides not only with communication with other fellow human beings, but also with a heightening of the intensity of such communication. This shows the advantages of a non-unitary vision of the subject. A depersonalisation of the self, in a gesture of everyday transcendence of the ego, is a connecting force, a binding force that links the self to larger internal and external relations. An isolated vision of the individual is of hindrance to such a process, as [...] Virginia Woolf knew all too well.[22]

Such a non-unitary vision of subjectivity is experienced, Braidotti claims, by Sackville-West in her reaction to reading *Orlando*. In her letters to Woolf, we can see that she embraces the character of Orlando not through passive self-reflection, but active and affirmative depersonalisation. Consider the following letter from 11th October 1928 when Sackville-West remarks: 'Darling, I don't know and scarcely even like to write so overwhelmed am I, how you could have hung so splendid a garment on so poor a peg. [...] Also, you have invented a new form of narcissism – I confess – I am in love with Orlando – this is a complication I had not foreseen.'[23] Whilst this might seem to strengthen Sackville-West's sense of self, Braidotti suggests that her reaction has 'nothing to do with narcissistic delight – it is actually a sort of yearning on Vita's part for potential that lies not so much in her, as in the encounter between herself and Virginia'.[24]

Approaching *Orlando* with this in mind is not to deny the biographical dimension to the novel, but to realise an 'apersonal' desire present in the text that 'does not coincide at all with the individual biographies of the protagonists' but 'actively reinvents them as they rewrite each other's lives, intervening energetically in its course'.[25] So when Braidotti claims that *Orlando* is 'one of the greatest love stories of all times'[26] there is an important difference from Nigel Nicolson's ubiquitously quoted assessment of it as the 'longest and most charming love letter in literature'.[27] The fictional 'story' goes beyond the biographical 'letter'; it is not simply that Orlando has become Vita, but that Vita becomes Orlando:

> Vita herself does justice to this process by accepting to become other than she is, engaging with great generosity with her own reflected image [...] she becomes a mere reader and not the main star of the process of

becoming-Orlando [. . .] she displays surprising skills of adaptation by letting her narcissism be gratified – 'I love myself as Orlando!' – but simultaneously blown to smithereens, not only in the sense of 'I will never have been as fascinating and complex as Orlando', but also 'Orlando is the literary creation of a woman who is much greater than I will ever be!'[28]

In other words, Sackville-West transforms negative into positive in an 'ethical moment' which rejects nihilism and an 'ascetic withdrawal from the world of negativity'. It is through 'shameful recognition of her failing' and 'destitution of the ego' that she charges the intensity that shapes their encounter.[29] Her reaction highlights the inadequacy of the relation, as it is conceived in psychoanalysis, between 'the empirical level (the real-life Vita) and its symbolic representation (the leading character in *Orlando*)' to account for the 'intense transformation that takes place around the field of forces that is activated by Virginia and Vita'.[30] The letters themselves are neither empirical biographical documents, nor symbolic fictional representations: 'The space of the letters is an in-between, a third party that does not fully coincide with either Virginia or Vita. It rather frames the space of their relationship. Read with Deleuze, it is a space of becoming.'[31]

The allusion to Deleuze in relation to Woolf is crucial, and Braidotti emphasises their connection and its influence on her thoughts on sexuality and desire in a 2006 interview with Rutvica Andrijasevic:

> I start from the idea that sexuality means relations, which are actualized in encounters. It's a matter of who, what, when, and where trigger the desire. This can be due to a thousand different modalities. Desire is not just about the choice of object, the sex or gender of the person involved. It has to do with the broader picture: the quality of the light at the moment of the meeting, the temperature of the air, and of course the hormonal level . . . What I am interested in talking about are the ways of destabilizing the categories of identity while regrounding them in a cartographic account of how actual instances of desire emerge. As I see it, they always emerge contextually, or territorially; they always emerge with a background; they always emerge rhizomatically across an infinite field of intensities of all kinds. Gilles Deleuze and Virginia Woolf write beautifully about this. For example, when Virginia Woolf writes about Vita Sackville-West, it's always about the organization of space around her incredibly attractive legs and the elongated shape of her aristocratic face. A loved face is a landscape of desire, so it is about your 'object' of desire, but fundamentally it's about something else – it is pure acceleration or speed.[32]

Braidotti's Deleuzian/Woolfian inspired theory is of desire as radically immanent, energised by a materialist 'polymorphous vitalism' that acts as 'a sort of geometry, a geology, and a meteorology of forces that gather round the actors (V & V), but do not fully coincide with them'.[33]

This 'polymorphous vitalism' offers the potential for a new queering of *Orlando* in that it espouses a sexuality and desire which departs from psychoanalytic models founded on lack, refuses to privilege language, is disentangled from identity politics and does not rely on a unified vision of the subject.

Braidotti herself does not much use the word *queer* in her work because of its association with a certain 'brand of identity politics',[34] but she does stress her openness to *queering* in the interview with Andrijasevic: 'It is absolutely true that my nomadic subject is very compatible with queering practices, so long as we agree on the terms and the structure of the exercise. Sexuality for me is not linguistically mediated, but rather an embodied practice of experimentation with multiple relations in an affirmative manner.'[35] Therefore, she adds, 'I would agree to talk about queer, if by queer we mean a verb, a process.'[36] What Claire Colebrook has recently termed 'queer vitalism', in an essay with the same title, may employ 'queer' as an adjective rather than a verb, but it might also have something to add to the Deleuzian/Woofian vitalism Braidotti describes. Queer vitalism involves the potential lines of flight from majoritarian politics towards a becoming-minoritarian, where part of this process is to 'approach the world as the unfolding of events' rather than see 'bodies in their general recognisable form, *as* this or that ongoing and unified entity'.[37] A queer/polymorphous, immanent vitalism lifts us out of a sexual politics which plays social constructivists off against biological determinists, where 'the relations between terms are neither exclusive (either male *or* female, either social/political *or* genetic, either real *or* constructed) nor transcendent (where such terms organise and differentiate life, and do so on the basis of some grounding value, whether that be genetics, reproduction, liberty or the human)'.[38] Queering vitalism is to acknowledge differences on a molar scale, but to avoid settling into identity groupings (whether constructed by social factors or biology) and instead 'signal the positive potentialities from which groups were formed: there could only be lesbian women because certain differences are possible (such as sexual difference, and difference in orientation), but that would then lead to further and further difference, not only to each individual but within each individual'.[39]

Throughout the remainder of this chapter my 'queering' is an attempt to find new patterns of desire in *Orlando* which include an array of non-human as well as human entanglements. By grounding my focus on non-human objects Orlando engages with – for example wedding rings and a motor-car – I hope to move towards the kind of 'post-anthropocentric theory of both desire and love' that Braidotti claims is required 'in order to do justice to the complexity of subjects of becoming': 'an intensive encounter that mobilizes the sheer quality of the light and the shape of the landscape [. . . includes] non-human cosmic elements in the creation of a space of becoming. This indicates that desire designs a whole territory and thus cannot be restricted to the mere human *persona* that enacts it.'[40] Challenging the anthropocentric and humanising impulses of much queer theory too,[41] this also involves the queering of 'queer' itself, a term that after all, Butler reminds us in *Bodies that Matter* (1993), is there precisely to be 'redeployed, twisted, queered'.[42] Indeed, as Eve Kosofsky Sedgwick recounts in *Tendencies* (1994), in its very etymology 'Queer is a continuing moment, movement, motive – recurrent, eddying, *troublant*. The word "queer" itself means across – it comes from the Indo-European root *–twerkw*, which also yields the german *quer* (transverse), Latin *torquere* (to twist), English *athwart*.'[43] *Queering* enacts a move from categorising noun to continuous, changing verb.[44]

As examples of this queering, Woolf and Sackville-West 'activate a process of becoming which goes beyond their psychological, amorous and sexual relationship. Something much more elemental, rawer, is at stake.'[45] 'Call it falling in love,' Braidotti writes, 'if you wish, but [. . .] if falling in love it is, it is disengaged from the human subject that is wrongly held responsible for the event.'[46] Woolf and Sackville-West may be entangled in a love story, but this story involves much more than the coming together of two individual women, for 'two is quite a crowd, when one is a multiple, complex and depersonalised entity to begin with'.[47] Whether we think of Orlando's relationships, or of Vita and Virginia, they are only 'accidental lovers'[48] involved in a materially embedded love story that is 'not entirely Virginia's or Vita's or my own, or yours [. . .] You can only share in the composition [. . .] in the company of others.'[49]

Queer/ring love

Whilst Woolf's relationship with Vita Sackville-West was the one that most influenced the composition of *Orlando*, on first reading Woolf's mock-biography one could argue that within the text itself, after Orlando's sex-change and various lovers, the love story ultimately becomes a conventional one, with the meeting of Orlando and Shelmerdine quickly resulting in marriage (and later a child). Indeed, this aspect of Woolf's mock-biography even irritated Sackville-West, despite the otherwise positive impact reading it had on her. In a letter to Harold Nicolson on 12th October 1928 she criticised Woolf for making Orlando 1) marry 2) have a child. Shelmerdine does not really contribute anything either to Orlando's character or to the problems of the story (except as a good joke at the expense of the Victorian passion for marriage) and as for the child it contributes less than nothing, but even strikes a rather false note. Marriage and motherhood would either modify or destroy Orlando, as a character: they do neither.[50]

Most critics are more sympathetic to Woolf's choice to marry Orlando and Shelmerdine, either playing on the humour that Sackville-West concedes and siding with Adam Parkes' view that Woolf 'mocks heterosexual romance' by making the marriage and childbirth 'relatively unremarkable features on the landscape of Orlando's journey through history',[51] or alternatively following Bowlby's suggestion that after exploring 'the interchangability in theory of masculine and feminine sexes' it might point 'to the actual dominance of the masculine and its construction of a femininity in or as its own image'.[52] But Orlando's marriage does not only serve as a mockery of heterosexual institutionalisation of love, or as a reminder of the very real psychological and material dominance of patriarchy after the theoretical playfulness of sex; rather, it is precisely and paradoxically through Orlando's marriage that Woolf points towards a subversion of heteronormative frameworks of sexuality. That is, this more conventional aspect of Woolf's text could actually be an equally crucial site of subversion as Orlando's sex-change and various lovers.

As a traditional symbol of heteronormative union, rings are central to *Orlando*'s queering of sexuality and desire in the context of engagement and marriage. This is evident when, following a 'repulsive' moment in which Orlando writes 'the most insipid verse she had ever read in her life', her body undergoes an 'extraordinary tingling and vibration' that reaches her 'toes' and 'marrow'. The description is more than suggestive of an erotic, polymorphous and vital experience, as we are told that 'she had the queerest sensations about her thigh bones. Her hairs seemed to erect themselves. Her arms sang and twanged'. But just when these vibrations appear to be reaching their climax, we learn that the queer sensation is located not so much in Orlando's physiology as in an external object: 'all this agitation seemed at length to concentrate in her hands; and then in one hand, and then in one finger of that hand, and then finally to contract itself so that it made a ring of quivering sensibility about the second finger of the left hand.' Finally it is revealed to be 'nothing but the vast solitary emerald which Queen Elizabeth had given her' (O 155–6). At first the 'second finger' with the ring on it is ambiguous, as it could indicate the middle finger (second finger after the thumb) or wedding finger (if counted from the other side),[53] but by the time Orlando questions 'was that not enough? [...] It was worth ten thousand pounds at least', the reader has been made aware that it is the former, and the wedding finger is ring-less:

> The vibration seemed, in the oddest way (but remember we are dealing with some of the darkest manifestations of the human soul) to say No, that is not enough; and, further, to assume a note of interrogation, as though it were asking, what did it mean, this hiatus, this strange oversight? till poor Orlando felt positively ashamed of the second finger of her left hand without in the least knowing why. (O 155)

The absence of a ring on her wedding finger is reinforced when Bartholomew, the housekeeper, appears and Orlando becomes conscious of something 'she had never noticed before – a thick ring of rather jaundiced yellow circling the third finger where her own was bare'. The importance given to this jaundiced ring is gently mocked as we witness Bartholomew's exaggerated reaction to Orlando's attempts to remove it:

> Bartholomew made as if she had been struck in the breast by a rogue. She started back a pace or two, clenched her hand and flung it away from her with a gesture that was noble in the extreme. 'No,' she said, with resolute dignity, her Ladyship might look if she pleased, but as for taking off her wedding ring, not the Archbishop nor the Pope nor Queen Victoria on her throne could force her to do that. Her Thomas had put it on her finger twenty-five years, six months, three weeks ago; she had slept in it; worked in it; washed in it; prayed in it; and proposed to be buried in it. In fact, Orlando understood her to say, but her voice was much broken with emotion, that it was by the gleam on her wedding ring that she would be assigned her station among the angels and its lustre would be tarnished for ever if she left it out of her keeping for a second.

Orlando is 'amazed' by the importance placed upon this ring in this Victorian era to the extent that 'it now seemed to her that the whole world was ringed with gold'. At dinner 'rings abounded', at church they 'were everywhere' (O 156) – in fact, rings abound so much in *Orlando* that in the book's title and the protagonist's name both begin and end with a ring-shaped 'O'.

To be sure, beauty is not the reason for the Victorian obsession with rings, but their symbolic attachment to marriage: 'thin, thick, plain, smooth, they glowed dully on every hand. Rings filled the jewellers' shops, not the flashing pastes and diamonds of Orlando's recollection, but simple bands without a stone in them.' Orlando also notices that these rings coincide with a more reserved public display of sexuality: meeting 'a boy trifling with a girl under a hawthorn hedge' has been replaced by couples who 'trudged and plodded in the middle of the road' (O 156) (by contrast we might wonder what exactly Orlando had been up to much earlier in the novel when alone he 'walked very quickly uphill through ferns and hawthorn bushes, startling deer and wild birds'!; [O 6]). Woolf clearly satirises this restrained behaviour of Victorian couples:

> Often it was not till the horses' noses were on them that they budged, and then, though they moved it was all in one piece, heavily, to the side of the road. Orlando could only suppose that some new discovery had been made about the race; that they were somehow stuck together, couple after couple, but who had made it, and when, she could not guess. It did not seem to be Nature. She looked at the doves and the rabbits and the elkhounds and she could not see that Nature had changed her ways or mended them, since the time of Elizabeth at least.

Such is the pervasive nature of this Victorian preoccupation with marriage and decency that Orlando comes to the swift conclusion that 'there was nothing for it but to buy one of those ugly bands and wear it like the rest' and then, following another failed attempt at writing, 'to yield completely and submissively to the spirit of the age, and take a husband'. Importantly, however, marriage is not held out as natural, and Orlando's decision to marry is itself 'against her natural temperament' (O 157–8).

One aspect that seems to concern Orlando in the above passages is the way in which marriage and the vibrancy of sexuality are conceived as mutually exclusive – this is reinforced both in the way that Orlando's experience of 'queerest sensations' is de-eroticised by the ring that reminds her of the one absent from her wedding finger, and also in the mocking of restrained public coupling at the expense of a quickie 'under a hawthorn hedge'. This concern is succinctly captured when Orlando recalls her previous desire for '"Life! A Lover!" not "Life! A Husband!"' Her pursuit of a lover led her to go 'to town and run about the world' but the 'antipathetic' nineteenth century replaces 'Lover' with 'Husband' and 'batters down' such desires. Her body is now far from vibrancy, 'dragged down by the weight of the crinoline which she had submissively adopted. It was heavier and more drab than any dress she had yet worn. None had ever so impeded her movements.' Where earlier Orlando experienced an 'extraordinary tingling and vibration' in her toes, marrow, and thigh bones, now her 'muscles had lost their pliancy' (O 158). But Orlando does not obey convention for long, as in one paragraph her feelings of loneliness and the need to find a husband to lean upon 'bore her down unescapably', and in the next her body is retuned to material vibrations and sensations: 'some strange ecstasy came over her. Some wild notion she had of following the birds to the rim of the world and flinging herself on the spongy turf.' Orlando now 'quickened her pace; she ran; she tripped; the tough heather roots flung her to the ground. Her ankle was broken. She could not rise' (O 160). Even though Orlando's movements once again appear to have been 'impeded' (O 158), her 'ecstasy' has not entirely disappeared:

> she lay content. The scent of the bog myrtle and meadow-sweet was in her nostrils. The rooks' hoarse laughter was in her ears. 'I have found my mate,' she murmured. 'It is the moor. I am nature's bride,' she whispered, giving herself in rapture to the cold embraces of the grass as she lay. (O 160–1)

As Orlando lies on the grass where her 'forehead will be cool always' and anticipates (erotic?) 'wild dreams' while 'slipping [the ring] from her finger', we seem to be witnessing an outright rejection of marriage. The fact this occurs on grass takes on added significance when we consider the belief that our earliest ancestors would literally 'tie the knot' whereby the man would tie cords of braided grass around the woman's wrists, ankles, and waist, which then became just the waist, and finally just the finger would be 'encircled with grass'.[54] Orlando's body is embedded, if not encircled, in grass in this moment of heightened sensation when she looks up at the clouds and sees 'camels' and 'mountains' and hears 'goat bells ringing'. But just as the vibrations that ran through her toes, marrow, and bones return now as 'the heart in the middle of the earth', the core of the material world, these turn out to be, of course, 'the trot of a horses hoofs' carrying Marmaduke Bonthrop Shelmerdine, Esquire, to whom Orlando becomes engaged 'a few minutes later' (O 162). It is here, then, at the very moment when the rejection of the desire for marriage appears to be most obvious that she decides that she will in fact get engaged.

The crucial point, and the reason this passage is in keeping with Woolf's disruption of sexual and gendered identities in *Orlando*, is that meeting and then marrying Shelmerdine allows Orlando to move beyond a concern with the opposition between 'Lover' and 'Husband', an opposition designed to uphold societal conventions with regard to sexuality. This is comically emphasised when we are told that Orlando did not actually learn of her new fiancé's name until the morning after their first night together 'as they sat at breakfast'. Orlando neither accepts the replacement of 'Husband' for 'Lover' nor rejects the idea of a husband entirely, refusing to uphold the opposition between the terms, and therefore refusing to submit to a dualistic conceptualisation of love that fully obeys the conventions of the time. It may initially seem as though the Victorian age gets the better of her, but by the time Orlando is married the ring does not symbolise union in the way it is depicted in the Victorian period of the novel – plodding down the middle of the street together – but rather signals a speed and intensity: 'She had been about to say, when Basket and Bartholomew interrupted with the tea things, nothing changes. And then, in the space of three seconds and a half, everything had changed [...] There was the wedding ring on her finger to prove it' (O 172). There is something incredibly present about the ring, a vital immediacy, added by the feeling that it might at any moment be removed by some force. In itself this demonstrates the queerness of her ring when we consider that she was 'broken off in the middle of a tribute to eternity' just prior to getting married; the ring is associated with intensity where traditionally it symbolises eternity.[55]

On the one hand the ring is the centre-piece of the satire in the passages that follow, as Orlando now takes care 'lest it should slip past the joint of her finger' (O 172) and 'doubts' are expressed about what marriage means (O 173), but on the other hand Orlando is now able to write, having performed a delicate negotiation and passed the 'examination successfully' of her time (O 174). The metaphor she draws in the description of her negotiation with her age is revealing in both its lightness and seriousness; she now performs

> a deep obeisance to the spirit of her age, such as – to compare great things with small – a traveller, conscious that he has a bundle of cigars in the corner of his suit case, makes to the customs officer who has obligingly made a scribble of white chalk on the lid. For she was extremely doubtful whether, if the spirit had examined the contents of her mind carefully, it would not have found something highly contraband for which she would have had to pay the full fine. (O 174)

What seems like a light-hearted comparison has a stark realism when we consider that the year in which the novel is now set, 1928, is a time when homosexuality was a criminal offence and also the year of the obscenity trial of Radclyffe Hall's *The Well of Loneliness* (1928) (with Woolf being one of those writers who appeared in court in support of the book's publication) – the material realities of the 'present moment' (O 195) are indeed brought to the fore. Like Lily in *To the Lighthouse*, Orlando escapes Victorian stricture 'by the skin of her teeth' (*TL* 200; O 174), just as Woolf narrowly avoided the censors with *Orlando*.[56] But where Lily rejects marriage in *To the Lighthouse*, Orlando realises, as Lily herself does in relation to her painting, that opposition is an inadequate design. As Burns puts it, 'she has conformed just enough to slip by unnoticed in the age, while she may also maintain a resistance to further constraint'.[57]

The queerest sensations caused by the absence of the wedding ring ultimately lead to Orlando wearing a distinctly queer ring; if it symbolises anything it is a queering of love and of desire. Woolf is not only queering the ring but queering how we theorise such material objects – objects that are no longer seen as either symbols that stand in for some transcendent realm of meaning, nor subjugated by the (hu)man who manipulates them for his own ends. There is a hint of this queering of both 'queer' and 'ring' in the etymology of 'ring' itself, coming from the Proto-Indo-European root '(s)ker-' meaning 'to turn, bend', where the root 'twerk-' for 'queer' also means 'to turn, twist' – it is Woolf's turning, bending, and twisting of convention that puts both the 'queer' and 'ring' in Woolf's 'queering'. Sara Ahmed has argued more recently in *Queer Phenomenology* (2006) that it is the inherent twists in the term 'queer' that make it possible for us 'to move between sexual and social registers, without flattening them or reducing them to a single line'. Using the term 'as a way of describing what is "oblique" or "off line"' – as Woolf's own use of the word in *Orlando* and elsewhere, coming before the additional social, political, and theoretical resonances 'queer' embodies in our contemporary context, often implies – is not so much a threat to the significance of 'queer' as describing certain sexual practices as it is an important reminder of 'what makes specific sexualities describable as queer in the first place: that is, that they are seen as odd, bent, twisted'.[58] By making Orlando marry and wear a wedding ring, Woolf not only demonstrates how pervasive the societal customs were of the time but reconceptualises marriage as a queer event created by a desire which turns, bends, and twists in order to flourish, just as the language and plot of the text itself. After all, as Parkes points out, 'the union with Shelmerdine could not have been more appropriate, for his sexual identity is as unstable as Orlando's',[59] which is of course highlighted by the well-known exchange between them: '"You're a woman, Shel!" she cried. "You're a man, Orlando!" he cried' (O 164). What Woolf manages to do so skilfully through her queering of love and of those 'queerest sensations' is to entangle them in a more complicated, intensive manner than an oppositional framework allows. Interestingly, this all chimes with a particular remark Woolf herself makes in a letter to Molly McCarthy as early as 1912, where she describes moving from an 'ideal' of marriage to a rejection of it before finally seeing a third way of thinking about it: 'I began life with a tremendous, absurd, ideal of marriage, then my bird's eye view of many marriages disgusted me, and I thought I must be asking what was not to be had. But that has passed too. Now I only ask for someone to make me vehement, and then I'll marry him!' (*L1* 492).

'Hail! natural desire!'

> Many variations can be played on the theme of sex, and with such happy results (*MB* 57)

The question of whether or not the choice to marry necessarily conflicts with a subversive, nonheteronormative conceptualisation of love and desire is something Deleuze remarks upon in his 'Letter to a Harsh Critic' – a wonderfully sarcastic letter he wrote in response to the critic Michel Cressole, who had contacted Deleuze whilst preparing publication of a highly critical book on him. After being accused by Cressole of being 'domestically trapped' because he was married and had children, Deleuze notes that what he calls 'nonoedipal love' is not simply a superficial rejection of social-familial structures, but comes about through 'experimenting on yourself' and 'opening yourself up to love and desire'. In other words to be married is not, *per se*, the problem, nor, as Deleuze stresses, is it about creating counter-categories: 'Non-oedipal love is pretty hard work. And you should know that it's not enough just to be unmarried, not to have kids, to be gay, or belong to this or that group, in order to get round the Oedipus complex':[60]

> We have to counter people who think 'I'm this, I'm that,' and who do so, moreover, in *psychoanalytic* terms (relating everything to their childhood or fate), by thinking in strange, fluid, unusual terms: I don't know what I am – I'd have to investigate and experiment with so many things in a non-narcissistic, non-oedipal way – no gay can ever definitively say 'I'm gay.' It's not a question of being this or that sort of human [. . .] but unraveling your body's human organization, exploring this or that zone of bodily intensity, with everyone discovering their own particular zones, and the groups, populations, species that inhabit them.[61]

What is 'unusual' and 'strange', what is queer, is directly set against the identification with either heterosexuality or homosexuality, so that for Deleuze – as, I have been arguing, for Woolf – we cannot judge subversiveness, or indeed queerness, simply based on whether someone is married and heterosexual, unmarried and homosexual, or married and homosexual or bisexual (and so on) and to think so is a conceptual misunderstanding of our materially embedded relations. While Deleuze and Guattari point to another modernist, Lawrence, as exemplary in exposing 'the poverty of the immutable identical images, the figurative roles that are so many tourniquets cutting off the flows of sexuality: "fiancée, mistress, wife, mother" – one could just as easily add "homosexuals, heterosexuals," etc. – all these roles are distributed by the Oedipal triangle, father-mother-me', we might well think of Woolf as also challenging these 'figurative roles', and of exploring desire as 'an infinity of different and even contrary flows'.[62]

Understanding sexuality through identifications with nouns such as 'homosexual', 'heterosexual', and even 'bisexual' confines desire within molar categories of identity, and defines it in relation to a majoritarian standard: '[Sexuality] is badly explained by the binary organization of the sexes, and just as badly by a bisexual organization within each sex. Sexuality brings into play too great a diversity of conjugated becomings, these are like *n* sexes.'[63] In *Anti-Oedipus* Deleuze and Guattari reinforce this point by stressing that the liberation of sexuality cannot be brought about solely through an identity politics which is 'caught up in a relation of exclusive disjunction with heterosexuality'; instead they are interested in the 'reciprocal inclusion and transverse communication' of homosexuality and heterosexuality which involves flows of desire as 'included disjunctions, local connections, nomadic conjunctions'.[64] Desire is 'apprehended below the minimum conditions of identity'[65] and consists everywhere of 'a microscopic transsexuality' that is not contained within a human subject. Their explanation of this microscopic transsexuality as 'resulting in the woman containing as many men as the man, and the man as many women, all capable of entering – men with women, women with men – into relations of production of desire that overturn the statistical order of the sexes'[66] echoes my reading of Woolf's androgyny in *A Room of One's Own*, as well as the kind of desire that created, and is created in, *Orlando*, a text where Woolf not only challenges binary models of sexuality but reformulates desire based on molecular connections rather than molar identities. It is a queering in and of *Orlando* that involves a Deleuzian form of 'vital desire that experiments with innumerable sexualities';[67] a polymorphous and queer vitalism, as detailed by Braidotti and Colebrook. Indeed, a similar frustration with the limitation of categorising desire in this way is evident in Woolf's observations on 'perversion', noted in a letter to Ethel Smyth on the 15th August 1930: 'Where people mistake, as I think, is in perpetually narrowing and naming these immensely composite and wide flung passions – driving stakes through them, herding them between screens. But how do you define "Perversity"? What is the line between friendship and perversion?' (*L4* 200) In her essay in *Queering the Non/Human* (2008), Patricia MacCormack's description of 'perversion' in Deleuze and Guattari's philosophy as 'the multiplicity at the heart of desire' could almost be used to describe Woolf's own theorising of desire, that is of 'queering desire rather than reifying any one form of sexuality as queer'.[68]

In the first two chapters of Woolf's fictional biography, the 'desire' of Orlando as a man is linked to a majoritarian will to possess and gain status, therefore upholding the broadly psychoanalytic structures of repression and lack that Deleuze so vehemently disavows: 'From the moment that we place desire on the side of acquisition, we make desire an idealistic (dialectical, nihilistic) conception, which causes us to look upon it as primarily a lack: a lack of an object, a lack of the real object.'[69] In the first appearance of the term 'desire' in the text, the biographer remarks that Orlando is destined to climb the social/professional hierarchy with ease and acquire status: 'From deed to deed, from glory to glory, from office to office he must go, his scribe following after, till they reach whatever seat it may be that is the height of their desire. Orlando, to look at, was cut out precisely for some such career' (O 4). Later, it is repeated that Orlando had a 'desire of Fame' (O 48) and Orlando's 'desire to make [Nick Greene's] acquaintance' (O 50) is based on this. But in chapter three, and significantly after the sex-change has taken place, we begin to see, through the narrator, a critique of this desire to attain or control: 'no passion is stronger in the breast of man than the desire to make others believe as he believes. Nothing so cuts at the root of his happiness and fills him with rage as the sense that another rates low what he prizes high' (O 94). One example of this is in political allegiances, a macro politics based on molar parties: 'Whigs and Tories, Liberal party and Labour party – for what do they battle except their own prestige? It is not love of truth, but desire to prevail that sets quarter against quarter and makes parish desire the downfall of parish' (O 94). Several pages later we see a further, and more direct, challenging of the 'desire to prevail'. This example is clearly linked to Orlando's new position as a woman, with an outsider's view of the majoritarian rule:

> She remembered how, as a young man, she had insisted that women must be obedient, chaste, scented, and exquisitely apparelled. 'Now I shall have to pay in my own person for those desires,' she reflected; 'for women are not (judging by my own short experience of the sex) obedient, chaste, scented, and exquisitely apparelled by nature. They can only attain these graces, without which they may enjoy none of the delights of life, by the most tedious discipline.' (O 99)

In a further passage, when the narrator begins to describe what happens when Nell, Prue, Kitty, and Rose join Orlando 'round the punch-bowl' to share 'fine tales' and 'amusing observations' (O 140), the desire of the (male) subject wishing to obtain an object even extends to the desire to possess desire itself:

> it cannot be denied that when women get together – but hist – they are always careful to see that the doors are shut and that not a word of it gets into print.

> All they desire is – but hist again – is that not a man's step on the stair? All they desire, we were about to say when the gentleman took the very words out of our mouths. Women have no desires, says this gentleman, coming into Nell's parlour; only affectations. Without desires (she has served him and he is gone) their conversation cannot be of the slightest interest to anyone. 'It is well known,' says Mr. S. W., 'that when they lack the stimulus of the other sex, women can find nothing to say to each other. When they are alone, they do not talk, they scratch.' (O 140–1)

The stuttering syntax here is gradually – first with a 'step of the stair', then entering the parlour, and finally through the direct speech of Mr S. W. – taken over by men who will not allow that women have desires of their own, men who cannot allow an understanding of desire that is not the compensation of men for what women 'lack'. But whilst the men succeed in silencing the women in this particular passage, Orlando has already moved beyond a majoritarian appropriation of desire; in an earlier passage we see the beginnings of a reconceptualisation of desire as she reflects that it is 'better to leave the rule and discipline of the world to others; better to be quit of martial ambition, the love of power, and all the other manly desires if so one can more fully enjoy the most exalted raptures known to the human spirit'. Named as one of these 'exalted raptures', 'love' is then opposed to 'manly desires' (O 102–3). Rather than being about the wished acquisition by the subject of an object, the frustrated attempt to satiate the lack, Orlando realises that desire is precisely the 'exalted rapture' which is the creation of new minoritarian connections and events. It is the conceptualisation of a desire as positive and productive, as simple as the creation of aggregates or contexts; a desire which is 'not bolstered by needs, but rather the contrary; needs are derived from desire'.[70]

By the final chapter this mode of desire is more fully realised in Woolf's text, and desire is conceived as an affirmative deterritorialisation of patriarchal Empire-building:

> Hail! natural desire! Hail! happiness! divine happiness! and pleasure of all sorts, flowers and wine, though one fades and the other intoxicates; and half-crown tickets out of London on Sundays, and singing in a dark chapel hymns about death, and anything, anything that interrupts and confounds the tapping of typewriters and filing of letters and forging of links and chains, binding the Empire together[.] (O 192)

In this passage there is no subjective 'I' attempting to capture an object, to satisfy a lack, illustrating Deleuze and Guattari's claim that, far from the psychoanalytic model of a subject's desire fuelled by the lack of an object, it is 'the *subject* that is missing in desire, or desire that lacks a fixed subject'.⁷¹ Objects, clearly named in this passage, are not lacking, yet are not possessed either; desire in *Orlando* is precisely what escapes 'filing', 'binding', and 'chains'. *Orlando* hints at more than just a critique or opposition to majoritarian desire, but a reconceptualisation of it – a minoritarian desire that has something in common with the kind of desire Jessica Berman finds in Woolf's fictional biography following Orlando's sex-change, where it 'becomes the principle of affiliation not in terms of a strict one-to-one, lover/beloved arrangement, but in a more open-ended social relationship'.⁷²

A history of bedrooms

This more social, minoritarian mode of desire has created Orlando's colourful history. In *A Thousand Plateaus* Deleuze and Guattari themselves comment on Woolf's *Orlando* as operating 'by blocks, blocks of ages, blocks of epochs, blocks of the kingdoms of nature, blocks of sexes, forming so many becomings between things, or so many lines of deterritorialization'.⁷³ The emphasis is placed on particular forms of history in becoming, and therefore in addition to those passages in the novel in which we can find specific allusions to autobiographical happenings, or which consider domestic and marital relations between characters, Deleuze and Guattari draw attention to Woolf's choice to set the novel over four centuries, engaging with a range of factual and fantastical detail. In *Machinic Modernism*, Beatrice Monaco's Deleuzian reading of *Orlando* illuminates instances where Woolf creates 'a kind of hyperbolic historical materialism: she draws a sweeping and vivifying outline of "moments" of cultural change in England over the course of three centuries and fills them with material detail'.⁷⁴ I would add that Woolf's theorising of desire in *Orlando* is bound up with this 'hyperbolic historical materialism'; that is, she emphasises the materiality of theory where the becoming-queer of *Orlando* is also the becoming of history.⁷⁵ As Deleuze and Guattari put it in *Anti-Oedipus*:

> through its loves and sexuality [. . .] the libido is continually re-creating History, continents, kingdoms, races, and cultures [. . .] our choices in matters of love are at the crossroads of 'vibrations', which is to say that they express connections, disjunctions, and conjunctions of flows that cross through a society, entering and leaving it, linking it up with other societies, ancient or contemporary, remote or vanished, dead or yet to be born [. . .] The desiring sexual relationships of man and woman (or of man and man, or woman and woman) are the index of social relationships between people. Love and sexuality are the exponents or the indicators, this time unconscious, of the libidinal investments of the social field. Every loved or desired being

serves as a collective agent of enunciation. And it is certainly not, as Freud believed, the libido that must be desexualised and sublimated in order to invest society and its flows; on the contrary, it is love, desire, and their flows that manifest the directly social character of the nonsublimated libido and its sexual investments.[76]

Desire is always already invested in the social field,[77] and history, as Deleuze and Guattari make clear in *What is Philosophy?*, is important to the creation of the 'new' that is becoming, but is never finally settled or *a priori*: 'History today still designates only the set of conditions, however recent they may be, from which one turns away in order to become, that is to say, in order to create something new.' They add: 'How could something come from history? Without history, becoming would remain indeterminate and unconditioned, but becoming is not historical.'[78] What we find in *Orlando* is a desire and a history filled with molecular events, where the particular moment in all its historical specificity becomes an accident of entangled agencies.[79] As Monaco puts it, 'in *Orlando* history is not just something we write and authorise, but something which acts for, and which changes, itself. History is a multiplicity, the whole nature of which changes with each localised modification.'[80]

The affirmation of desire, and of history, as multiplicity is also seen in the novel through the depiction of the house Orlando was born in which 'had 365 bedrooms and had been in the possession of her family for four or five hundred years'. Orlando makes the mistake of assuming her own ancestry of 'earls, or even dukes' as the oldest, truest example of an 'ancient and civilised race', but the multiplicity and scope of history is emphasised as Orlando comes to realise that Rustum and the other gypsies she is with judged a

> descent of four or five hundred years only the meanest possible. Their own families went back at least two or three thousand years. To the gypsy whose ancestors had built the Pyramids centuries before Christ was born, the genealogy of Howards and Plantagenets was no better and no worse than that of the Smiths and the Joneses: both were negligible. (O 93)

The desire to build and possess hundreds of bedrooms was 'vulgar' to the gypsies, and Orlando acknowledges that

> from the gipsy point of view, a Duke [. . .] was nothing but a profiteer or robber who snatched land and money from people who rated these things of little worth, and could think of nothing better to do than to build three hundred and sixty-five bedrooms when one was enough, and none was even better than one. She could not deny that her ancestors had accumulated field after field; house after house; honour after honour [. . .] Nor could she counter the argument (Rustum was too much of a gentleman to press it, but

she understood) that any man who did now what her ancestors had done three of four hundred years ago would be denounced – and by her own family most loudly – for a vulgar upstart, an adventurer, a *nouveau riche*. (O 94)[81]

Whilst Orlando does not entirely give up her defence of her own particular ancestry – 'had none of them been saints or heroes, or great benefactors of the human race' – significantly she now speaks of how 'four hundred and seventy-six bedrooms mean nothing to them' (O 94). The specificity of her history becomes muddled and an extra 111 bedrooms are added to her previous dwelling place.[82] Rather than strengthening the fact of Orlando's history, such quantitative detail appears to be satirised; the number of bedrooms becomes arbitrary or accidental. Once again Orlando refuses dichotomous choices; she neither wants to return to her old life nor to remain with the gypsies: 'To leave the gipsies and become once more an Ambassador seemed to her intolerable. But it was equally impossible to remain for ever where there was neither ink nor writing paper, neither reverence for the Talbots nor respect for a multiplicity of bedrooms' (O 95).

By creating a 'multiplicity of bedrooms' that appears to be numerically arbitrary, *Orlando* brings to light the distinction between two kinds of multiplicity – quantitative and qualitative – that we find in Deleuze's philosophy, where the former is homogeneous and numerical and the latter is heterogeneous and intensive. Multiplicity, Deleuze and Guattari explain in *A Thousand Plateaus*, 'was created precisely in order to escape the abstract opposition between the multiple and the One, to escape dialectics, to succeed in conceiving the multiple in the pure state, to cease treating it as a numerical fragment of a lost Unity or Totality or as the organic element of a Unity or Totality yet to come, and instead distinguish between different types of multiplicity'.[83] Deleuze and Guattari's emphasis on multiplicity is especially influenced by Bergson's *durée* as a form of multiplicity that is 'qualitative and fusional' as distinct from 'metric multiplicity or the multiplicity of magnitude',[84] and in *Bergsonism* Deleuze outlines Bergson's importance in offering multiplicity as a way out of dialectical thought which deals with abstract concepts that are overblown and empty 'like baggy clothes':

> There are many theories in philosophy that combine the one and the multiple. They share the characteristic of claiming to reconstruct the real with general ideas. We are told that the Self is one (thesis) and it is multiple (antithesis), then it is the unity of the multiple (synthesis). Or else we are told that the One is already multiple, that Being passes into nonbeing and produces becoming. [. . .] To Bergson, it seems that in this type of *dialectical* method, one begins with concepts that, like baggy clothes, are much too big. The One in general,

the multiple in general, nonbeing in general ... In such cases the real is recomposed with abstracts.

As Deleuze stresses, the dialectic is a *'false movement'* because 'the concrete will never be attained by combining the inadequacy of one concept with the inadequacy of its opposite. The singular will never be attained by correcting a generality with another generality.'[85] What is truly transgressive, whether concerned with sexuality or otherwise, is that which escapes a dialectical orientation.

In *Transpositions*, Braidotti helpfully discusses these distinctions between two types of multiplicity in relation to her theory of nomadic, non-unitary subjectivity by describing the distinction between 'quantitative pluralities' that represent 'merely a multiple of One', and 'qualitative multiplicities' which 'trace patterns of becoming' and 'express changes not of scale, but of intensity, force, or *potentia* (positive power of expression)'.[86] Seen in this light, the multiplicity of Orlando's bedrooms is not so much a celebration of a plurality of lovers as it is a kind of qualitative polyamory, which depends not on one or many lovers but on a realisation that love is always already a question of intensity that involves much more than two human subjects from the beginning, whether you stay in one bedroom or explore many, precisely because each individual, and each bedroom, is already a multiplicity. After all, as Deleuze puts it in *Dialogues* with Claire Parnet,

> What a depressing idea of love, to make it a relation between two people, whose monotony must be vanquished as required by adding extra people. [...] The question about sexuality is: into the vicinity of what else does it enter to form [...] particular relations of movement and rest? [...] it is not simply from one to the other of the two 'subjects' that this vicinity or combination takes place; it is in each of the two that several fluxes combine to form a bloc of becoming which makes demands on them both [...] Not the man and woman as sexual entities, caught in a binary apparatus, but a molecular becoming[.][87]

Queering in *Orlando* is precisely this move from quantitative plurality to qualitative multiplicity, entering into and creating molecular events together in the company of others – human and nonhuman, bodies and environments: 'making love is not just becoming as one, or even two, but becoming as a hundred thousand. Desiring-machines or the nonhuman sex: not one or even two sexes, but *n* sexes.'[88]

The queering of Orlando's bedrooms, then, has as much to do with the queer nature of history as it does Orlando's queer sex and sexuality. Neither her own personal history or that of the gypsies is appealing as

Orlando realises that these histories are not determined by quantitative measures that can be retraced, but by qualitative creation. Orlando's desired return to England is not sparked by an attempt to find a lost object, but rather her desire produces a new England, where nature is part of a shared agency rather than reduced to a passive background; a qualitative event which cannot be reduced to its parts:

> And then Nature, in whom she trusted, either played her a trick or worked a miracle [...] Suddenly a shadow, though there was nothing to cast a shadow, appeared on the bald mountain-side opposite. It deepened quickly and soon a green hollow showed where there had been barren rock before. As she looked, the hollow deepened and widened, and a great park-like space opened in the flank of the hill. Within, she could see an undulating and grassy lawn; she could see oak trees dotted here and there; she could see the thrushes hopping among the branches. She could see the deer stepping delicately from shade to shade, and could even hear the hum of insects and the gentle sighs and shivers of a summer's day in England. (O 95)

In this passage the 'undulating' grass, the 'hopping' thrushes, the 'stepping' deer and the humming insects all combine in Orlando's desiring-England, a non/human desiring which shares something of the 'transsexual communications' with both organic and inorganic materials and objects that Deleuze finds in Proust's writing – what he calls 'an intensive continuum of substances'.[89] It is another clear example in Woolf's writing of Nature's 'queer tricks', of the entanglement between human bodies and nonhuman environments where 'the most ordinary moment in the world, such as sitting down at a table and pulling the inkstand towards one, may agitate a thousand odd, disconnected fragments' (O 46).

Of course in *Orlando* such non/human entanglements have a much more fantastical dimension than in *To the Lighthouse* or, as I discuss in the following chapter, in *Flush*, and this is emphasised in a passage much earlier in Woolf's mock-biography where following Sasha's departure there is a flood and the melting of the ice, and the river becomes what Julia Briggs refers to as 'a figure for time itself, carrying away a bizarre medley of human and non-human life':[90]

> The river had gained its freedom in a night. [...] All was riot and confusion. The river was strewn with icebergs. Some of these were as broad as a bowling green and as high as a house; others no bigger than a man's hat, but most fantastically twisted. [...] For furniture, valuables, possessions of all sorts were carried away on the icebergs. Among other strange sights was to be seen a cat suckling its young; a table laid sumptuously for a supper of twenty; a couple in bed; together with an extraordinary number of cooking utensils. (O 35–6)

This particular non/human collection, infused with humour, is 'at once the most imaginative and the most violent of Woolf's moments of rupture'. Significantly, it follows the departure of Sasha, 'the impossible and perfect love object'.[91] Following such events in *Orlando*, desire is irreducible to real-life figures such as Sackville-West and Woolf or indeed any of the characters or objects in Woolf's text. 'Desire', affirms Deleuze, 'is revolutionary because it always wants more connections', and in *Orlando* such connections are not regulated by lack or limited to the human.[92]

Multiplicity in a motor-car and 'Monday or Tuesday'

It is in the throes of 'the present moment' that Orlando cruises through and out of London in her motor-car (O 195), demonstrating a queering of subjectivity, time, and space, so that what results is a multiplicity of agencies which involve the nonhuman as much as the human. Indeed, 'changing her selves as quickly as she drove', Woolf's protagonist somewhat frantically contemplates so many selves to the point that it becomes 'an open question in what sense Orlando can be said to have existed at the present moment' (O 201):

> 'What then? Who then?' she said. 'Thirty-six; in a motor car; a woman. Yes, but a million other things as well. A snob am I? The garter in the hall? The leopards? My ancestors? Proud of them? Yes! Greedy, luxurious, vicious? Am I? (here a new self came in). Don't care a damn if I am. Truthful? I think so. Generous? Oh, but that don't count (here a new self came in). Lying in bed of a morning listening to the pigeons on fine linen; silver dishes; wine; maids; footmen. Spoilt? Perhaps. Too many things for nothing. Hence my books (here she mentioned fifty classical titles; which represented, so we think, the early romantic works that she tore up). Facile, glib, romantic. But (here another self came in) a duffer, a fumbler. More clumsy I couldn't be. And – and – (here she hesitated for a word and if we suggest 'Love' we may be wrong, but certainly she laughed and blushed and then cried out –) A toad set in emeralds! Harry the Archduke! Blue-bottles on the ceiling! (here another self came in). But Nell, Kit, Sasha? (she was sunk in gloom: tears actually shaped themselves and she had long given over crying). Trees, she said. (Here another self came in.) I love trees (she was passing a clump) growing there a thousand years. And barns (she passed a tumble-down barn at the edge of the road. She carefully avoided it). And the night. But people (here another self came in). People? (she repeated it as a question.) I don't know. Chattering, spiteful, always telling lies. (Here she turned into the High Street of her native town, which was crowded, for it was market day, with farmers, and shepherds, and old women with hens in baskets.) I like peasants. I understand crops.' (O 203)

In this remarkable passage Orlando's variegated selves are described as 'truthful', 'spoilt', 'romantic', and 'clumsy' to name only a few. But this is much more than a case of different adjectives being used to describe different aspects of one queer personality. The striking spatial and temporal dimension to this passage brings together form and content, where the brackets become a doorway through which 'another self came in', disrupting the temporal rhythm of the reader and the spatial flow of the text. When the parentheses are not introducing 'another self' they are updating the reader on the movement of the car, emphasising the motion and physicality of these changes (we are not to read this passage as presenting the transcendent powers of the imagination): 'she passed a tumble-down barn', 'she turned into the High Street', for example. After all, she was 'changing her selves as quickly as she drove – there was a new one at every corner' (*O* 202). Further examples – 'lying in bed of a morning listening to the pigeons on fine linen' and 'I love trees (she was passing a clump) growing there a thousand years' – foreground both time and place, stretching from a specific morning to a millennium. As Andrew Thacker observes in *Moving Through Modernity* (2003), in this passage the boundaries are being crossed between 'psychic identity and physical place' as 'the words in brackets somehow exist embedded in the landscape through which Orlando travels, propping up when her gaze alights upon them, or flashing back from the landscape to the viewer'.[93]

Of all Woolf's other writings, this scene from *Orlando* most clearly shares similarities with her short posthumously published essay 'Evening Over Sussex: Reflections in a Motor Car' (1942), where the narrator describes how 'the self splits up' whilst driving through and perceiving the Sussex landscape. Along the way, we are introduced to four selves, one of which 'is eager and dissatisfied and the other stern and philosophical', a third self is then 'aloof and melancholy' (*E6* 454), and a fourth 'erratic and impulsive' (*E6* 455). Reading these texts together in the historical and cultural context of the development of the motor-car in the first decades of the twentieth century and Woolf's own changing response to this, including her personal experiences of driving, Minow-Pinkney shows that 'the link between motoring experience and aesthetic practices is not just a matter of trope or analogy but motoring, together with other experiences distinctive to the modern age of technology, affects the human sensory organization itself'.[94] Of 'Evening Over Sussex', she places emphasis on the car's movements, rather than those of the human mind or body, in the creation of multiple images evident in Woolf's essay: 'a haystack; a rust red roof; a pond; an old man coming home with his sack on his back; [. . .] Gone, gone; over, over; past and done with, past and done with. I feel life left behind even as the road is left behind' (*E6* 454). Here the '"I" has no control over the concatenation of the images; the rhythm and the visual impression effected by the list of words, the use of commas and semicolons, coveys the sensation of the compulsive, fast movement.' Woolf's aesthetic imagination 'extends itself to the future and to a nonanthropomorphous vision'.[95] To conclude this chapter I would like to suggest that along with 'Evening Over Sussex', a further intertext for the above passage from *Orlando*, and one which emphasises precisely this nonanthropomorphous, and indeed nonanthropocentric, vision is another of Woolf's short pieces, 'Monday or Tuesday'. Crucially though, in this short sketch such a vision is conceived directly in relation to 'desire'.

Written in 1920, 'Monday or Tuesday' is without an identifiable narrator, and, while offering an imagined insight into what the point of view of the 'heron' in the story might be, Woolf is careful not to fully anthropomorphise this bird: 'Lazy and indifferent, shaking space easily from his wings, knowing his way, the heron passes over the church beneath the sky' (*CSF* 137). There is no 'I' in the story and the only personal pronoun is 'his', which is used twice in the first sentence to refer to the heron. What is immediately striking looking at 'Monday or Tuesday' alongside the above passage of Orlando in her motor-car, is their similar use of textual space, with bracketed parentheses concerned with both spatial and temporal movement in the surrounding environment:

> Desiring truth, awaiting it, laboriously distilling a few words, for ever desiring – (a cry starts to the left, another to the right. Wheels strike divergently. Omnibuses conglomerate in conflict) – for ever desiring – (the clock asseverates with twelve distinct strokes that it is midday; light sheds gold scales; children swarm) – for ever desiring truth. (*CSF* 137)

In her wonderfully titled short article 'Woolf's Verb Impersonators (and Other Deviants)', Molly McQuade describes how this story has the movement of poetry but with 'brilliantly concrete language'.[96] She points in particular to Woolf's 'deviant verbs', occurring at a more frequent ratio than is often found in prose (McQuade counts one in every six words as verbs in the story; this is even more than the above passage from *Orlando*, which on my count stands at a ratio of one in eight words), as well as Woolf's use of dashes which combine to 'introduce furious speed into her prose'.[97] But I want to suggest that what is really central to the intensity of this piece is Woolf's use of the gerund 'desiring', the putting into continuous movement of desire, which punctuates the whole of the second paragraph. That we find a 'desiring truth' transposed through movement so vividly in a text without a definitive human presence – simply 'children', 'men's feet and women's feet' and

'Miss Thingummy' (*CSF* 137) – is further evidence of Woolf creating the kind of nonhuman connections Braidotti and Deleuze see as part of desire (desire which we might also see evinced in the above passage from *Orlando* where nonhuman movements are pronounced, this time alongside the human, but queering, Orlando). After all, as Deleuze states in *Dialogues*, 'Do you realize how simple a desire is? Sleeping is a desire. Walking is a desire. Listening to music, or making music, or writing, are desires. A spring, a winter, are desires.'[98] Woolf's 'desiring' is both her deviant verb and her queering verb.

If Orlando's cruising out of London in her motor-car puts into motion a range of desires seen in the connections different selves make as every corner is turned, then we need not view these selves as simply plural versions of Orlando's identity; indeed, recalling the distinction between quantitative pluralities and qualitative multiplicities, we might say that *Orlando* transports subjectivity from plurality to multiplicity. The idea of countable selves is satirised both here and with the changing and seemingly arbitrary (and inconsistent) numerical speculations as to how many selves one has – similar to Orlando's 'multiplicity of bedrooms'. For example, over just four pages we are told that 'a biography is considered complete if it merely accounts for six or seven selves, whereas a person may well have as many thousand' (O 202), that 'there may be more than two thousand' (O 205), 'if there are (at a venture) seventy-six different times all ticking in the mind at once, how many different people are there not – Heaven help us – all having lodgement at one time or another in the human spirit' (O 201),[99] and Orlando might be 'a million other things as well' (O 203). We are left in little doubt about the inadequacy of trying to quantify these selves: 'she had a great variety of selves to call upon, far more than we have been able to find room for' (O 202). This move from quantity to quality, from plurality to multiplicity, is perfectly summed up when we read that 'still the Orlando she needs may not come; these selves of which we are built up, one on top of another, as plates are piled on a waiter's hand, have attachments elsewhere, sympathies, little constitutions and rights of their own, call them what you will (and for many of these things there is no name)' (O 201). The quantitatively measured figuration of plates 'piled on a waiter's hand' proves insufficient and so the sentence continues into a further clause, as if in realisation that these selves are already forming qualitative connections that cannot be counted, balanced, or gathered together; they have 'attachments elsewhere, sympathies, little constitutions' – a description that has more in common with Deleuze and Guattari's statement that 'everyone is a little group'[100] than it does a simile involving the piling of plates. The point is that one does not *have* any selves in the sense of being contained within or by a 'Captain Self' who 'amalgamates and controls' all these different selves and has 'the power to desire' (O 202). The motor-car scene, like Woolf's queering of desire throughout *Orlando*, contradicts the possibility of this controlling (dominant) self, already undermined a few sentences later when we are told: 'in this we may well be wrong' (O 203). Even this hesitation, then, is an affirmative destabilising of majoritarian control, freeing desire to create new twists and turns.

Notes

1. Braidotti, *Transpositions*, p. 191.
2. Raitt, *Vita and Virginia*, p. 1.
3. Ibid., p. 17. See also Sproles, *Desiring Women*.
4. See Marcus, 'Storming the Toolshed'.
5. Raitt, *Vita and Virginia*, p. 4.
6. Knopp, 'If I Saw You', p. 27.
7. Hankins, 'Switching Sex', p. 26.
8. Meese, 'When Virginia Looked at Vita', p. 472. Louise DeSalvo sees the humour in *Orlando* as another example of 'Woolf's continuing inability to give full acknowledgement to her own lesbianism'. See DeSalvo, 'Lighting the Cave', p. 207. All of these readings add weight to Diana Swanson's suggestion that 'it is impossible to separate biography and literary analysis completely in discussions of Woolf and lesbianism'. See Swanson, 'Lesbian Approaches', p. 190.
9. Coffman, 'Woolf's *Orlando*'. The mining for signs of lesbian desire is more fruitful when focused primarily on Woolf's texts rather than her biography. For example, Kathryn Simpson's uncovering of signs of same-sex eroticism in Woolf's work opens up questions of sexuality rather than foreclosing them. Simpson focuses on Woolf's mermaid metaphors: 'In embodying woman-centred eroticism, whilst refusing to explicitly name or define this desire, Woolf's writing of desire between women maintains a radically queer evasion of precise definition as, like a "queer fish" itself, it remains on the borderlines and refuses binary oppositions or categorizations.' Simpson, 'Queer Fish', p. 80. See also Simpson, 'Pearl-diving', pp. 37–58, and Kohn, 'Erotic Daydreams', pp. 185–8.
10. Braidotti, *Transpositions*, p. 192.
11. Kaivola teases out the less fixed sexual identities of Woolf and Sackville-West in 'Virginia Woolf, Vita Sackville-West', pp. 18–40.
12. Ramsey, 'Producing Queer Affiliations', p. 280.
13. Cohen and Ramlow, 'Pink Vectors'.
14. See Chapter 5, n.65.
15. Braidotti, *Transpositions*, p. 196.
16. Ibid., p. 196.
17. Ibid., p. 191.
18. Ibid., p. 196.

19. Minow-Pinkney, *Virginia Woolf*, p. 129.
20. Burns, 'Re-dressing', p. 350.
21. DiBattista, *Virginia Woolf*, p. 120.
22. Braidotti, *Transpositions*, p. 197.
23. Sackville-West, *The Letters of*, pp. 288–9.
24. Braidotti, *Transpositions*, p. 195.
25. Ibid., p. 194.
26. Ibid., p. 198.
27. Nicolson, *Portrait*, p. 186.
28. Braidotti, *Transpositions*, p. 197.
29. Ibid., p. 198.
30. Ibid., p. 195.
31. Ibid., p. 192.
32. Braidotti, *Nomadic Subjects*, 2nd edn, p. 289. This interview took place in August 2006 in Lodz, Poland, during a conference which included plenaries by both Braidotti and Butler. For a summary of this event see 'Transformative Thresholds'.
33. Braidotti, *Transpositions*, p. 191.
34. Braidotti, *Nomadic Subjects*, 2nd edn, p. 293. See also Braidotti and Butler, 'Feminism'. As well as her concerns with queer identity politics, Braidotti claims that aspects of queer theory conflict with her nomadic feminism founded on embodied sexual difference. Whilst I share these concerns (the reason why I emphasise that this chapter is interested in a 'queering' of, rather than identifying as 'queer', *Orlando*) and yet also see some problems in her model of sexual difference (discussed in Chapter 2), I find that Braidotti's reading of Vita and Virginia in *Transpositions*, and her view of sexuality and desire, goes beyond the limitations of both positions.
35. Braidotti, *Nomadic Subjects*, 2nd edn, p. 291.
36. Ibid., p. 293.
37. Colebrook, 'Queer Vitalism', p. 83.
38. Ibid., p. 84.
39. Ibid., p. 86. With Deleuze underpinning Colebrook's thought, she argues elsewhere that 'Queer encounters, from a Deleuzian perspective, are not affirmations of a group of bodies who recognise themselves as other than normative, but are those in which bodies enter into relations where the mode of relation cannot be determined in advance'. Colebrook, 'How Queer', p. 30. As Tamsin Lorraine has recently put it: 'On Deleuze and Guattari's view, a personal self or identity as a totalised point of origin to which to refer all desire operates as a kind of stranglehold on the individual and the capacities it could unfold'. Lorraine, 'Feminist Lines of Flight', p. 75.
40. Braidotti, *Transpositions*, p. 197.
41. See Giffney and Hird, 'Queering', pp. 6–7.
42. Butler, *Bodies That Matter*, p. 228.
43. Sedgwick, *Tendencies*, p. xii.
44. For an illuminating summary of the 'queer' in queering/queer theory see Giffney and Hird, 'Queering', pp. 4–6.
45. Braidotti, *Transpositions*, p. 191.

46. Ibid., p. 197.
47. Braidotti, *Transpositions*, p. 195. This echoes Deleuze and Guattari's opening sentences to *A Thousand Plateaus*: 'The two of us wrote *Anti-Oedipus* together. Since each of us was several, there was already quite a crowd'. Deleuze and Guattari, *A Thousand Plateaus*, p. 3.
48. Cf. Braidotti's insistence in *Nomadic Subjects* that sexual difference is 'not accidental'. Braidotti, *Nomadic Subjects*, p. 186.
49. Braidotti, *Transpositions*, pp. 194–5.
50. Cited in Moore, 'Orlando', p. 349.
51. Parkes, 'Lesbianism', p. 450.
52. Bowlby, *Feminist Destinations*, p. 53.
53. It has not always been the case that wedding rings were placed on what we now call the 'wedding finger', or indeed on the left hand. See Gad, *Wedding Rings*, pp. 38–44.
54. Ibid., p. 18.
55. Indeed rings have symbolised eternity from the moment they were first exchanged as objects of love in 2800 bc in Egypt. Ibid., p. 19.
56. For more on *The Well of Loneliness* trial and *Orlando*'s escape from the censors see Parkes, 'Lesbianism'.
57. Burns, 'Re-dressing', p. 355.
58. Ahmed, *Queer Phenomenology*, p. 161.
59. Parkes, 'Lesbianism', p. 450
60. Deleuze, *Negotiations*, p. 10.
61. Ibid., p. 11.
62. Deleuze and Guattari, *Anti-Oedipus*, p. 385. For an insightful discussion of Lawrence and Deleuze see Masschelein, '"Rip the veil"', pp. 23–39.
63. Deleuze and Guattari, *A Thousand Plateaus*, p. 307.
64. Deleuze and Guattari, *Anti-Oedipus*, p. 384.
65. Ibid., p. 385.
66. Ibid., p. 325.
67. Conley, 'Thirty-six Thousand', p. 26. Nonetheless, Conley does point to potential limitations of Deleuze and Guattari here, and how some of their thoughts have perhaps become out-dated (34).
68. MacCormack, 'Necrosexuality', pp. 339–40. Several contemporary theorists and critics have referred to Deleuze's theorising as a form of queering: see Nigianni and Storr (eds), *Deleuze and Queer Theory*. Of all French philosophers, Verena Andermatt Conley argues, it is 'especially in the the writings of Gilles Deleuze and Félix Guattari that the question of homosexuality as queering, that is, as becoming and as an ongoing differing of difference, is raised.' Conley, 'Thirty-six Thousand', p. 24.
69. Deleuze and Guattari, *Anti-Oedipus*, p. 26.
70. Ibid., p. 28.
71. Ibid., p. 28.
72. Berman, *Modernist Fiction*, p. 134.
73. Deleuze and Guattari, *A Thousand Plateaus*, p. 324.
74. Monaco, *Machinic Modernism*, p. 156.
75. For a discussion of the relationship between queering and history in *Between the Acts* see Delsandro, '"Myself – it was impossible"', p. 94.
76. Deleuze and Guattari, *Anti-Oedipus*, p. 386.

77. For more on this, including a discussion of misreadings of Deleuze's conceptualisation of desire by Butler among others, see Smith, 'The Inverse Side', pp. 646–7; 650. See Butler, *Subjects of Desire*, pp. 214–15.
78. Deleuze and Guattari, *What is Philosophy?*, p. 96.
79. Monaco, *Machinic Modernism*, p. 157.
80. Ibid., p. 157.
81. Kirstie Blair focuses on the gypsies in *Orlando* and in correspondences between Vita and Virginia as evidence of 'an undercurrent [. . .] a tug towards "gypsiness" that functions [. . .] as a hint of same-sex desire'. See Blair, 'Gypsies', p. 142. For more on the link between Vita and gypsies see French, 'Peeling the Gypsy'.
82. These extra 111 bedrooms also take us away from the specificity of Vita's history, where Knole has 365 rooms. See Adams, *Shaggy Muses*, p. 224.
83. Deleuze and Guattari, *A Thousand Plateaus*, p. 36.
84. Ibid., pp. 533–4. Deleuze and Guattari also discuss how their conceptualisation of multiplicity is influenced by Riemann, Meinong, and Russell, amongst others, and they propose a whole range of ways to conceptualise these different multiplicities, using terms I reference throughout this book including aborescent and rhizomatic multiplicities, macro- and micro-multiplicities, that 'constantly construct and dismantle themselves in the course of their communications, as they cross over into each other at, beyond, or before a certain threshold' (36–7; See also 532).
85. Deleuze, *Bergsonism*, p. 44.
86. Braidotti, *Transpositions*, p. 94.
87. Deleuze and Parnet, *Dialogues*, pp. 75–6.
88. Deleuze and Guattari, *Anti-Oedipus*, p. 325.
89. Deleuze, *Desert Islands*, p. 287. See also Deleuze, *Proust and Signs*.
90. Briggs, *Reading Virginia Woolf*, p. 134.
91. Ibid., p. 134.
92. Deleuze and Parnet, *Dialogues*, p. 58.
93. Thacker, *Moving Through Modernity*, p. 179.
94. Minow-Pinkney, 'Virginia Woolf and the Age of Motor Cars', p. 163. In a later essay Leena Kore-Schröder also draws fruitful comparisons between this passage from *Orlando* and 'Evening Over Sussex', arguing that 'the experience of driving offered Woolf an *embodied* knowledge of time and space'. Kore-Schröder, 'Reflections', p. 146.
95. Minow-Pinkney, 'Virginia Woolf and the Age of Motor Cars', pp. 177–8.
96. McQuade, 'Woolf's Verb Impersonators', p. 6.
97. Ibid.
98. Deleuze and Parnet, *Dialogues*, p. 71.
99. It is lines such as this that have prompted Bergsonian readings of time in *Orlando*. See for example Gillies, *Henri Bergson*, pp. 124–6.
100. Deleuze and Guattari, *Anti-Oedipus*, p. 396.

Chapter 4

The Question of the Animal in *Flush*

As Woolf's underdog book, *Flush: A Biography* has recently received increased levels of critical attention and gained entry into Woolf's modernist canon, although it is still by no means afforded the same scrutiny as her more famous fictional biography, *Orlando*. Indeed, *Flush*'s (re)creation of Elizabeth Barrett Browning's cocker spaniel – from his early life in the country to a rear bedroom in London's Wimpole Street, dognapping and incarceration in Whitechapel, a journey abroad to Florence, and finally his death on Barrett Browning's lap – has often been written off as a relatively trivial escapade, with Woolf's own description in December 1932 of the project as 'just a little joke' frequently presented as justification for this (*L5* 140). To use this remark as evidence of the text's unimportance is, however, to overstate its significance; it must be remembered that Woolf is writing here to Ethyl Smyth, the very person she had earlier worried would 'hate' the book (*L5* 108). Similarly, Woolf refers to *Flush* again as being 'by way of a joke' in January 1933, but does so when writing to her American publisher, Donald Brace, apprehensive of his reaction (*L5* 155). By contrast, Woolf seems genuinely thrilled in a letter to Lady Colefax, in reaction to her praise for the book: 'I'm so glad that you liked *Flush*. I think it shows great discrimination in you because it was all a matter of hints and shades, and practically no one has seen what I was after, and I was elated to Heaven to think that you among the faithful firmly stood – or whatever Milton said' (*L5* 236).

Even when critics have taken Woolf's fictional biography seriously, they have not necessarily taken Flush *the dog* seriously. Susan Squier, for example, considers Flush as a 'stand-in for the woman writer';[1] for Michael Rosenthal he is a 'satiric device' there to illuminate Elizabeth Barrett Browning's escape from familial and class oppression;[2] to Pamela Caughie *Flush* is 'an allegory of canon formation and canonical value';[3] and for David Eberly the dogginess of Flush is merely a decoy, allowing

Woolf to 'bring to the surface the repressed emotional narrative of her childhood' (in particular, her experience of sexual abuse).[4] When it does seem as though the critical focus may be turning towards Woolf's canine protagonist, it is often only gestural. This is evident when Ruth Vanita comments on Mr Browning's introduction and 'Flush's silent suffering, his feelings of neglect, loneliness and helplessness' being 'movingly evoked', but then shifts immediately to focus on the role of jealousy in Woolf's own relationships with other women, with Flush's role again to act as a 'metaphor'.[5] Such readings are at risk of displaying what Craig Smith terms an 'anthropocentric bias', where critics claim that Woolf *uses Flush* (and its eponymous protagonist) for allegorical ends and is therefore 'accepted as a serious object of study only to the extent that it may be represented as being not really about a dog'.[6] Without wishing to deny that these critics offer insightful political, social, cultural, and biographical interpretations of Woolf's text, it might be argued that none of their readings shift the focus further from the human than Jean Guiguet did in his classic book-length study of Woolf's writings. In Guiguet's view, Flush is a mirror reflecting his owner's life, where his own experiences are of little importance: 'Flush's incapacity either to interest us in his own story or to tell us his mistress's effectively, leads one to wonder why Virginia Woolf chose this subject and this point of view.'[7] Indeed he doubts the place in literature altogether of this branch of the Canidae family tree: 'Flush's inarticulate and primitive reactions, however penetrating, are incompatible with the resources of literature. After all, this was never meant for dogs.' For Guiguet *Flush* is interesting because of 'the limits it seems to set to the author's theories' rather than opening up a space in which these theories can be discussed.[8] Perhaps the most interesting part of his commentary comes, however, when he refers to 'Flush's mind and sensibility',[9] but fails to ask questions of the extent to which we can think of dogs as having such a mind and sensibility, let alone what the possible effects could be of representing Flush as having these faculties and what questions this may pose for the assumed human/animal divide. This is similar to the way in which Rosenthal unflinchingly refers to 'the richness of [Flush's] memory' and yet does not retain a focus on Flush for long enough to reflect upon what Woolf's canine protagonist may reveal about dogs, or about the question of the animal.[10]

Following my discussion in previous chapters of some of the ways in which human bodies and nonhuman environments and objects are entangled in Woolf's theorising, it is precisely to this question of Woolf's treatment of animals in *Flush* that I now turn. Focusing on Woolf's exploration of animals entails a consideration of the role allegory and anthropomorphism has played in critical approaches to *Flush*, but Woolf's text also explores issues of animal nudity, gaze, and nonverbal communication, allowing for various theoretical perspectives on the material relations between species to be considered. Whilst these matters have predominately been seen to divide human and animal, they are central to Woolf's challenging of our preconceived notions of species distinctions, and her reconceptualisation of the complex spaces shared by human and nonhuman animals.

After allegory and anthropocentrism

Where certain critics have more recently directed their focus on canine matters, Woolf has been criticised for displaying anthropomorphism in her depiction of Barrett Browning's cocker spaniel. Jutta Ittner's comparison of *Flush* and Paul Auster's *Timbuktu* (1999), for example, raises concerns that Woolf fails to fulfil the 'radical potential' in presenting animals in literature and concludes that Woolf's anthropomorphic depiction leaves Flush as 'a creature that is doubly instrumentalized':

> First, because he has been created by Woolf as a conscious and emotive animal in order to tell a familiar story from an unusual angle, he has no agency of his own [...] Flush is constructed less for the purpose of creating complexity or contrast than for amusement while reinforcing societal values. In fact, all the different layers of this anthropomorphic construct are human- rather than animal-oriented [...] Second, the mock agency granted to Flush is Woolf's ironic critique of Victorian constructs of class, rank, and gender relationships [...] animal existence is diminished to an anthropomorphized caricature – animal alterity turned into a literary device. Flush's inner and outer world as constructed by Woolf does not challenge the reader to reconceptualize animalness but rather reaffirms human projections in a loving, if ironic and often condescending, way.[11]

Ittner is too quick to dismiss the subversive potential of Woolf's exploration of nonhuman animals, but her reading does point to the potential danger of anthropomorphism in subsuming the animal within a human 'world' without taking on board the different experiences specific to different species. In *The Open: Man and Animal* (2004), Giorgio Agamben comments on this danger by turning to German ethologist Jakob von Uexküll's concept of *Umwelt* (referring to each animal's specific 'environment-world'). We must not fall into the assumption, he writes,

> that the relations a certain animal subject has to the things in its environment take place in the same space and in the same time as those which bind us to

the objects in our human world. This illusion rests on the belief in a single world in which all living beings are situated [. . .] The fly, the dragonfly, and the bee that we observe flying next to us on a sunny day do not move in the same world as the one in which we observe them, nor do they share with us – or with each other – the same time and the same space.[12]

Agamben rightly warns against too easily judging an animal's sensory-perceptual world based on our own.

My reading will at various points focus on instances in *Flush* that could be viewed as anthropomorphic, and I may at times run the risk faced by readers of projecting anthropomorphic significance onto animals. But whilst it is important to keep in mind the potential pitfalls in accounting for nonhuman animals through a human perspective, it is crucial not to dismiss the subversive potential of what might on first reading appear to be a straightforward case of anthropomorphism. As Dan Wylie has pointed out, those aspects of texts like *Flush* that some critics have labelled as 'anthropomorphic' actually function in more complex ways. It is important to remember, for instance, that Woolf is fully aware as she writes of the limitations of trying to represent a dog's life through human language.[13] For Wylie anthropomorphism does have its limits, but

> anthropomorphic writing nevertheless seems to embody the proposition that animals – or at least certain animals – are in some sense understandable, and have enough in common with us to demand an ethically equivalent response and sense of responsibility from humans [. . .] the use of the spaniel's perspective seems more than merely instrumental or allegorical. Woolf also seems interested in the actuality of an animal's consciousness.[14]

In this view, then, it is the very process of imagining that is most revealing; the implications of this possible animal consciousness and of a 'new kind of society' that is 'inclusive of dogs and humans' is what matters: 'the issue is not whether or not anthropomorphising is "true," but that it is both imaginatively possible and fruitful. [. . .] This is the ethic of anthropomorphism.'[15]

This ethic of anthropomorphism has something in common with what Marjorie Garber describes in *Dog Love* (1996) as 'The New Anthropomorphism' in science: 'a new wave of "neo-anthropomorphists" has arisen: animal behaviourists who believe that anthropomorphism can actually help them "do their science," as scientists like to say. "Anthropomorphism is just another word for empathy," they claim.'[16] At the very least anthropomorphism can lead to a willingness to consider that the animal is more capable than we ordinarily conceive. We might note here the significance of Woolf's short story 'The Widow and the Parrot: A True Story'[17] when Mrs Gage talks to the Parrot, James, 'as though he were a human being' but in doing so thinks that 'the creature has more meaning in its acts than we humans know' (*CSF* 167). More recently Jane Bennett, whose theory of 'vital materialism' I discuss in the next chapter in relation to Woolf's materialist, immanent theory of 'life' in *The Waves*, has argued that 'an anthropomorphic element in perception can uncover a whole world of resonances and resemblances – sounds and sights that echo and bounce [. . .] revealing similarities across categorical divides', thereby helping to challenge human claims to privilege over nonhuman worlds. It may be, then, that a little anthropomorphism does not necessarily lead to an anthropo*centric* outlook; that, in fact, the outright rejection of any sign of anthropomorphism allows the human/animal divide to remain unchallenged, limiting the sense to which nonhumans and humans are materially, socially, and emotionally co-involved. As animal research scientist Jonathan Balcombe argues, it is possible to 'use our own experiences as a useful template for interpreting the emotions of other beings' without falling into the false and problematic assumption – not least because we already know that sensory systems work differently between species – that 'human capacity for feeling' is 'the "gold standard" by which all other species should be measured'.[18]

A more sympathetic reading of Woolf's modernist canine aesthetics in this respect is provided by Smith who sets *Flush* apart from earlier novels that placed an animal as protagonist – for example, Anna Sewell's *Black Beauty* (1877) and Jack London's *The Call of the Wild* (1903) – by claiming that it 'is neither specifically humane nor specifically humanist in its agenda'. Instead of this, he argues that Woolf maps 'a canine subjectivity, as an experiment worth performing for its own sake'.[19] Rather than shirking further consideration of the capacity of the dog's mind or richness of the dog's memory, Smith takes examples such as the episode where Flush dreams in order to argue that rather than being written-off as anthropomorphic, Woolf's depictions may not be so implausible. As she writes in *Flush*:

> He slept as dogs sleep when they are dreaming. Now his legs twitched – was he dreaming that he hunted rabbits in Spain? Was he coursing up a hot hillside with dark men shouting 'Span! Span!' as the rabbits darted from the brushwood?[20] Then he lay still again. And now he yelped, quickly, softly, many times in succession. Perhaps he heard Dr Mitford egging his greyhounds on to the hunt at Reading. Then he wagged his tail sheepishly. Did he hear old Miss Mitford cry 'Bad dog! Bad dog!' as he slunk back to her, where she stood among the turnips waving her umbrella? (*F* 104)

Woolf's use of questions in this passage reveals a humble mode of speculation that leaves her strikingly close to the general consensus among animal researchers that dogs do indeed dream and that it is the precise content we are unaware of: 'the assumption that canine dreams like human ones emerge from a mixture of memory, anxiety, and desire, is as valid as any'.[21] Again Woolf turns our focus towards the dog in this story rather than allegorical interpretations centred on his human owner, where notably the dream does not contain any memories of Barrett Browning.[22] Consequently, if *Flush* is taken 'as an intuitive, clear-eyed attempt to represent a nonhuman subject', we might see it as 'one of Woolf's most original and forward-looking achievements [...] making a substantial gesture toward crossing the gulf of understanding between human and nonhuman subjects, and toward understanding the relationship between the two'.[23]

Whilst I am wary of Smith's interchangeable use of the term 'subject', the salient point for my argument in this chapter is the emphasis his reading places on the possibility of viewing *Flush* in nonhumanist terms, especially if we accept the growing claims among animal theorists that it is the humanist tradition which has upheld the human/animal distinction, and consequent marginalisation of (and violence against) animals. In *Zoographies* (2008), for example, Matthew Calarco's project is to disassociate the pro-animal discourse from the 'rights' based agenda of liberal humanism and instead cast it against the pervasive anthropocentrism internal to a liberal humanist politics.[24] In his carefully argued book, Calarco exposes the 'blind spots' of 'implicit anthropocentrism' at the heart of the contemporary debates in continental philosophy, and argues that it is essential to turn to thinkers such as Derrida and Deleuze in order to counter humanist discourses. These include the refusals seen in the works of neo-Marxist and neo-Lacanian thinkers such as Slavoj Žižek and Alain Badiou to abandon the subject as a ground for thought where

> even if this concept of subjectivity functions [...] as a means of opening onto something other than metaphysical *humanism*, it is not at all clear that it opens onto something other than metaphysical *anthropocentrism*. When these theorists [Žižek and Badiou] speak of the subject as being called into being as a response to an event of some sort, it is always a human subject that is being described, and it is always an *anthropogenic* event that gives rise to the human subject.[25]

Defending Derrida and Deleuze against accusations that their different critiques of subjectivity result in an ineffective and weakened political agency, Calarco argues that their work is useful in that it points to the complicity between the metaphysics of humanism and anthropocentrism. The nonanthropocentrism found in the writings of Derrida and Deleuze should not be ignored amidst 'a hasty retrieval of anthropocentric subjectivity toward supposedly radical political ends'.[26]

Arguing that *Flush* is indeed one of Woolf's most forward-looking texts, this chapter will go on to read her fictional canine biography alongside both Derrida and Deleuze, as well as Haraway. Taking the dog in this text seriously as well as the text itself – therefore worrying over, as Goldman puts it, the 'dogginess of the dog'[27] – I am interested in the ways in which Woolf's modernist canine experiment anticipates and intervenes in the wider context of our own contemporary debates on the question of the animal in literary studies, theory/philosophy, and posthumanities more broadly. The aim of this approach is not to empty Woolf's text of humour, but rather to ask whether the humour is not aimed at the ways in which we take our own human position too certainly – an effort, in Woolf's words, to 'caricature the pomposity of those who claim that they are something' (*F* 89). As Pamela Caughie suggests, 'to take *Flush* as a joke might not be to dismiss it but to keep from taking oneself too seriously as a leader or figure, to keep from taking a firm position'.[28] Rather than attempting to reach a definitive conclusion as to whether Woolf's writing is either anthropocentric or illustrative of a truly animal agency, I want to suggest some of the ways in which *Flush* opens up a space where we may (re)think the animal/human relation, and where there are more than these two options – anthropocentric allegory or animal agency – available to us.

Derrida's cat and Woolf's denuded dog

> It is generally thought [. . .] that the property unique to animals, what in the last instance distinguishes them from man, is their being naked without knowing it. Not being naked therefore, not having knowledge of their nudity[.][29]

At the beginning of *The Animal That Therefore I Am* (2008), Derrida reminds us that one issue upholding the human/animal distinction in Western philosophy is a two-fold assumption concerning nudity; that the animal is naked, and the animal is unaware of this nakedness: 'They wouldn't be naked because they are naked. In principle, with the exception of man, no animal has ever thought to dress itself. Clothing would be proper to man, one of the "properties" of man.' In the world, therefore, humans dress, adorning themselves with a layer of cultural expression and performance, where animals are reduced to their biological wear: 'The animal, therefore, is not naked because it is naked. It doesn't feel its own nudity. There is no nudity "in nature."'[30] Naked in his bathroom and facing his cat, Derrida uses the realisation of his own nudity to launch his philosophical treatise on the nature of the human/animal relationship. Before going on to consider Derrida's main concerns in the essays in *The Animal That Therefore I Am* (where/how this human/animal distinction should be drawn, and the ethical implications of animal suffering), I want to stay with this much-discussed encounter between Derrida and his cat: 'Before the cat looks at me naked', he asks, 'would I be ashamed *like* a beast that no longer has the sense of its nudity? Or, on the contrary, *like* a man who retains his sense of nudity?' What is interesting in this remark is not only the focus on shame (something we will return to), but Derrida's emphasised simile which suggests that from the start he is unwilling to go along with simple assumptions concerning animal nudity, as if he is not quite settled upon his own humanity/animality. From the beginning, from the double-meaning of the French *je suis* ('I am' and 'I follow'), Derrida is asking us to consider the ontological uncertainty of both himself and his cat: 'Who am I, therefore? Who is it that I am (following)?' And these are questions not only for him to ask of himself: 'Whom should this be asked of if not of the other? And perhaps of the cat itself?'[31]

In *Flush*, cats themselves figure only as figures of speech (or rather, of silence) as their sole appearance in the text is when we are told that Flush 'came to prefer the silence of the cat to the robustness of the dog' (F 32).[32] Through her own rich portrayal of the canine, however, Woolf engages with the type of philosophical questions at the heart of Derrida's naked encounter with his own silent cat, and perhaps goes even further in her literary rendering of a cocker spaniel than Derrida does in his philosophical consideration of the cat's perspective in all of this. One key moment which invites a comparison between *Flush* and Derrida's bathroom encounter with his cat comes towards the end of Woolf's text when a fully clothed (as far as we can tell) Mr Browning clips off Flush's fur whilst in Florence – a result of 'red and virile' fleas that 'scourged' him, that 'nested in Flush's fur' and 'bit their way into the thickest of his coat' (F 88). Rather than Flush's coat signalling his natural status as naked, he appears to be clothed by his fur and it is the fleas that are reduced to their 'virile', unkempt nature. It is also suggested that Flush's coat, perhaps like human clothing, is seen as a sign of his status:

> He carried his pedigree on his back. His coat meant to him what a gold watch inscribed with the family arms means to an impoverished squire whose broad acres have shrunk to that single circle. It was a coat that Mr Browning now

proposed to sacrifice. He called Flush to him and, taking a pair of scissors, clipped him all over into the likeness of a lion. (*F* 89)

The comparison of Flush's coat to a watch and his now denuded body to that of a lion subtly hints at both human-animal likenesses as well as animal-animal differences. We learn that 'as the travesty of quite a different animal rose round his neck, Flush felt himself emasculated, diminished, ashamed' (*F* 89). The claim that Flush being purged of his coat qualifies as animal nudity should not simply be read as an anthropomorphic projection; this is precisely one instance, as with Woolf's description of canine dreams, where a perceived anthropomorphism might in fact lead us to, at the very least, pose important questions that might otherwise be left unasked.

Such imaginative possibilities are considered when the narrative informs us that it is Flush who this time ponders: 'What am I now? he thought, gazing into the glass. And the glass replied with the brutal sincerity of glasses, "You are nothing". He was nobody. Certainly he was no longer a cocker spaniel' (*F* 89). Importantly, Flush's aforementioned shame does not triumph over curiosity and he begins to feel positively about his changed appearance so that he gazes not once but twice in the mirror:

> as he gazed, his ears bald now, and uncurled, seemed to twitch. It was as if the potent spirits of truth and laughter were whispering in them. To be nothing – is that not, after all, the most satisfactory state in the whole world? He looked again [...] there could be no doubt that he was free from fleas. He shook his ruff. He danced on his nude, attenuated legs. His spirits rose. (*F* 89–90)

Flush appears to revel in his nudity, indeed to 'caricature the pomposity of those who claim that they are something'. Challenging the notion that an animal cannot experience nudity, and that the very questioning of such an experience need involve a human at all, Flush recognises his changed appearance in a mirrored encounter with his denuded self rather than with Mr Browning.[33] Derrida reminds us that these questions of animal nudity and of recognition are ones that 'philosophical thinking [...] has never touched on'. Emphasising the heterogeneity within the category 'animal', he notes that 'one of the structural differences among animals is drawn there, between those who have some experience of the mirror and those who don't have any at all'.[34] As one of those animals who appears to have some experience of the mirror, does Flush's encounter with his denuded body show that Woolf is beginning to imagine in literature what philosophy has failed to do? The excerpt cited above is not the only moment in the text where Flush is faced with himself in a mirror. In an earlier scene Miss Barrett makes Flush 'stand with her in front of the looking-glass and ask him why he barked and trembled. Was not the little brown dog opposite himself? But what is "oneself"? Is it the thing people see? Or is it the thing one is? So Flush pondered that question too' (F 32). This passage has been traced to a letter Barrett wrote to her friend Hugh Stuart Boyd in which she comments that Flush 'can't bear me to look into a glass, because he thinks there is a little brown dog inside every looking glass, and he is jealous of its being so close to *me*' (F 122, n.32). In *Dog Love*, Garber emphasises the significance of the fact that Woolf's Flush is described differently in front of the mirror than Miss Barrett had originally put it: 'Where Barrett's Flush sees "another" dog, and is jealous, Woolf's Flush sees "himself," and ponders the problem of reality.'[35] By re-writing Barrett's interpretation of Flush's mirrored gaze, Woolf again turns the focus away from the human and towards the animal.

With her re-creation of Miss Barrett's canine companion, then, Woolf not only asks the questions, 'Can one speak of the animal? Can one approach the animal?', nor does she simply consider – and this would already be going further, according to Derrida, than the majority of Western philosophical tradition – whether 'one from the vantage of the animal [can] see oneself being looked at naked?'[36] Instead, Woolf seems to ask whether the animal 'can see *itself* naked', a question that according to Derrida 'is never asked'.[37] Derrida posits: 'The animal looks at us, and we are naked before it. Thinking perhaps begins there.'[38] Is Woolf opening up the possibility that Flush looking at himself naked (regardless of whether a denuded human is present) may be where thinking begins? After being cured of fleas, like a beautiful woman freed from 'clothes and cosmetics' or a clergyman whose collar has been thrown 'into the dustbin', Flush is let off his leash: '"Flush," Mrs Browning wrote to her sister, "is wise." [. . .] The true philosopher is he who has lost his coat but is free from fleas' (F 90). When Flush returns to London with his coat growing back, we are told that he falls asleep one afternoon as the sun 'burn[t] through his fur to the naked skin' (F 103). This is the moment when Flush dreams, but it is also the moment where the suggestion is reinforced that Flush is not, as an animal, always and already naked – his 'naked skin' being covered by his fur.

By describing Flush's denuded encounter with the mirror, focusing on his (self-) gaze, Woolf may invite accusations of anthropomorphism, but in the process she also points to limitations in Derrida's own consideration of the animal, nudity, and the mirror. At the end of the first essay in *The Animal That Therefore I Am*, which shares the same title, Derrida introduces a 'full-length mirror [une psyché]' as a segue into his next discussion, 'But as for me, who am I (following)?':

> Wherever some autobiographical play is being enacted there has to be a psyché, a mirror that reflects me naked from head to toe. The same question then becomes whether I should show myself but in the process see myself naked (that is, reflect my image in a mirror) when, concerning me, looking at me, is this living creature, this cat that can find itself caught in the same mirror? Is there animal narcissism? But cannot this cat also be, deep within her eyes, my primary mirror?[39]

In passages such as these, the extent to which Derrida is ultimately concerned with the animal is in question. Haraway picks Derrida up on precisely this issue in *When Species Meet*, insisting that whilst he 'understood that actual animals look back at actual human beings [. . . and] he was in the presence of someone, not of a machine [. . .] he did not seriously consider an alternative form of engagement either, one that risked knowing something more about cats and *how to look back*, perhaps even scientifically, biologically, and *therefore* also philosophically and intimately.'[40] For Haraway, then, despite coming 'right to the edge of respect', where his cat was concerned 'Derrida failed a simple obligation of companion species; he did not become curious about what the cat might actually be doing, feeling, thinking, or perhaps making available to him in looking back at him that morning [. . .] he missed a possible invitation'.[41] Unlike Flush, Derrida is perhaps more concerned with the shame of his own nudity, and the shame of Western philosophy, than curiosity about his cat:[42] 'in all this worrying and longing, the cat was never quite heard from again'.[43] Calarco holds a similar frustration that, given Derrida's careful and rigorous probing of the human/animal distinction on ethical as well as ontological grounds, and despite his taking Heidegger to task elsewhere for his insistence on an 'abyssal' gulf between human and animal (for example in his 1985 essay 'Geschlecht II: Heidegger's Hand'), Derrida himself falls back on 'a definitive division, or rather a series of divisions, between human beings and animals'.[44]

Nonetheless, in his autobiographical and theoretical inquiry into the animal, Derrida does pose a range of important questions that he feels have been neglected, some of which Woolf engages with, to a greater or lesser degree, in *Flush*:

> The question 'Does the animal dream?' is, in its form, premises, and stakes, at least analogous to the questions 'Does the animal think?' 'Does the animal produce representations?' a self, imagination, a relation to the future as such?

Does the animal have not only signs but a language, and what language? Does the animal die? Does it laugh? Does it cry? Does it grieve? Does it get bored? Does it lie? Does it forgive? Does it sing? Does it invent? Does it invent music? Does it play music? Does it play? Does it offer hospitality? Does it offer? Does it give? Does it have hands? eyes? etc.? modesty? clothes? and the mirror?[45]

To this we can add Haraway's question: 'can I learn to play with *this* cat? Can I, the philosopher, respond to an invitation or recognize one when it is offered'?[46] And we could contrast Derrida's naked encounter with his cat here with a similar meeting described by Balcombe in *Second Nature* (2010), when sitting in the bath he uses suds to change his hairstyle into one upright peak (to which his cat Mica looked relaxed) and then form two horns (to which Mica's 'stare intensified, his pupils began to dilate, and he lowered himself gradually into a crouching position'). What is noticeably different in Balcombe's bathroom encounter with his cat is his sense of curiosity for what the cat may be feeling, leading Balcombe to think of experiments 'to test cats' responses to familiar faces with various horns, some of which do and do not resemble those of real animals'. For Balcombe, his own nudity is far from the focus of his reflections.[47] Indeed, this touches on a further question posed by Haraway: 'what if the question of how animals engage *one another's* gaze *responsively* takes center stage for people?'[48] Perhaps it is a variation of this last question posed by Haraway – a question that we are left asking – which is also raised by comparing the encounters between Derrida and his cat and Woolf's depiction of Elizabeth Barrett Browning's denuded dog: what would happen if Flush's gaze were to be directed towards Derrida's cat?

On four gazes: face-to-face with companion species

> We are face-to-face, in the company of significant others, companion species to one another. That is not romantic or idealist but mundane and consequential in the little things that make lives.[49]

Regardless of the extent to which it might be argued that Derrida is in the end more concerned with shame than curiosity, he insists that we do not generalise his cat, or elevate it into some mythical creature: 'the cat I am talking about is a real cat, truly, believe me, a *little cat*. It isn't the *figure* of a cat. It doesn't silently enter the bedroom as an allegory for all the cats on the earth, the felines that traverse our myths and religions, literature and fables.'[50] In his insistence that we recognise his cat's 'unsubstitutable singularity', Derrida is keen to reinforce that we can not think of animals in one generalised and homogeneous grouping. In responding to his cat's gaze, he is unwilling to assume that it is only he (and all humans) who have the capacity for response, whilst his cat (representing all animals) would only have the ability to react: 'When it responds in its name (whatever "respond" means, and that will be our question), it doesn't do so as the exemplar of a species called "cat," even less so of an "animal" genus or kingdom.'[51] It is interesting to note here that a similar emphasis on the singularity of her dog is evident in Elizabeth Barrett Browning's 'To Flush, My Dog' (1843), which was a source for Woolf's fictional biography and where it is repeated on several occasions that the poem is about 'This dog' as opposed to 'Other dogs', with eight lines beginning with one of these two phrases.[52] In her later 'Flush or Faunus' (1850), also a source for Woolf, the first line again repeats the demonstrative pronoun as specific marker of 'this dog', albeit that Flush is here elevated in his association to the part-man, part-beast mythical creature of the Faunus or Pan.[53]

Derrida distinguishes between his cat and Alice's cat in *Alice in Wonderland* (1865), which, he posits, ends with 'Alice's very Cartesian statement' that '"On this occasion the kitten only purred: and it was impossible to guess whether it meant "yes" or "no."'' He emphasises:

> my real cat is not Alice's little cat [. . .] because I am certainly not about to conclude hurriedly [. . .] that one cannot speak with a cat on the pretext that it doesn't reply or that it always replies the same thing [. . . It] comes down to knowing not whether the animal speaks but whether one can know what *respond* means. And how to distinguish a response from a reaction.[54]

This raises its own questions in relation to Woolf's novel: is the singularity we are speaking of named Flush capable of responding? Does Flush's gaze shed any light on the questions Derrida asks following the gaze of his cat? Are we capable of responding to his response? In *Flush* there are four key moments where Flush and Miss Barrett gaze at each other, moments that provide examples, as shown below, of mutual recognition and response of various forms.

'For the first time Flush looked at the lady lying on the sofa'

After Miss Mitford gives Flush to Miss Barrett as a gift, the first face-to-face encounter between Flush and his new 'owner' occurs: '"Oh Flush!" said Miss Barrett. For the first time she looked him in the face. For the first time Flush looked at the lady lying on the sofa' (*F* 18).

Immediately, we are left in no doubt that Flush has a 'face',[55] but we are not yet certain that Flush is actually looking at Miss Barrett's, as his gaze is described here as non-specific, directed simply 'at the lady'. In the next paragraph, as the narrator has described the similarities of their appearance – Miss Barrett's 'heavy curls', 'large bright eyes' and 'large mouth' reflecting Flush's 'heavy ears', 'large and bright' eyes, and 'wide' mouth – it is confirmed that this is indeed a face-to-face gaze. Whilst their mutual 'surprise' registers recognition of 'a likeness between them', it is soon their differences, of species as well as of sex, that are focused on: 'As they gazed at each other each felt: Here am I – and then each felt: But how different! [. . .] Between them lay the widest gulf that can separate one being from another. She spoke. He was dumb. She was woman; he was dog. Thus closely united, thus immensely divided, they gazed at each other' (F 18–19). Even here, however, when we are reminded of Miss Barrett's access to human speech as opposed to Flush who is 'dumb', Woolf's use of free indirect discourse refuses to mark the voice of Miss Barrett. The use of the semi-colon too is important in signalling an openness to the boundaries between them, and the possibility that what they are 'divided' by is not essential and finally determined. Moreover, the response to this (mis)recognition is for Flush to join his new companion on the sofa, 'on the rug at Miss Barrett's feet'. Ironically, just as we are told that 'the widest gulf' lay between them, it is simply a matter of feet between Miss Barrett and Flush. What is important here is not the reinforcing of difference between human and animal, but the fact that there has been a moment of mutual recognition, that Flush seems to have responded, and that the narrative has at least posed the possibility of inter-species connection: 'Broken asunder, yet made in the same mould, could it be that each completed what was dormant in the other?' (F 18) According to Derrida, there are 'two types of discourse regarding the animal', the first formed by writers 'as if they themselves had never been looked at, and especially not naked, by an animal that addressed them', an animal that is 'something seen and not seeing', and the second by those 'who admit to taking upon themselves the address that an animal addresses to them', those who Derrida does not yet know of: 'I have found no such representative, but it is in that very place that I find myself, here and now, in the process of searching.' Simply asking the above question, showing the face-to-face recognition, allows us, from this first instance, to consider that Woolf is also in this place with Derrida, experimenting and 'searching'.[56]

'large bright eyes shone in hers'

The connection between Flush and Miss Barrett is also illustrated in their second reciprocal gaze, which this time, we are left in no doubt, is eye-to-eye (or eye-in-eye) as Flush's 'large bright eyes shone in hers'. Rather than this providing an example of Miss Barrett subsuming Flush, it is clear that she responds to his look, that it changes her mood and impacts upon her sense of reality as she is 'transformed' into 'a Greek nymph' being kissed by that 'bearded god' named 'Flush, or was it Pan?' (*F* 27) Mirroring the early phrase that 'she was woman; he was dog' (*F* 19), in this moment 'she was a nymph and Flush was Pan' (*F* 27). What is additionally interesting is the way in which Flush appears to respond to her response: 'So, too, Flush felt strange stirrings at work within him' (*F* 27). Just as Miss Barrett imagines a time and place when they could be, perhaps, closer, so does Flush: 'he longed for the day when his own rough roar would issue like hers in the little simple sounds that had such mysterious meaning' (*F* 28). We might draw a comparison here with the 'little language such as lovers use, words of one syllable such as children speak' that Bernard desires in *The Waves*. In fact, Bernard barely wants to sound human at all when he declares 'I need a howl; a cry [. . .] I have done with phrases' (*W* 246), and at one point he even specifies that what one really needs is 'a bark' (*W* 210). We might say that both Flush and Bernard display a longing to, as Deleuze and Guattari put it, 'stammer language, be a foreigner in one's own tongue'.[57] Indeed, in a 1985 interview with Antoine Dulaure and Claire Parnet, Deleuze claims Woolf's writing as one example of an author styling a 'new syntax' which breaks with dominant and conventional modes and creates 'a foreign language within the language'.[58]

If imagining Flush and Miss Barrett as Pan and a nymph is to imagine some state which blurs the human/animal distinction, then so is Flush's description of this longing to communicate with her on different terms. Importantly, however, this is not a wish for anthropomorphism, as he does not long to understand or speak the human language, but rather 'innumerable sounds', 'little simple sounds' with 'mysterious meaning' (*F* 28). Indeed a specifically human language is charged as hindering communication rather than aiding it: 'The fact was that they could not communicate with words, and it was a fact that led undoubtedly to much misunderstanding. Yet did it not lead also to a peculiar intimacy? [. . .] do words say everything? Can words say anything? Do not words destroy the symbol that lies beyond the reach of words?' (*F* 27) As Garber puts it, commenting on this same passage, 'precisely because our dogs cannot speak, we are able to hear – with uncanny and uncanine skill – what they have to say'.⁵⁹ In emphasising the inadequacies of language and suggesting that it is not a necessary component of close companion species bonding, Woolf posits the animal's apparent lack of speech as not in fact a lack at all. As Derrida challenges: 'It would not be a matter of "giving speech back" to animals but perhaps of acceding to a thinking, however fabulous and chimerical it may be, that thinks the absence of the name and of the word otherwise, and as something other than a privation.'⁶⁰ Perhaps Flush is pointing us towards Deleuze and Guattari's statement that 'language is not life; it gives life orders. Life does not speak; it listens and waits.'⁶¹ *Flush* would seem to imply that it is not sufficient to tie response to language, and therefore claim that humans 'respond' and animals simply 'react' in these terms.⁶²

'Miss Barrett refused even to meet his eyes'

Whilst in the two examples so far Flush meets Miss Barrett's gaze, there is a revealing scene later in the text in which Miss Barrett momentarily refuses to do so: 'though Flush might look, Miss Barrett refused even to meet his eyes. There she lay on the sofa; there Flush lay on the floor' (*F* 46). Chastised after his jealous attack on Mr Browning, Flush is relegated to the floor, and his status is lowered to such a state that Miss Barrett refuses to respond. But the semi-colon again seems important here, signalling that although Miss Barrett is angry there is still the possibility of reconciliation, and Flush does indeed respond even to this refusal to respond:

> exiled, on the carpet, he went through one of those whirlpools of tumultuous emotion in which the soul is either dashed upon the rocks and splintered or, finding some tuft of foothold, slowly and painfully pulls itself up, regains dry land, and at last emerges on top of a ruined universe to survey a world created afresh on a different plan. (*F* 47)

The narrator ponders this unsettling moment in Flush's life: 'Which was it to be – destruction or reconstruction? That was the question.' Going against the stereotype of animalistic, mindless reaction, Flush opts for reconstruction, his response is the realisation that 'things are not simple but complex. If he bit Mr Browning he bit her too. Hatred is not hatred; hatred is also love. Here Flush shook his ears in an agony of perplexity. He turned uneasily on the floor. Mr Browning was Miss Barrett – Miss Barrett was Mr Browning; love is hatred and hatred is love' (*F* 47).

Woolf's narrative refuses here to fall into the type of assumptions about the limitations of animal psychology that would lead to accusations of a problematic anthropomorphism. Consistent with the representations of response we have already seen, the most important point being made is that 'things are not simple but complex'. To emphasise the complex intertwining of their relationship, Miss Barrett does, after looking at Flush again, respond by forgetting her idea 'to buy a muzzle' (*F* 47) and, 'la[ying] down her pen' (as if to signal once again that language is secondary to their connection) 'she forgave him'. What follows is the description a few days later when Flush and Miss Barrett seem intimately connected in communication as Flush chooses to eat the cakes Mr Browning had previously brought because they were now 'symbols of hatred turned to love' (*F* 48). As Miss Barrett explains to Flush that he should not try to bite Mr Browning again, Flush's response suggests an inter-species communication that crosses over this supposed abyss between them: 'Flush solemnly repeated, in his own language, the words she had used – he swore to love Mr Browning and not bite him for the future' (*F* 49).

'he leapt on the sofa and thrust his face into hers'

As it turns out, Flush's ability to respond to his owner's gaze is only denied by death. In the closing moments of the text, we have the fourth and final example of human and dog meeting face-to-face. As Miss Barrett, by now of course Mrs Browning, responds to Flush jumping on the sofa and 'thrust[ing] his face into hers' by recalling her sonnet 'Flush or Faunus', they seem to be connected by more than just their gaze (if you like they are not just face-to-face but face-in-face, recalling the eye-in-eye gaze above) (*F* 105). As Haraway notes, we now know that the 'molecular record' of humans and dogs contain traces of each other,[63] and if this material, molecular intermingling is being emphasised in Woolf's text, then it is fitting that this should occur – as a reminder of the importance of Flush's life on the shaping of his companion – moments before his demise. Woolf could not, of course, have been aware of today's advances in molecular biology, but it is as though she wants to emphasise that Flush should not be thought of as some symbolic canine figure that stands for all dogs (just as Derrida insists with his cat) let alone as mere allegory for a strictly human concern. If he is a figure at all, he illustrates those of Haraway, where 'figures are not representations or didactic illustrations, but rather material-semiotic nodes or knots in which diverse bodies and meanings coshape one another'.[64] Indeed, such nodes or knots also seem to be evident in a short unfinished sketch written by Woolf entitled 'The Dog' (1989): 'She attached herself [. . .] she would not let me out of her sight. She became like a supplementary limb – a tail, something attached to my person. I never had to call her. I had great difficulty in detaching her' (*CSF* 334–5).[65]

The fact that the closing lines of *Flush* echo the description used when Flush and Miss Barrett first looked at each other is also revealing. We will recall that in the first example we read: 'Broken asunder, yet made in the same mould, could it be that each completed what was dormant in the other? She might have been – all that; and he – but no. Between them lay the widest gulf that can separate one being from another. She spoke. He was dumb. She was woman; he was dog' (*F* 18–19). And in the final paragraph we read: 'Broken asunder, yet made in the same mould, each, perhaps, completed what was dormant in the other. But she was woman; he was dog' (*F* 105). Woolf is not simply reinforcing the gulf between Flush and his human companion one final time – as with the earlier passage the semi-colon appears to leave the possibility of boundary crossing open. More tellingly, however, this latter passage is different from the former in two important respects: firstly, the possibility that each 'completed what was dormant in the other' is no longer followed by a question mark – although Woolf uses the word 'perhaps', she seems to be more certain of their connection across species, and perhaps also across sexes, by the end of the book; secondly, instead of the sharp 'But no. Between them lay the widest gulf', the conjunction Woolf uses at the end of the book is far softer. In this instance the 'but' may not be in forceful contradiction to the statement preceding it, but might simply present the anomaly that Woolf's text has illuminated: here is a human and a cocker spaniel whose lives are intertwined beyond language 'But' they belong to different species (we might note that this latter passage does not reinforce the statement concerning who could speak and who was 'dumb'). As we read that Mrs Browning 'looked at Flush again' and that 'he did not look at her' we are aware that this must not be due to an incapacity of his species for response or an abyssal gulf between human and dog (indeed the very fact she expected Flush to return her gaze emphasises their inter-species connection) but rather because 'he had been alive; he was now dead. That was all' (*F* 105–6).

Does seeing the relationship between Flush and his human companion through their shared gaze in these four examples point us towards the 'mortal world-making entanglements' that Donna Haraway terms 'contact zones'?[66] It is certainly true that Woolf's examples of reciprocal gaze between human and dog turn out to anticipate current scientific research. In 'The Secret Life of the Dog', a BBC *Horizon* documentary, we see animal behaviour scientist Daniel Mills' experiment into dog recognition of human emotions, which previous research has shown to be expressed asymmetrically so that when humans look at a face they have a left-gaze bias (i.e., they look at the right-hand side of the person's face). The findings are fascinating: while dogs look randomly at pictures of objects or of other dogs, they also display a left-gaze bias when looking at a human face. Later in the documentary, cognitive psychologist Juliane Kaminski conducts an experiment which shows that dogs are even attuned to the direction of the human gaze, something not achieved by our closest ancestor, the chimpanzee. Moreover, these skills are specifically developed through the co-evolutionary stories of humans and dogs (dogs do not show these abilities with their own species, for example).[67] Rather than emphasising 'The Great Divides' between animals (in nature) and humans (in culture), here differences appear to, as Haraway would put it, 'flatten into mundane differences – the kinds that have consequences and demand respect and response',[68] the kinds that are evinced in 'naturecultures' where 'we are training each other'.[69] In *Flush*, these learned and materially embedded capabilities for human-dog communication display 'material-semiotic dancing in which all partners have face, but no one relies on names. [. . .] Non-linguistic embodied communication [which] depends on looking back and greeting significant others, again and again.'[70] By asking us to respond to Flush's responses, Woolf reminds us that we cannot adequately account for the relations between companion species 'if the fleshly historical reality of face-to-face, body-to-body subject making across species is denied or forgotten in the humanist doctrine that holds only humans to be true subjects with real histories'.[71] Even in Wimpole Street – 'the heart of civilisation' (*F* 20) – we are reminded, as Haraway writes in *The Companion Species Manifesto* (2003), that 'conceiving of "nature" and "culture" as either polar opposites or universal categories is foolish [. . .] Instead of opposites, we get the whole sketchpad of the modern geometrician's fevered brain with which to draw relationality.'[72]

From Spaniel Club to Animalous Society

In *The Companion Species Manifesto*, Haraway alludes to *A Room of One's Own* when arguing that 'categorically unfixed dogs' – what we might call 'mongrels', 'random bred dogs', 'mixed breeds, or just plain dogs' – need 'A Category of One's Own': 'Woolf understood what happens when the impure stroll over the lawns of the properly registered.'[73] Whilst Haraway makes links between 'unregistered' dogs and Woolf's feminist concerns in *A Room of One's Own*, in *Flush* Woolf can be seen to re-draw precisely this relation between the 'properly registered' and 'unregistered'.⁷⁴ And although her protagonist is a cocker spaniel, Woolf does this no where more so than in her critique of the 'Spaniel Club' in the opening pages, where the dogginess of the dog is decided by a distinctly hierarchical and exclusive (we might say 'properly registered') organisation:

> By that august body it is plainly laid down what constitute the vices of a spaniel, and what constitute its virtues. Light eyes, for example, are undesirable; curled ears are still worse; to be born with a light nose or a topknot is nothing less than fatal. The merits of a spaniel are equally clearly defined. His head must be smooth, rising without a too-decided stoop from the muzzle; the skull must be comparatively rounded and well developed with plenty of room for brain power; the eyes must be full but not gozzled; the general expression must be one of intelligence and gentleness. (F 7)

Membership of The Spaniel Club (established since 1885 as an offshoot of The Kennel Club, itself founded in 1873)⁷⁵ depends on categorisation based on physiology. It is not only a question of who is a member and who is not; behind the humour and elegance of Woolf's prose is a matter of life itself: 'the spaniel that exhibits these points is encouraged and bred from; the spaniel who persists in perpetuating topknots and light noses is cut off from the privileges and emoluments of his kind'. Perhaps most telling, however, is the fact that standing at the top of this hierarchy, firmly on two legs, is always a human judge 'laying down the law, impos[ing] penalties and privileges which ensure that the law shall be obeyed' (F 7). Indeed, Linden Peach has pointed out that The Spaniel Club's focus on the 'pure bred' takes on an added significance when we consider the publication history of *Flush* – this section of Woolf's text appeared in the first instalment in the October 1933 issue of *Atlantic Monthly* alongside a review of Adolf Hitler's *Mein Kampf* by Alice Hamilton.⁷⁶

If Woolf is opening up a space in *Flush* which offers the possibility of a more fluid and varied relation between species, then this space is quite different from the exclusive organisation of The Spaniel Club. The close relationship between companion species would seem to challenge the objectifying, hierarchical organisation of dogs, as well as between human and dog. For Haraway, it should never be a question of one species or being having control over another, but rather multiple stories of cross-species entanglements: 'less a category than a pointer to an ongoing "becoming with"'.⁷⁷ As Susan McHugh explains, 'companion species' is a term used 'to inscribe people, animals, places, and technologies in relations that at their best inspire an ongoing sense of curiosity and reciprocity'.⁷⁸ Claiming to be a 'creature' (and philosopher) 'of the mud',[79] Haraway is the self-styled choreographer of 'a multipartner mud dance' where 'the partners do not precede their relating; all that is, is the fruit of becoming with: those are the mantras of companion species'.[80] But whilst Haraway's mud philosophy is important for emphasising the multiple ways in which our lives today – in domestic settings and in a coevolutionary sense[81] – are bound up with those of dogs (and other companion species), and also for shedding light on the specific ways in which animals are (mis)treated in our contemporary stories, her insistence on the 'ordinary' and 'domestic' has its own blind spots when it comes to how we think about the human/animal divide – limitations which fail to explain the whole story of *Flush*.

Haraway's emphasis on 'molecular differences'[82] and 'becoming with' echoes Deleuze and Guattari's concept of 'becoming-animal', which I discuss further below but will briefly define here as the shared event of becoming different, of becoming entangled with the other in a 'creative line of escape' from traditional ontological categories of human and animal.[83] But despite acknowledging in *When Species Meet* (albeit tucked away in a footnote of further criticisms) the influence of Deleuzian 'assemblages' on her thought,[84] Haraway is emphatic in her dislike of Deleuze and Guattari's 'becoming-animal': 'I want to explain why writing in which I had hoped to find an ally for the tasks of companion species instead made me come as close as I get to announcing, "Ladies and Gentlemen, behold the enemy!"'[85] Focusing on *A Thousand Plateaus*, what appears to make Haraway 'so angry' is what she sees as their 'scorn for all that is mundane and ordinary', for the 'homely'[86] and – in a more polemical version of her criticism of Derrida – 'profound absence of curiosity about or respect for and with actual animals'.[87] According to Haraway, they lack 'the courage to look [. . .] a dog in the eye':[88] 'This is a philosophy of the sublime, not the earthly, not the mud.'[89] She goes on to accuse Deleuze and Guattari's becoming-animal of demonstrating one of the clearest displays in all philosophy of 'misogyny, fear of aging, incuriosity about animals, and horror at the ordinariness of flesh, here covered by the alibi of an anti-Oedipal and anticapitalist project'.[90] If Haraway is engaged in a mud dance with her dogs, the problem, perhaps, is that she is also throwing mud. More pragmatically, Braidotti has suggested that what is shared between Haraway and Deleuze, and also her own 'nomadic subject', is a deep 'alliance' in presenting theories which are 'materialist' and 'neo-literal', and therefore not limited to the 'textual' and 'resolutely not metaphorical': 'Haraway shares with Deleuze two key features: serious neo-foundational materialism on the one hand and a rigorous theory of relationality on the other.'[91]

Although Haraway has taken issue with Deleuze and Guattari, then, a combination of her focus on domestic and coevolutionary stories and Deleuze and Guattari's disruption of human-centred relations is important when considering the question of the animal in Woolf's text. As Calarco, whose entire project in *Zoographies* is focused on the rejection of 'human chauvinism',[92] notes, Deleuze and Guattari provide a rare example in Western philosophy of a non-anthropocentric treatment of the animal.[93] In contrast to Haraway's accusation that they lack a curiosity for animals, for Calarco they demonstrate a

> 'fascination' for the animal and other nonhuman perspectives that are at work in becoming-animal; for them, it is this fascination that motivates revolutionary literature and progressive discourses on animals [. . .] a fascination for something 'outside' or other than the human and dominant perspectives (and this 'outside' might well lie within human beings, for example, in an inhuman space at the very heart of what we call human).[94]

The point then is not that Deleuze and Guattari are incurious as Haraway has charged, but that they are *more* than curious. Their real *fascination* is not limited to animals in their 'molar' (that is, unified and fixed) form but concerns the 'molecular' changes and intensive co-involvement of species. It is in this sense that fascination sparks becoming, where 'in the experience of becoming, when one is fascinated by something before oneself, when one contemplates something before oneself, one is *among* it, *within* it, together in a zone of proximity'.[95] In *Flush* this type of fascination actually occurs within a domestic setting, evident in the human/animal gaze shared by Flush and Miss Barrett. If we recall the example where Flush thrusts his face into Miss Barrett's, we could perhaps think of this not simply as a 'representational relation' between molar forms, but a becoming-molecular. As Leonard Lawlor notes, 'it is this gaze from the singular animal and its cries that place the animal *within* me: one in the other'.[96]

Turning to Deleuze and Guattari can therefore help to expand upon and complicate the domestic, material-semiotic entanglements between Woolf's canine protagonist and his owner.[97] In *A Thousand Plateaus*, Deleuze and Guattari outline three ways in which we can distinguish animals – the first two anthropomorphic and a third which challenges anthropocentric conceptualisations. First, there are the 'Oedipal animals [. . .] "my" cat, "my" dog.' Importantly it is here, in their criticism of the ways in which this view of animals 'draws us into a narcissistic contemplation' and reinforces the tendency for anthropomorphism, that Deleuze and Guattari make the comment which Haraway finds particularly distasteful: that '*anyone who likes cats or dogs is a fool*'! This is indeed a startling statement, but taking this comment out of context, Haraway risks giving the impression that Deleuze and Guattari are cruelly dismissive of animals, when in fact they are exposing the ways in which such animals have been reduced to mere psychoanalytic facades with 'a daddy, a mommy, a little brother behind them';[98] they are attempting to unsettle and complicate our conceptualisation of human/animal relations.[99] In Deleuze and Guattari's model, the second kinds of animals are 'State animals', those 'with characteristics or attributes' that fit them into 'divine myths'. Here there seems to be an affinity with recognising Derrida's real cat, rather than generalising and mythologising. Finally, there are the more nomadic 'pack or affect animals that form a multiplicity, a becoming'.[100] This third way of approaching the animal is to take into account their own capacity for world-making rather than assimilating them into an anthropocentric arrangement. Indeed, Deleuze and Guattari playfully invoke Woolf when clarifying that their emphasis on 'pack animals' is not a comment on the fact 'that certain animals live in packs' or such 'evolutionary classifications':

> Virginia Woolf experiences herself not as a monkey or a fish but as a troop of monkeys, a school of fish, according to her variable relations of becoming with the people she approaches. [. . .] What we are saying is that every animal is fundamentally a band, a pack. That it has pack modes, rather than characteristics, even if further distinctions within these modes are called for. It is at this point that the human being encounters the animal. We do not become animal without a fascination for the pack, for multiplicity.[101]

Whilst it is beyond the scope of this chapter to expand upon the relations between Woolf and monkeys or fish (!),[102] the important point here is the emphasis placed on moving away from individuated subjectivity (of humans or animals) and towards affect and movements of intensely interwoven multiplicitous agencies.

In order to explore the full extent of Woolf's fascination for animals in *Flush*, it is important not to abandon Deleuze and Guattari as 'the enemy', but to take on board their concerns about Oedipal and symbolic animals, and to ask whether this third kind of animal – the one that provides the line of flight from anthropocentrism – is located in Woolf's novel. After all, 'cannot any animal be treated in all three ways? [. . .] Even the cat, even the dog.'[103] Even, we might add, Flush. Again, Deleuze and Guattari allude here to Woolf – this time to her 'thin dog', which Woolf actually takes from Katherine Mansfield's diary (*E4* 447), to exemplify the symbiotic relations formed between the different elements that combine in an 'event' or 'haecceity': 'Climate, wind, season, hour are not of another nature than the things, animals, or people that populate them, follow them, sleep and awaken within them. This should be read without a pause: the animal-stalks-at-five-o'clock [. . .] Five o'clock is this animal! This animal is this place! "The thin dog is running down the road, this dog is the road," cries Virginia Woolf. That is how we need to feel.'[104]

Although Flush spends most of his time in a Victorian domestic setting, and although he is on a couple of occasions compared to Pan, he ultimately evades rather than conforms to the model of an 'Oedipal' or 'State' animal. Rather than settling into the domestic order or mythological associations, he has a central role in Woolf's reimagining of the earthly space shared by humans and animals, where hierarchies are flattened and species categories blurred. Take, for example, the description of how the previous domestic order had created a gulf fuelled by hatred between Flush and his human companions, likened to 'an iron bar corroding and festering and killing all natural life beneath it'. After 'the cutting of sharp knives and painful surgery, the iron has been excised' and what results is a kind of material-semiotic alliance between Flush and Miss Barrett, the fleshly reconceptualisation of human/dog relations:

> Now the blood ran once more; the nerves shot and tingled; flesh formed; Nature rejoiced, as in spring. Flush heard the birds sing again; he felt the leaves growing on the trees; as he lay on the sofa at Miss Barrett's feet, glory and delight coursed through his veins. He was with them, not against them, now; their hopes, their wishes, their desires were his. (*F* 49)

Complicating any view that the text presents another human appropriation of the dog, once again Woolf's use of free indirect speech encompasses a more collective, connected arrangement. We might see the passage as pointing towards a 'naturalcultural assemblage', to put together key terms used by both Deleuze and Haraway, where Flush's singularisation is intermingled with 'birds' and 'trees', as well as a pair of human 'feet' – which had earlier signalled the so-called 'gulf' and hierarchical order as he sat 'on the rug at Miss Barrett's feet' (*F* 18). Moreover, he

> could have barked in sympathy with Mr Browning now. The short sharp words raised the hackles on his neck. 'I need a week of Tuesdays,' Mr Browning cried, 'then a month – a year – a life!' I, Flush echoed him, need a month – a year – a life! I need all the things that you both need. We are all three conspirators in the most glorious of causes. We are joined in sympathy. We are joined in hatred. We are joined in defiance of black and beetling tyranny. We are joined in love. (*F* 49)

This evokes the image of Cam and James in the boat with Mr Ramsay in *To the Lighthouse* resolving to 'track down and stamp out – tyranny, despotism' (*TL* 209), the scene of their becoming-molecular together. Just as the tyranny they were defying was patriarchal chauvinism that divided women and men in hierarchical terms, here we see 'some dimly apprehended but none the less certainly emerging triumph' (*F* 50) against the human chauvinism that divides humans and animals, and seeks to classify animals based on biologistic qualities (*à la* The Spaniel Club), deprived of their place in an exclusively human culture.

But rather than simply providing another example of where dogs, as Haraway writes, are 'partners in the crime of human evolution',[105] Flush and his companion species move here towards Deleuzian becoming which prefers the term 'involution' and is not so much about 'descent and filiation' as it is about 'alliance' and 'transversal communications': 'to involve', they clarify, 'is to form a block that runs its own line "between" the terms in play and beneath assignable relations'.[106] Rejecting an understanding of evolution as signalling a process towards a more and more distinct organism or perfectly differentiated category of being, the term 'involution' best captures the symbiotic but never fixed relations between species; the alliance between Miss Barrett and Flush forms a shared becoming-other that involves human and animal at the same time as working between these terms and beneath species characteristics. Importantly, Miss Barrett's becoming-animal is not a matter of her growing a tail, nor is Flush's becoming-other a matter of walking on two legs – it is a case of neither resemblance nor imitation, nor is it simply a metaphor. As Deleuze and Guattari stress in *Kafka*, 'there is nothing metaphoric about the becoming-animal. No symbolism, no allegory.' Rather, 'it is an ensemble of states [. . .] a creative line of escape that says nothing other than what it is. [. . .] it constitutes a single process, a unique method that replaces subjectivity'.[107] Or as they write in *A Thousand Plateaus*, the important question becomes:

> which reality is at issue here? For if becoming animal does not consist in playing animal or imitating an animal, it is clear that the human being does not 'really' become an animal any more than the animal 'really' becomes something else. Becoming produces nothing other than itself. We fall into a false alternative if we say that you either imitate or you are. What is real is the becoming itself, the block of becoming, not the supposedly fixed terms through which that which becomes passes [. . .] becoming lacks a subject distinct from itself[.][108]

If the aforementioned passage from Woolf's text is a moment of 'deterritorialization', a moment of Flush and his human companions becoming-minoritarian, it is followed by 'reterritorialization', as predicated by Deleuze and Guattari's conceptual paradigm. The reterritorialisation in this instance is the dognapping of Flush, the blocking of his line of flight.[109] This moment of deterritorialisation is therefore not absolute but relative, and seems to be an example of what Deleuze and Guattari term 'negative' deterritorialisation where it is 'immediately overlaid by reterritorializations on property, work, and money':[110] as Flush is dognapped we are reminded of his position in an anthropocentric and capitalist culture whereby he becomes a piece of property to be bargained over by humans – the gulf is reinforced as the agents are reterritorialised in their hierarchical positions. But as Deleuze and Guattari are keen to emphasise, deterritorialisation has 'highly varied forms', and in Woolf's text what initially appears to be 'negative' soon becomes a 'positive' deterritorialisation which 'prevails over the reterritorializations, which play only a secondary role'.[111] This is seen in the fact that this traumatic incident when Flush is captured and taken to Whitechapel leads to a discussion of Wimpole Street and its dangers, and in Miss Barrett's resistance to the dominant, majoritarian viewpoint (of her husband and father) that they should not save Flush: 'For her it was madness. So they told her. Her brothers, her sisters, all came round her threatening her, dissuading her [...] But she stood her ground. At last they realised the extent of her folly. Whatever the risk might be they must give way to her' (*F* 66). The dognapping of Flush throws 'doubts upon the solidity even of Wimpole Street itself', undermining its 'apparent solidity and security' as the hub of Victorian civilisation (*F* 51).

Woolf ironically uses the moment where the human most obviously and cruelly exerts its power over the animal in order to elucidate human failings; that there is no natural order of things. When Flush does return to Miss Barrett their reterritorialisation does not dominate their deterritorialisation. After Flush is 'led out into the open air' and returned to Wimpole Street, it is a setting that now exposes the myth of itself as the safe an untouchable haven of civilisation: 'The old gods of the bedroom – the bookcase, the wardrobe, the busts – seemed to have lost their substance. This room was no longer the whole world; it was only a shelter' (*F* 67). We are told that 'everything was different' and that 'everything in the room seemed to be aware of change' (*F* 69). Miss Barrett's becoming-animal leads her to recognise and respond to the violence enacted against her companion species as she hears 'the howls of tethered dogs, the screams of birds in terror'. Flush, too, realises his perilous position as dog amongst men: having previously felt Mr Browning was with him in fighting against tyranny, 'behind those smiling, friendly faces' of Mr Browning and Mr Kenyon 'was treachery and cruelty and deceit' (F 67). The 'becoming with', to use Haraway's preferred term, of Miss Barrett and Flush is a becoming-minoritarian with, as they are closer now having somehow found a line of flight from the illusion of human superiority: 'They had been parted; now they were together. Indeed they had never been so much akin. Every start she gave, every movement she made, passed through him too.' Uncomfortable in her human skin, Miss Barrett 'seemed now to be perpetually starting and moving'. Intriguingly, she also hides the 'pair of thick boots' (presumably made from the hides of cattle) that are delivered (F 68), and it was 'great boots [. . .] stumbling in and out' (F 55), 'hard, horny boots' (F 57) that had haunted Flush when he was captive in Whitechapel. Miss Barrett's act of hiding these boots at once signals her alliance with Flush at the same time as reinforcing the notion that becoming-animal is not about imitation – she would be just as uncomfortable in an anthropomorphised animal skin as she is now in her human skin. Tellingly, their communication is now carried out non-verbally, in 'tremendous silence' (F 71).

This all leads to a more literal fleeing, as Flush and his companion escape to Italy 'leaving tyrants and dog-stealers behind them'. Both Flush and Miss Barrett 'had changed' (F 75), and with the latter now married and Flush 'independent' his relationship with Mr Browning also improves. Mr Browning, like Mr Ramsay in *To the Lighthouse*, appears to have been swept up in their becoming, so that 'he and Flush were the best of friends now' that Flush 'was his own master'. The deep empathy shared between Miss Barrett and Flush in their escape from hierarchies of oppression is reinforced here also: 'Fear was unknown in Florence; there were no dog-stealers here and, she may have sighed, there were no fathers' (F 78). The events immediately before and following Flush's dognapping therefore illuminate lines of flight that cross the human/animal divide, and attempt to show a less hierarchical relation between companion species. In *Dialogues*, Deleuze describes the process of becoming-animal as 'the picking-up of a code where each is deterritorialized',[112] and true to their positive deterritorialisation Flush 'had revised his code accordingly' so that this 'new conception of canine society' (note again the mixing of canine and society, of nature and culture), is one where dogs are more liberated: 'Where was "must" now? Where were chains now? Where were park-keepers and truncheons? Gone, with the dog-stealers and Kennel Clubs and Spaniel Clubs of a corrupt aristocracy!' We learn that Flush 'was the friend of all the world now. All dogs were his brothers. He had no need of a chain in this new world; he had no need of protection' (F 77). With the equality of dogs pronounced, this reads like an earlier canine version of Woolf's famous statement in *Three Guineas* concerning the role of women as members of an 'Outsiders' Society' and therefore not being controlled within any nationalistic boundaries: '"For," the outsider will say, "in fact, as a woman, I have no country. As a woman I want no country. As a woman my country is the whole world"' (*TG* 313). Ultimately, Flush too seems to fit better with an Outsider's Society as opposed to The Spaniel Club; it may well be true that on one level *Flush* acts as an allegory for, as Woolf puts it in *A Room of One's Own*, the 'dog's chance' women writers have been given in patriarchal culture (*RO* 141), but it also offers a specifically nonanthropocentric version of such an Outsider's Society – what I term in my sub-heading an 'An*i*malous Society'.

Anna Snaith has commented that *Flush* is 'a text whose supposed anomalousness has often caused it to be read out of context – or not to be read at all'.[113] Arguing that this book is not so anomalous after all, Snaith's reading makes an important and convincing case for taking *Flush* the text seriously as 'part of Woolf's anti-fascist writing of the 1930s'.[114] But focusing on the question of the animal, I am suggesting that it is precisely the anomalous status of Woolf's canine protagonist that enables us to explore a more entangled and non-hierarchical relation between human and nonhuman. In *A Thousand Plateaus*, Deleuze and Guattari's definition of the 'anomalous' has much in common with their understanding of an 'Outsider' – the anomalous is a 'phenomenon of bordering [. . .] a position or set of positions in relation to a multiplicity' that is distinct from the 'abnormal' which 'can be defined only in terms of characteristics, specific or generic'.[115] To be anomalous, an Outsider, the unregistered, is not as simple as failing to embody a purebred standard; as Joshua Delpech-Ramey notes, 'the anomalous is the cutting edge, the edge of "deterritorialization" of the group itself. What is anomalous is not that which is outside of the group or divergent within it, but that individual who forms a porous border between the group and its Outside.'[116] We are therefore reminded of the opening pages of *Flush*, when Woolf lays out the etymology of the word 'Spaniel', dog of 'Hispania' which 'derives from the Basque word *espana*, signifying an edge or boundary' (*F* 5). My neologism 'An*i*malous Society' implies that the anomalous and animal in Woolf's text are coextensive; Flush, as a dog who 'would meet with the approval of the Spaniel Club' as 'a purebred Cocker of the red variety marked by all the characteristic excellences of his kind' (*F* 10) but also becoming with and becoming-animal with his human companions, should not be seen as simply an 'exceptional individual' trapped within the confines of his role as 'the family animal or pet',[117] but as transforming human/animal relations and becoming nomadic even within his domestic arena. In *Flush*, the ordinary and extraordinary are intermingled to launch becomings-animal, the becoming-anomalous through the animal: a becoming-an*i*malous. For if the anomalous functions to draw us into 'a movement away from our molar identity' and moves us towards a 'zone of new ways of relating [. . .] of novelty and possibilities' then it would seem that this could also describe Flush.[118] Taking account of the anomalous in *Flush* is not then a question of the abnormal and rejected or normal and included, nor is it about anomalies *within* a group; instead it is the creation of gaps in the divide, and the invitation to trespass those divides, *between* inside and outside, culture and nature, registered and unregistered.

Conclusion? It's a cow's life

When theorising a new relation between animal and human, it is important to emphasise their 'fleshly historical reality' as Haraway puts it.[119] That is, Woolf's cocker spaniel is not to be read simply as 'an alibi for other themes'[120] nor does our reading of *Flush* lead us to some sublime escape from reality, but draws out the complexity of materially involved entanglements between companion species, which includes the possibility for the movements of becoming rather than a fixed and defined dividing line. Whether or not there are moments in *Flush* that can be read as anthropomorphic, I have argued that it challenges anthropocentric concerns and demonstrates a curiosity, or fascination, for animals (including humans) living together. As Jeanne Dubino has pointed out, these animals include more than simply cocker spaniels: 'Woolf populates *Flush* with wild and tamed species – a menagerie of cats and lions and tigers, partridges and parrots and rooks, elephants and fish and fox, black beetles and blue bottles, hares and fleas, and dogs.'[121] Missing from this list are cows, and I end this chapter by briefly turning to Woolf's description of this particular species in order to consider further issues of flesh and suffering.[122]

Following Jeremy Bentham's famous plea for animal rights, Derrida claims that 'the *first* and *decisive* question would [. . .] be to know whether animals *can suffer*'.[123] Whilst Haraway has pointed out the limitations of focusing our philosophical and ethical concern for animals primarily on this question of suffering, she nonetheless accepts it as an important issue amongst others.[124] In addition, Calarco argues that rather than using Bentham's question to launch an empirical investigation into the capacity animals have to experience pain and suffering, Derrida's use has a more profound proto-ethical purpose, where he broaches the issue of 'the embodied exposure of animals, their finitude and vulnerability [. . .] the question points toward and contains within itself the trace of something more basic: an interruptive encounter with animal suffering that calls for and provokes thought'.[125] In Woolf's fictional biography, after Flush's dognapping from Wimpole Street and before we learn of his suffering in the seedy Whitechapel where he is held for ransom, we are presented with just such an interruptive encounter which highlights the 'embodied exposure of animals' and their 'vulnerability' when the narrator invokes Thomas Beames' 1852 book *The Rookeries of London*:

> he was shocked. Splendid buildings raised themselves in Westminster, yet just behind them were ruined sheds in which human beings lived herded together above herds of cows – 'two in each seven feet of space'. He felt that he ought to tell people what he had seen. Yet how could one describe politely a bedroom in which two or three families lived above a cow-shed, when the cow-shed had no ventilation, when the cows were milked and killed and eaten under the bedroom? (F 52)

Whilst much of the remainder of the paragraph goes on to focus on the suffering of the human beings living in these and similar conditions, it is significant that Woolf's narrative expands on the pronounced and exposed vulnerability of these cows, and that the sentence she quotes directly, 'two in each seven feet of space', refers to them. Indeed, this phrase is taken from the Hon. Frederick Byng's 1847 pamphlet addressed to the inhabitants of St. James, Westminster, which is quoted at length by Beames:

> Two of these sheds are situated at the angle of Hopkins and New Streets (*real Rookeries*), and range one above the other, within a yard of the back of the houses in New Street. Forty cows are kept in them, two in each seven feet of space. There is no ventilation save by the unceiled tile roof, through which the ammoniacal vapours escape to the destruction of the health of the inmates. Besides the animals, there is, at one end, a large tank for grains, a store-place for turnips and hay, and between them a receptacle into which the liquid manure drains, and the solid is heaped. At the other end is a capacious vault with a brick partition, one division of which contains mangold-wurzel, turnips, and potatoes; and the other a dirty liquid, called brewers' wash, a portion of which is pumped up, and mixed with the food of the cows.[126]

A report compiled by a medical practitioner, Mr Anselbrook, concludes: 'From the above-mentioned facts it is obvious, that much of the milk sold at the West End of the Metropolis is elaborated in the udders of animals unnaturally treated, and kept in an atmosphere impregnated with gases detrimental to common health.'[127]

Instead of experiencing 'the recognition of an animal's "ability" or "capacity" for suffering', this passage from *Flush* is most disturbing to the reader because it describes 'an encounter with an animal's *in*ability or *in*capacity to avoid pain, its fleshly vulnerability and exposure to wounding'.[128] What is so difficult for Beames to describe in the above passage, and what is most troubling for the reader, is the way in which these cows are already reduced to food and drink by the humans with whom they share such close living quarters. Beames himself argues that this is overwhelming evidence that cow-sheds, including underground sheds in Whitechapel which 'reek with an abominable odour', are 'dens of destitution' and a 'disgrace to our age'.[129] Woolf, it seems, was also thoroughly convinced by the evidence. Moreover, when Flush's experience of his dognapping is then detailed by Woolf, we are confronted with not only Flush's suffering, but his vulnerability which led to him being moved so easily and so quickly from his home to the 'complete darkness', the 'chillness and dampness' of his dognappers' lair in Whitechapel. As if to emphasise the inability of the animal to avoid this plight, we are told that 'the floor was crowded with animals of different kinds', including 'dogs of the highest breeding [. . .] like himself' (*F* 55). In Wimpole Street a dog's vulnerability is doubled – either kept on a leash, or stolen. Indeed, comparing Flush's later migration to Italy with the fact that Mrs Carlyle's dog Nero 'leapt from a top-storey window' and was later run over by a Butcher's cart (*F* 92; 113, n.8), Dubino points out that the two options ultimately become 'death or escape'.[130]

The key in all of this is not to stop at pity, but to explore, as I have claimed Woolf does in *Flush*, the way in which these encounters create a new relation between, and conceptualisation of, human and animal. As Deleuze and Guattari note in *What is Philosophy?*, 'the slaughter of a calf remains present in thought not through pity but as the zone of exchange between man and animal in which something of one passes into the other'.[131] In *Francis Bacon* Deleuze argues that Bacon's paintings draw our attention to the fact that:

> meat is not dead flesh; it retains all the sufferings and assumes all the colours of living flesh. It manifests such convulsive pain and vulnerability, but also such delightful invention, colour, and acrobatics. Bacon does not say, 'Pity the beasts,' but rather that every man who suffers is a piece of meat. Meat is the common zone of man and the beast, their zone of indiscernibility.[132]

Deleuze goes on to discuss the eighteenth-century German writer Karl Philipp Moritz and his novel *Anton Reiser* (1785–1790), citing a particular passage which leads Deleuze to write that 'animals are part of humanity [. . .] we are all cattle': 'a calf, the head, the eyes, the snout, the nostrils ... and sometimes he lost himself in such sustained contemplation of the beast that he really believed he experienced, for an instant, the *type of existence* of such a being ... in short, the question if he, among men, was a dog or another animal had already occupied his thoughts since childhood'.[133] For Deleuze, this reveals 'the reality of becoming', which is not a question of resemblance between man and animal but 'a zone of indiscernibility more profound than any sentimental identification: the man who suffers is a beast, the beast that suffers is a man'. 'What revolutionary person', asks Deleuze, 'in art, politics, religion, or elsewhere – has not felt that extreme moment when he or she was nothing but a beast, and became responsible not for the calves that died, but *before* the calves that died?'[134]

Flush's multiple experiences – his gazing and his playing as well as his denuding and his dognapping – added to Beames' encounter with these cows, demonstrate the 'various ways', as Calarco states, 'in which animals might interrupt us, challenge our standard ways of thinking, and call us to responsibility'.[135] By highlighting the specificities of Flush's varied lives against the backdrop of the plight of other animals – be it cows or humans – Woolf is resisting the homogenisation of animality/humanity at the same time as challenging any straightforward distinction between animalities and humanities. In this sense she seems to be offering a way out of what we could perhaps see as the false dichotomy ultimately presented by Derrida, where he places 'heterogeneities and abyssal ruptures as against the homogeneous and continuous';[136] to put it simply, the choice here appears to be between maintaining the human/animal distinction at the same time as exploring heterogeneities, or subverting the distinction and reducing everything to homogeneity. Focusing on this issue at the end of *Zoographies*, Calarco argues that

> there is another option available beyond philosophical dualism, biological continuism, and Derrida's deconstructive approach [. . .] *we could simply let the human-animal distinction go* or, at the very least, not insist on maintaining it [. . .] Might not the challenge for philosophical thought today be to proceed altogether without the guardrails of the human-animal distinction and to invent new concepts and new practices along different paths?[137]

For Haraway this different path would be one of 'naturecultures', of non-hierarchical entanglements of companion species in assemblages that do not privilege a notion of a human culture or an animal nature, and in the next chapter such naturecultures are explored further in the context of quantum 'philosophy-physics' and the matter of life in *The Waves*. What remains up for debate here, however, is how convincing Calarco's call to simply 'let the distinction go' is. For example, John

Llewelyn has recently responded by arguing that in following Calarco's lead in letting the distinction go, we actually maintain it: 'Must we not hang on to the distinction if we are to let it go? For even if we decide to avoid making this distinction in what we say, must we not, in order to carry out this resolution, retain the distinction in what we think?'[138] It may well be going too far to claim that *Flush* takes us beyond *all* thoughts of a human/animal distinction, but it does provide crucial instances of the materiality of Woolf's nonanthropocentric theorising; a careful and playful consideration of the question of the animal that involves, to borrow Haraway's words, 'transposing the body of communication; remolding, remodelling; swervings that tell the truth [. . .] Woo[l]f'![139]

Notes

1. Squier, *Virginia Woolf and London*, p. 124.
2. Rosenthal, *Virginia Woolf*, p. 206.
3. Caughie, *Virginia Woolf and Postmodernism*, p. 146. Caughie convincingly argues that 'reading *Flush* can show us that readings, texts, and canons are always mixed, never pure, and that we give them the illusion of purity, permanence, and prestige by reading efficiently, separating off the excess that would expose this rather messy and conflicted system' (163).
4. Eberly, 'Housebroken', p. 24.
5. Vanita, '"Love Unspeakable"', p. 252; p. 254.
6. Smith, 'Across the Widest Gulf', p. 349. Smith also notes that such bias exists against studies of animal consciousness in science.
7. Guiguet, *Virginia Woolf*, p. 347.
8. Ibid., p. 348.
9. Ibid., p. 346.
10. Rosenthal, *Virginia Woolf*, p. 211.
11. Ittner, 'Part Spaniel', p. 189.
12. Agamben, *The Open*, p. 40.
13. Wylie, 'The Anthropomorphic Ethic', p. 116.
14. Ibid., pp. 116–17.
15. Ibid., p. 122.
16. Garber, *Dog Love*, p. 31. For a thorough discussion of anthropomorphism in animal studies see Daston and Mitman (eds), *Thinking with Animals*, 2005.
17. This story was written in the 1920s for the Bell children's newspaper, *The Charleston Bulletin*, but the precise date is unknown.
18. Balcombe, *Second Nature*, p. 47.
19. Smith, 'Across the Widest Gulf', p. 349.
20. Woolf is here referring back to the beginning of the novel when she lays out the etymology of the word 'Spaniel' (*F* 5). See section 'From Spaniel Club to Animalous Society' later in this chapter.
21. Smith, 'Across the Widest Gulf', p. 357.

22. Ibid., p. 357.
23. Ibid., p. 359.
24. Calarco, *Zoographies*, p. 6. The limitations of 'animal rights' that are based on a liberal humanist model are also discussed by Haraway: 'We do not get very far with the categories generally used by animal rights discourses, in which animals end up permanent dependents ("lesser humans"), utterly natural ("nonhuman"), or exactly the same ("humans in fur suits").' Haraway, *When Species Meet*, pp. 66–7. See also Calarco, *Zoographies*, p. 128 and Derrida, *The Animal*, pp. 87–8.
25. Calarco, *Zoographies*, p. 12.
26. Ibid., p. 13.
27. Goldman, '"When Dogs Will Become Men"', p. 180.
28. Caughie, *Virginia Woolf and Postmodernism*, p. 154.
29. Derrida, *The Animal*, pp. 4–5.
30. Ibid., p. 5.
31. Ibid.
32. Elsewhere Woolf herself is praiseworthy of cat qualities other than silence, seen when she describes Katherine Mansfield: 'It struck me that she is of the cat kind: alien, composed, always solitary and observant.' Woolf empathises with this, and there is a connection between them: 'And then we talked about solitude, and I found her expressing my feelings, as I never heard them expressed' (*D2* 44). Whilst beyond the scope of this current chapter, it might also be fruitful to compare Derrida's cat to Woolf's depiction of the Manx cat who appears in *A Room of One's Own* as a 'queer animal' without its tail (*RO* 16).
33. In a passing reference to Flush in his poem 'How It Strikes a Contemporary', the poem from which Woolf took the title for her 1925 essay, Robert Browning describes him as 'bald'. See Adams, *Shaggy Muses*, p. 44.
34. Derrida, *The Animal*, p. 59. Various studies into animal cognition have attempted to tackle this question of animals' self-recognition in relationship to the mirror. Such experiments have tended to have a very simple design (developed by Gordon Gallup Jnr in 1970 and commonly known as 'The Mirror Test'), usually involving putting a mark somewhere on the animal's body that could only be seen with the use of a mirror, and seeing whether the animal responds to this mark by touching or exploring it on their own body. John Pearce has provided an overview of research in this area which has indicated that such mirror-recognition is evident in some great apes, dolphins, and elephants. See Pearce, *Animal Learning*, pp. 319–25. It may be, however, that self-recognition extends beyond mammals, as Jonathan Balcombe has argued in *Second Nature*, pp. 65–7. Whilst these studies have not indicated that dogs can pass the mirror test, they are important in emphasising that we must not only think of humans as having a relationship to the mirror, and that Woolf was ahead of her time in imagining that a nonhuman animal may have such a relationship. In addition, Balcombe and Pearce both note the relatively simple design of this study and the limitations of drawing conclusions about the inner lives of animals based on behaviour, and so future studies are needed to reveal more about animals' relationships with the mirror, and what these relationships may reveal about self-recognition.

35. Garber, *Dog Love*, p. 47. Garber goes on to draw parallels between Flush's mirrored encounter and Lacan's 'mirror-stage' formulation. Jacqui Griffiths has complicated this reading of Flush by arguing that unlike the infant in Lacan's theory – or the child without language, 'the child at the *infans* stage' – Flush's 'encounter cannot be characterized as infantile in a pre-Oedipal sense'. Griffiths argues that whilst Flush 'occupies the subordinate position of a child in the family structure, he is obviously at an advanced (i.e., post-Oedipal) stage of childhood development'. But where Griffiths suggests this episode shows Woolf's 'anthropomorphic use of the Oedipalized dog as a human substitute', I would argue that we again see an example of anthropocentric bias in the critic, who is primarily focused on 'the child' in this story. See Griffiths, 'Almost Human', p. 166.
36. Derrida, *The Animal*, p. 21.
37. Ibid., p. 59.
38. Ibid., p. 29.
39. Ibid., pp. 50–1.
40. Haraway, *When Species Meet*, p. 20.
41. Ibid.
42. Ibid., pp. 22–3.
43. Ibid., p. 20.
44. Calarco, *Zoographies*, p. 146.
45. Derrida, *The Animal*, pp. 62–3. For Jonathan Balcombe, 'the question is no longer Do animals think? But What do animals think?' Balcombe takes issue with the way that science has often placed 'the burden of proof on those who would ascribe thoughts and feelings to animals rather than on those who would deny animals these attributes'. Once again, Woolf's decision to ascribe thoughts and feelings to a dog may not be evidence of an anthropocentric attitude that doesn't take into account the singularity of Flush, but rather 'humbly allow[ing] the likelihood that animals have more going on in their minds than our limited vantage points allow us to appreciate'. See Balcombe, *Second Nature*, p. 29.
46. Haraway, *When Species Meet*, p. 22.
47. Balcombe, *Second Nature*, pp. 45–6.
48. Haraway, *When Species Meet*, p. 22.
49. Ibid., p. 93.
50. Derrida, *The Animal*, p. 6.
51. Ibid., p. 9. My aim in this section is not to answer definitively what constitutes a response, but to suggest that through Flush we are presented with a 'response' that it is not reserved for the human in direct opposition to a hard-wired, fixed 'reaction' of the animal.
52. Barrett Browning, 'To Flush, My Dog', pp. 12–15.
53. Barrett Browning, 'Flush or Faunus', p. 188.
54. Derrida, *The Animal*, p. 8.
55. The pity evoked in the dog led Emmanuel Levinas to conclude that the dog 'has a face', although he remained 'agnostic' on how far this would extend to other animals. See Calarco, *Zoographies*, p. 67. Carrie Rohman argues that Derrida's cat has a face: 'The cat looks at me and, Derrida insists, *addresses* me. We might say, at the very least, that Derrida asymptotically approaches the claim in these moments that animals have a face,

that faciality as an ethical demand extends beyond the human.' Rohman, 'On Singularity', p. 66.
56. Derrida, *The Animal*, p. 14.
57. Deleuze and Guattari, *A Thousand Plateaus*, p. 148.
58. Deleuze, *Negotiations*, p. 133.
59. Garber, *Dog Love*, p. 117.
60. Derrida, *The Animal*, p. 48.
61. Deleuze and Guattari, *A Thousand Plateaus*, p. 84.
62. And to dogs, of course, life smells. In several passages Woolf describes how 'a variety of smells interwoven in subtlest combination thrilled [Flush's] nostrils' (*F* 11; see also 20, 85). Focusing on the importance the dog's scent-centred world, Allen McLaurin argues that 'it is true in a sense that language "deforms" sensation, for the dog's sense of smell is much richer and more concrete than the words "smell" and "aroma".' McLaurin, *Virginia Woolf*, p. 46. For more on olfaction in *Flush* see Booth, 'The Scent', pp. 3–22.
63. Haraway, *Companion Species*, p. 31.
64. Haraway, *When Species Meet*, p. 4. Recently, Jane Goldman's work on Woolf's canine tropes has taken a turn in precisely this direction, and she calls upon Haraway to suggest that in the opening pages of *The Years* Mira, Lulu, and the Colonel form 'a material-semiotic node of knotted beings, canine and human'. Goldman therefore posits that the identity of the humans in this knot, the Colonel and Mira, and the dog, Lulu, are not easily disentangled. See '"When Dogs Will Become Men"', p. 186.
65. This sketch is thought to have been written in 1939 (*CSF* 341).
66. Haraway, *When Species Meet*, p. 4.
67. 'The Secret Life of the Dog.' First broadcast on the BBC, 6th January 2010.
68. Haraway, *When Species Meet*, p. 15.
69. Ibid., p. 16. Haraway's 'naturecultures' are influenced by Bruno Latour: 'Nature and Society are not two distinct poles, but one and the same production of successive states of societies-natures, of collectives.' Latour, *We Have Never Been Modern*, p. 139.
70. Haraway, *When Species Meet*, pp. 26–7.
71. Ibid., pp. 66–7.
72. Haraway, *Companion Species*, p. 8.
73. Ibid., p. 88.
74. Woolf herself was especially fond of mongrels, and Grizzle, the Woolfs' dog between 1922 and 1926, was a mixed breed terrier. Indeed, as Maureen Adams has shown, when Grizzle died Woolf 'assigned Pinka – despite her aristocratic breeding and appearance – the role of the scruffy mongrel companion'. See *Shaggy Muses*, p. 229. Pinka was a model for Flush and was photographed for the front cover of the first edition (239).
75. See <http://www.thespanielclub.co.uk>; <http://www.thekennelclub.org.uk> (accessed 8 October 2012).
76. Peach, 'Editing Flush', pp. 203–4.
77. Haraway, *When Species Meet*, pp. 16–17.
78. McHugh, 'Queer (and) Animal', p. 159.
79. Haraway, *When Species Meet*, p. 2, p. 28.

80. Ibid., p. 16.
81. In her discussion of canine history in *Flush*, Jeanne Dubino argues that Woolf's text is 'informed by a deep appreciation and knowledge of Darwinism'. Dubino, 'Evolution, History, and *Flush*', p. 148.
82. Haraway, *Companion Species*, p. 5.
83. Deleuze and Guattari, *Kafka*, p. 17.
84. Haraway, *When Species Meet*, p. 314, n.37.
85. Ibid., p. 27.
86. Ibid., p. 29.
87. Ibid., p. 27.
88. Ibid., p. 29.
89. Ibid., p. 28.
90. Ibid., p. 30. Haraway notes that her reading of Deleuze is largely influenced by Rosi Braidotti, and some of the criticisms of 'becoming-woman' that I have discussed in Chapter 2. See *When Species Meet*, p. 315, n.39. Yet, as noted above, Braidotti has pointed to important shared concerns of Haraway and Deleuze.
91. Braidotti, 'Posthuman', p. 200. Braidotti makes brief reference to *Flush* as evidence of Woolf's exploration of the 'vitality of the living world' being focused on the nonhuman or animal life. See *Transpositions*, pp. 103–4.
92. Calarco, *Zoographies*, p. 35.
93. In *The Beast and the Sovereign*, Derrida speaks of Deleuze and Guattari's 'great, rich chapter' on becoming-animal (in *A Thousand Plateaus*) and urges students to read Deleuze's writings on the animal '*in extenso*': 're-read it all', he recommends. Derrida, *The Beast, Volume 1*, pp. 141–2.
94. Calarco, *Zoographies*, pp. 42–3. Despite Calarco's interest in Deleuze and Guattari's writings on the animal, however, they are only discussed in a few pages of his book. Calarco instead concentrates on Heidegger, Levinas, Agamben, and Derrida.
95. Lawlor, 'Following the Rats', p. 176.
96. Ibid., p. 176.
97. Demonstrating further the links between them, the emphasis on 'material-semiotic' that we see in Haraway is also central to Deleuze and Guattari's philosophy: 'As matters of expression take on consistency they constitute semiotic systems, but the *semiotic* components are inseparable from *material* components and are in exceptionally close contact with molecular levels.' See Deleuze and Guattari, *A Thousand Plateaus*, p. 369.
98. Deleuze and Guattari, *A Thousand Plateaus*, p. 265.
99. Susan McHugh has also recently disagreed with Haraway's harsh dismissal of Deleuze and Guattari's 'becoming-animal'. See McHugh, *Animal Stories*, p. 14.
100. Deleuze and Guattari, *A Thousand Plateaus*, p. 265.
101. Ibid., p. 264.
102. Kathryn Simpson does, however, discuss Woolf's 'queer fish'. See Simpson, 'Queer Fish'. See also Chapter 3, n.9.
103. Deleuze and Guattari, *A Thousand Plateaus*, pp. 265–6.
104. Ibid., p. 290. Goldman weaves this passage into the introduction to '"Ce chien est á moi"', which digs up and chases down Woolf's canine meta-

phors, focusing particularly on *A Room of One's Own*. See also Chapter 1, n.22.
105. Haraway, *Companion Species*, p. 5.
106. Deleuze and Guattari, *A Thousand Plateaus*, p. 263.
107. Deleuze and Guattari, *Kafka*, pp. 35–6.
108. Deleuze and Guattari, *A Thousand Plateaus*, p. 262.
109. Elizabeth Barrett Browning's Flush was actually stolen three times in total (in 1843, 1844, and 1846), as Woolf herself notes (*F* 109), and this was not an uncommon occurrence at the time. See Adams, *Shaggy Muses*, pp. 26–8; pp. 36–8, and Snaith, 'Of Fanciers', p. 620.
110. Deleuze and Guattari, *A Thousand Plateaus*, p. 560.
111. Ibid., p. 560.
112. Deleuze and Parnet, *Dialogues*, p. 33.
113. Snaith, 'Of Fanciers', p. 615.
114. Ibid., p. 632.
115. Deleuze and Guattari, *A Thousand Plateaus*, p. 269.
116. Delpech-Ramey, 'Deleuze, Guattari', p. 13.
117. Deleuze and Guattari, *A Thousand Plateaus*, p. 269.
118. Brown, 'Becoming-Animal in the Flesh', p. 266. Reading becomings-animal alongside Barbara Smut's empirical documentations of her interactions with companion species – and therefore refusing to write-off Deleuze and Guattari's concept as being in opposition to the daily 'becomings with' of the kind Haraway emphasises – Lori Brown suggests that we can read Smuts' description of her dog, Safi, as being 'more attuned and aware than perhaps many other animals, including humans' (270).
119. Haraway, *When Species Meet*, p. 66.
120. Haraway, *Companion Species*, p. 5.
121. Dubino, 'The Bispecies Environment', p. 151.
122. In 'Outlines', Woolf suggests that 'our brilliant young men might do worse, when in search of a subject, than devote a year or two to cows in literature' (*CR1* 184).
123. Derrida, *The Animal*, p. 27.
124. Haraway, *When Species Meet*, p. 22.
125. Calarco, *Zoographies*, p. 117.
126. Beames, *The Rookeries*, pp. 214–15.
127. Ibid., p. 215.
128. Calarco, *Zoographies*, p. 118.
129. Beames, *The Rookeries*, p. 213, p. 214, p. 216.
130. Dubino, 'Evolution, History, and *Flush*', p. 148. Woolf's efforts to stress the traumatic experience of dogs stolen in this period are emphasised by the fact she turns the focus on Flush where in Elizabeth Barrett Browning's letters the focus is primarily on the upset Flush's disappearance caused her. See Adams, *Shaggy Muses*, p. 238.
131. Deleuze and Guattari, *What is Philosophy?*, p. 109.
132. Deleuze, *Francis Bacon*, p. 17. For a fascinating reading of Deleuze's becoming-animal in relation to Art, and specifically Francis Bacon's dogs, see Baker, *The Postmodern Animal*, p. 137–52.
133. Deleuze, *Francis Bacon*, p. 18.
134. Ibid., p. 18.

135. Calarco, *Zoographies*, p. 120.
136. Derrida, *The Animal*, p. 30.
137. Calarco, *Zoographies*, p. 149.
138. Llewelyn, 'Where to Cut', p. 187.
139. Haraway, *Companion Species*, p. 21.

Chapter 5

Quantum Reality and Posthuman Life: *The Waves*

'This table [. . .] about to undergo an extraordinary transformation' (*W* 97)

In *The Phantom Table* (2000) Ann Banfield sets Woolf's 'table' as the meeting place for her writings and the philosophy of Bertrand Russell and the Cambridge Apostles. As 'the paradigmatic object of knowledge' in the tradition of British Empiricism, the table is 'planted squarely in the centre of Woolf's novelistic scenery';[1] a place where Woolf can gather together her thoughts on 'subject and object and the nature of reality' (*TL* 28) and, according to Banfield, a place that aligns Woolf with Russell's theory of knowledge. In a recent article Timothy Mackin also discusses Woolf's tables as central to her engagement with philosophy, but argues that she is not, like Russell, 'trying to provide the foundation for a realist epistemology' so much as she is attempting to work through a relation between internal emotions and the external world.[2] Whilst these studies provide important insights into Woolf's philosophical engagement with her own contemporaries, I am interested in aspects of Woolf's exploration of epistemology and ontology, internal and external, subject and object, life and matter, which extend beyond Russell's theory of knowledge and Bloomsbury philosophy and can be thought about more broadly through what Karen Barad refers to in *Meeting the Universe Halfway* as a quantum 'philosophy-physics' born out of Planck's discovery of quanta in December 1900 (did human character change then, perhaps?), Bohr's atom (1913) (and Bohr is the central focus for Barad), Einstein's special theory (1905) and general theory (1916) of relativity, and the work on wave and particle theories of Heisenberg, de Broglie, and Schrödinger amongst others.[3] In their own distinct contributions, these scientific theories have been hugely influential in more recent debates on materiality and posthumanist life, revealing, as Coole and Frost have put it, 'that the empirical realm we stumble around in does not capture the truth or essence of matter in any ultimate sense and that matter is thus amenable to some new conceptions that differ from those upon which we habitually rely'.[4] Following my focus on Woolf's exploration of human and nonhuman animals in Chapter 4, it is the philosophical implications of this new conception of matter, as it relates to both human and nonhuman life in Woolf's writing, that I explore in this chapter.

Several critics have suggested routes through which Woolf may have had access to long-standing debates and contemporaneous developments in philosophy and physics. Regarding philosophy, Banfield points out that Woolf would have been introduced to Descartes, Locke, Berkeley, and Hume (whom she also read) by her father's *History of English Thought in the Eighteenth Century* (1876) and other books,[5] and Jaakko Hintikka has noted that Woolf learned Plato's dialogues as a child.[6] In relation to the new physics, Gillian Beer has shown how Woolf assimilated ideas from the bestsellers by Arthur Eddington and James Jeans, whom she was reading whilst writing *The Waves*,[7] and Sue Sun Yom notes that Woolf would have learned about wave-particle duality and other aspects of light through newspapers such as *The Times* and *The Saturday Evening Post*,[8] as well as the *Listener*.[9] In addition to these sources, we know that Woolf often listened to scientists on the radio,[10] and she would have been exposed to both philosophy and science through the table talk of those around her: 'Woolf, we might say, had a knowledge *ex auditu* of philosophy.'[11] Regardless of which particular source most influenced her thinking, several critics have argued that insights provided by the new physics coalesced with Woolf's own developing philosophical ideas.[12] In particular, Woolf's use of 'atoms' is often highlighted,[13] and one key example Whitworth draws attention to is from the '1908' section of *The Years*, when Eleanor contemplates the atomic formation of a cup, whilst pointing to the 'vast gaps' and 'blank spaces' in her knowledge: 'take this cup for instance; she held it out in front of her. What was it made of? Atoms? And what were atoms, and how did they stick together? The smooth hard surface of the china with its red flowers seemed to her for a second a marvellous mystery' (Y 134). Of particular relevance to this current chapter, another revealing occurrence is in Woolf's diary entry from 28th November 1928, when she is at the early stages of conceiving what will become *The Waves* – at this point 'The Moths' – and thinking about her 'position towards the inner & the outer' and that 'some combination of them ought to be possible'. Woolf writes that she wants to

> saturate every atom. I mean to eliminate all waste, deadness, superfluity: to give the moment whole; whatever it includes. Say that the moment is a combination of thought; sensation; the voice of the sea. Waste, deadness, come

> from the inclusion of things that don't belong to the moment; [. . .] I want to put practically everything in: yet to saturate. That is what I want to do in The Moths. It must include nonsense, fact, sordidity: but made transparent. (D3 209)

The significance of this passage in particular is emphasised by Deleuze and Guattari when in *A Thousand Plateaus* they link it to their concept of 'haecceities', which I discuss later in this chapter when turning to Woolf's conceptualisation of life itself.

The extent to which Woolf's writing explores the more radical philosophical implications of quantum physics is the subject of Paul Tolliver Brown's recent work on Woolf, Leslie Stephen, and Einstein. Brown points out that while several studies on Woolf have suggested correlations between her writing and the new physics, critics 'have yet to establish the specific ways in which the ideas she shared with the preeminent subatomic scientists of her time work into the characters and themes of some of her most important novels'.[14] In an attempt to do just this Brown neatly presents how two tables in *To the Lighthouse* – one associated with Mr Ramsay and the other with Mrs Ramsay – signal Woolf's move from the theory of relativity to some of the more profound aspects of quantum mechanics that Einstein found so difficult to accept:

> The difference between Woolf's viewpoint and that of her father and Einstein makes itself apparent through the contrast between the table as an object of permeability and connectivity versus the table as an object of independence and separation. The dinner table that acts as Mrs. Ramsay's primary domain of influence and unification is juxtaposed in the novel with Mr. Ramsay's kitchen table that represents the isolated and unperceived object [. . .] Mr. Ramsay's table exists independently of its observation, whereas Mrs. Ramsay's table is a participatory 'object,' interacting and changing with the forces of her consciousness.

Crucially, Mrs Ramsay is aligned with a quantum reality whereby the 'holistic relationship to the world around her [. . .] confounds the notion that subjects and objects are specifically located and bounded'.[15] This would seem to go further than simply refusing to see the world as 'an unbroken whole' or having 'not one table, but many', as Banfield puts it;[16] it is a world that 'cannot be explained by any attempt at reducing them to their parts'.[17] Instead of choosing between wholeness and the fragmentation of this whole, the debate is already elsewhere – beyond arguments that depend upon a Cartesian or *a priori* subject/object split. Brown points to Niels Bohr's famous assertion that 'we are both onlookers and actors in the great drama of existence'[18] and argues that Bohr shares Woolf's sentiments that reality is not contained within a single perceptual consciousness, nor does it exist as a collection of multiple but rigidly divided perceptual consciousnesses [. . .] The reality depicted in *To the Lighthouse* seems to be composed of multiple interpenetrating consciousnesses interconnected with one another and loosely housed within fluid subjectivities and objectivities that interactively create, as well as observe, their environment.[19]

Mrs Ramsay's relationship with objects therefore reveals, I would add, what Barad has described as 'the heart of the lesson of quantum physics: *we are a part of that nature that we seek to understand*'.[20]

Intra-action and the entanglement of agency

Materiality is always something more than 'mere' matter: an excess, force, vitality, relationality, or difference that renders matter active, self-creative, productive, unpredictable.[21]

Quantum physics takes us away from a reality of dis/connecting individualities, where there is a leap beyond both traditional Newtonian realism (what Heisenberg calls 'dogmatic realism'[22]) and Einsteinian realism.[23] In *Meeting the Universe Halfway*, Barad outlines her notion of an 'agential realism' which, influenced by Bohr, is not reliant on 'subject-object, culture-nature, and word-world distinctions'.[24] Drawing on the work of Haraway, Butler, and Foucault in her reading of Bohr's 'philosophy-physics',[25] Barad's 'posthumanist performative'[26] approach to realism is one in which 'agency is not an attribute' of a being or thing, subject or object, but is entangled in 'the ongoing reconfigurations of the world'.[27] Barad's neologism 'intra-action' captures the new terms of debate brought about by quantum philosophy-physics:

'intra-action' *signifies the mutual constitution of entangled agencies*. That is, in contrast to the usual 'interaction,' which assumes that there are separate individual agencies that precede their interaction, the notion of intra-action recognizes that distinct agencies do not precede, but rather emerge through, their intra-action. It is important to note that the 'distinct' agencies are only distinct in a relational, not an absolute, sense, [. . .] *agencies are only distinct in relation to their mutual entanglement; they don't exist as individual elements*.[28]

Barad reaches this conceptualisation of reality by distinguishing Bohr's philosophy-physics from the work of Heisenberg, locating their difference in the matter of epistemology and ontology. Heisenberg's uncertainty is based on 'disturbance' and primarily concerned with epistemology (in other words, whilst we cannot know the value of a particle's momentum due to the disturbance that measurement entails, it is nonetheless 'assumed to exist independently of measurement'),[29] whereas 'Bohr is making a point about the nature of reality, not merely our knowledge of it':[30]

> For Bohr, the real issue is one of *indeterminacy*, not uncertainty [...] He understands the reciprocal relation between position and momentum in *semantic* and *ontic* terms, and only derivatively in epistemic terms (i.e., we can't know something definite about something for which there is nothing definite to know.) Bohr's indeterminacy principle can be stated as follows: *the values of complementary variables (such as position and momentum) are not simultaneously determinate*. The issue is not one of unknowability per se; rather, it is a question of what can be said to simultaneously exist.[31]

Whilst critics working on Woolf's relationship to the new physics have been keen to indicate examples of these ideas in her writings, it is often Heisenberg's 'uncertainty' that is focused on. For example, Zucker speaks of Woolf's 'uncertainty principle of language', whereby her 'literary "experiments"' are characterised by 'disrupted syntax, ambiguous referents, apparent contradictions' among other features.[32] In addition, there is sometimes the very confusion between uncertainty and indeterminacy that Barad warns against – this is seen when Sun Yom talks of Heisenberg's 'indeterminacy principle' (with no mention of Bohr)[33] and also when Louise Westling comments on 'the indeterminacy of our access to accurate knowledge, which Heisenberg's Uncertainty Principle clearly established early in the century'.[34] The fact that Brown, in the aforementioned study, therefore aligns Woolf with Bohr is important, and the reality he finds in *To the Lighthouse* where 'fluid subjectivities and objectivities [...] interactively create, as well as observe, their environment'[35] seems to point towards this notion of 'intra-action'.

In all of Woolf's writing the mutual entanglement of agency created by (and creating) intra-actions is perhaps most clearly evident in Bernard's summing up in *The Waves* when he attempts 'to break off, here at this table, what I call "my life", it is not one life that I look back upon; I am not one person; I am many people; I do not altogether know who I am – Jinny, Susan, Neville, Rhoda, or Louis; or how to distinguish my life from theirs' (W 230). It seems more than a coincidence that Bernard is accompanied by a table here as this key distinction between inter- and intra-action is brought to the fore, where the former is associated with epistemological uncertainty (there are six beings, I just do not know which one I am) and the latter with ontological indeterminacy (I cannot know which of these beings I am, because we are not distinct and separated). It is several pages later, however, that the question of whether Bernard is describing a purely epistemic concern or an ontological one becomes clearer. Bernard, now 'begin[ning] to doubt the fixity of tables',[36] asks: '"Who am I?" I have been talking of Bernard, Neville, Jinny, Susan, Rhoda and Louis. Am I all of them? Am I one and distinct?' As Bernard concludes 'I do not know' (W 240), there is a sense in which there is no clear answer to know other than where 'knowing is a matter of intra-acting [. . .] not a bounded or closed practice but an ongoing performance of the world'.[37] Such a network of intra-action is reinforced when Bernard 'cannot find any obstacle separating us. There is no division between me and them. As I talked I felt, "I am you". This difference we make so much of, this identity we so feverishly cherish, was overcome' (W 241). As Deleuze and Guattari write about *The Waves*: 'each of these characters, with his or her name, its individuality, designates a multiplicity [. . .] is simultaneously in this multiplicity and at its edge, and crosses over into the others'.[38]

Bernard goes on to describe 'patterns of marks on bodies'[39] caused by the intra-active dynamism of his friends: 'Here on my brow is the blow I got when Percival fell. Here on the nape of my neck is the kiss Jinny gave Louis. My eyes fill with Susan's tears. I see far away, quivering like a gold thread, the pillar Rhoda saw, and feel the rush of the wind of her flight when she lept' (W 241). That Jinny does not actually kiss Bernard or that his eyes cannot in reality be filled with 'Susan's tears' does not mean that this is all in his imagination. It is possible to think of them as markings of intra-action where 'connectivity does not require physical contiguity. (Spatially separate particles in an *entangled state* do not have separate identities but rather are part of the same phenomena.)'[40] As Barad clarifies, with an example especially relevant to Eleanor's china cup in *The Years*: 'physics tells us that edges or boundaries are not determinate either ontologically or visually. When it comes to the "interface" between a coffee mug and a hand, it is not that there are x number of atoms that belong to a hand and y number of atoms that belong to the coffee mug.'[41] When Bernard 'come[s] to shape here at this table between [his] hands the story of [his] life' (W 241), his conclusion returns us to his statement near the beginning of the novel that 'when we sit together, close [. . .] we melt into each other with phrases. We are edged with mist' (W 11). Not only is the 'interface' between his hand and the table indeterminate, but that between he and his friends too.

Naturalcultural phenomena

Rather than a reality consisting of individuated subjects and objects, a quantum philosophical reading of *The Waves* emphasises a reality consisting of 'phenomena', as foundational units which include all features in a given experimental arrangement, with no ontologically predetermined separation:

> Phenomena are constitutive of reality. Parts of the world are always intra-acting with other parts of the world, and it is through specific intra-actions that a differential sense of being – with boundaries, properties, cause, and effect – is enacted in the ongoing ebb and flow of agency. There are no preexisting, separately determinate entities called 'humans' that are either detached spectators or necessary components of all intra-actions. Rather, to the extent that 'humans' emerge as having a role to play in the constitution of specific phenomena, they do so as part of the larger material reconfiguration, or rather the ongoing reconfiguring, of the world. [...] 'Humans' are emergent phenomena like all other physical systems.[42]

Shared among agencies that can only be locally determined,[43] this notion of reality is posthumanist, where

> refusing the anthropocentrisms of humanism and antihumanism, *posthumanism* marks the practice of accounting for the boundary-making practices by which the 'human' and its others are differentially delineated and defined [...] it refuses the idea of a natural (or, for that matter, a purely cultural) division between nature and culture, calling for an accounting of how this boundary is actively configured and reconfigured.

Posthumanism challenges the hierarchical arrangement of the materiality of life which would place humans at the summit: 'Posthumanism does not presume that man is the measure of all things [...] Posthumanism doesn't presume the separateness of any-"thing," let alone the alleged spatial, ontological, and epistemological distinction that sets humans apart.'[44] Where the previous chapter turned away from an anthropocentric relation between humans and animals, the issue here is a move away from a human-centred form of interaction between individual things and beings and towards a posthuman form of intra-actions of 'emergent phenomena' where 'it is through such practices that the differential boundaries between humans and nonhumans, culture and nature, science and the social, are constituted'.[45]

If intra-action depends upon the naturalcultural entanglements[46] of agencies both human and nonhuman (and beyond this distinction), then from the beginning of *The Waves* there are examples of such a reality.

Louis' embodiment seems to be erotically intertwined with the earth at the same time as it is marked by Jinny's kiss:

> I am rooted to the middle of the earth. My body is a stalk. I press the stalk. A drop oozes from the whole at the mouth and slowly, thickly, grows larger and larger. Now something pink passes the eye-whole. Now a beam is slid through the chink. Its beam strikes me. I am a boy in a grey flannel suit. She has found me. I am struck on the nape of the neck. She has kissed me. (W 8)

With this kiss the nature/culture distinction is 'shattered' (W 8), and the humanist privilege given to individualism challenged, as Louis wishes to escape his other-ised identity – as Rhoda would say, having 'to go through the antics of the individual' (W 186) – and 'be unseen' (W 8). This is emphasised a few pages later when Louis, again aware of his Australian accent, does not privilege knowledge over nature; the fact that he 'know[s] the lesson by heart', including the grammatical rules of 'cases' and 'genders', and his (admittedly egotistical) view that he 'could know everything in the world', is less important than the sense that his 'roots are threaded, like fibres in a flower-pot, round and round about the world' (W 14). Significantly, the friend he then attempts to 'imitate' is 'Bernard softly lisping Latin'. Rather than choosing Neville, with his belief that words and grammatical systems show 'there is an order in this world; there are distinctions' (W 15), in Bernard he has chosen to imitate the character most attuned to the complexity and instability (later to be inadequacy) of language with words that 'flick their tails' as he speaks them, 'now this way, now that way, moving all together, now dividing, now coming together' (W 14). Indeed, Bernard later appears to reject the primacy of human knowledge and instead evokes a suitable description of quantum-inspired intra-action: 'To speak of knowledge is futile. All is experiment and adventure. We are forever mixing ourselves with unknown quantities' (W 97).[47]

Being rooted to the earth does not mean being rooted in a fixed and eternal way to a solid and external earth; rather, being 'rooted' here is to be entangled in 'material-discursive' intra-acting[48] – perhaps what Jinny describes when she states 'I am rooted, but I flow' (W 83). In other words, the entanglement of materiality and meaning is not to be found in the combination of parts which nonetheless remain distinct and fixed entities (for instance 'the earth' and 'the human'), rather 'everything [even the "hard ground"] dances – the net, the grass; your faces leap like butterflies; the trees seem to jump up and down. There is nothing staid, nothing settled, in this universe. All is rippling, all is dancing; all is quickness and triumph' (W 35). Later, when Louis' body is this time linked to his being identified as 'the best scholar in the school', it is 'unenviable' – thus when the body is not conceived of in its dynamic intra-actions it is an unwanted relic of individualism, of the self that defines Louis as an outsider because of his accent. Importantly, this does not mean that Louis wishes to escape the material world and delve into some mystic otherworldliness;[49] on the contrary it is in 'put[ting] off' this particular image of the body that he can 'inhabit space' (W 41). Perhaps Louis is again following Bernard, who perfectly captures this move from representation (and identity) to intra-action: 'I am only superficially represented by what I was saying tonight. Underneath, and, at the moment when I am most disparate, I am also integrated' (W 62). To intra-act is to be 'inextricably involved' (W 60); to be 'integrated' at the same time as 'disparate' is to feature within Bohrian phenomena. We can also think here about the narrative style of *The Waves*, the way in which direct speech is used for each character and a new paragraph is always taken before a new character speaks, and yet these monologues seem to be integrated.

That Neville, arguably the character most attached to the idea of individuality and fixity, is involved in one of the clearest affirmations of intra-action in *The Waves* gives weight to the view that Woolf is engaging with this notion of reality. Having earlier 'hate[d] wanderings and mixing things together' (W 11), Neville then laments that the choice to follow this identity or that leads to the conclusion that 'change is no longer possible. We are committed.' Now seeing past the 'narrow limits' of the identity he (thinks he) is known by, he is 'immeasurable; a net whose fibres pass imperceptibly beneath the world'. Similar to Louis' body and the earth, what is at stake here is not two distinct elements – one being 'the world' and the other the 'net' (or himself); rather the net captures Neville's intra-actions with/in the world, the 'net is almost indistinguishable from that which it surrounds' (W 178). Again there is no fixed internal and external in this material-discursive world; or, as Susan says, 'I cannot be divided, or kept apart' (W 79) – a comment which echoes Heisenberg's view that quantum physics 'makes the sharp separation between the world and I impossible'.[50] The 'I' in Susan's statement is already more than a defined, distinct human individual:

> I am the field, I am the barn, I am the trees; mine are the flocks of birds, and this young hare who leaps, at the last moment when I step almost on him. Mine is the heron that stretches its vast wings lazily; and the cow that creaks as it pushes one foot before another munching; and the wild, swooping swallow; and the faint red in the sky, and the green when the red fades; the silence and the bell; the call of the man fetching car-horses from the fields. (W 78)

As in *Between the Acts*, 'sheep, cows, grass, trees, ourselves – all are one. If discordant producing harmony' (*BA* 157). What Susan cannot be divided from then is a multiplicitous 'I' which includes creaking cows and an array of other nonhuman elements: 'I am not a woman, but the light that falls on this gate, on this ground. I am the seasons, I think sometimes, January, May, November; the mud, the mist, the dawn' (*W* 79). Blurring the boundaries between human and nature in order to refuse any settled concept of human nature, Woolf is here providing an image of intra-action which rejects the notion of hierarchical distinctions between human and nonhuman, culture and nature.

It is important that all of the characters in *The Waves* are part of these naturalcultural intra-actions, even if their feelings about such entanglements differ. Writing of Woolf's 'mood waves', John Briggs links the novel to both chaos theory and neuroscience (in particular the non-linearity of the brain) in order to emphasise that in Woolf's vision of reality 'it is not the mood itself that matters, but the way in which a mood – whether positive or negative – punctures the surface of everyday life, shatters for an instant habits of mind and emotion'.[51] Taking on board the (often sudden) fluctuations from exultation to depression in the novel, Briggs posits that

> Woolf's mood waves function at *different scales*: on the level of the novel as a whole, within sections, within sentences [...] Like real waves – which even as they are rising and seem coherent, are, in fact, dissipating and incipient with the very disorder that will soon bring them down – Woolf's mood waves contain wavelets, and wavelets within wavelets, a fractal structure. This rhythmic action – and the rhythmic eddying action within action – imbues her work with its paradoxical atmosphere of both infinite variety and wholeness.[52]

The description here of 'action within action' reads a lot like intra-action, and the 'paradoxical atmosphere of both infinite variety and wholeness' might be the reality of entanglements which do not adhere to an internal/external logic, but are always, as Barad writes, concerned with 'exteriority within'.[53] In relation to the characters in *The Waves*, the point is not that they are the *same*, with consistent emotions and reactions, but neither should they be thought of as fully distinct and separate individuals simply *inter*acting with one another and with their external environment. But if *The Waves* describes the material entanglement of agencies that do not adhere to the opposition between subject/object and internal/external, to what extent is Woolf engaging with an ontology of 'life itself', and with the relationship between life and matter?

Life and the living

> Life is that tendency, *in matter itself*, to prolong, delay, detour, which means that matter, 'an undivided flux,' is as alive, as dynamic, as invested in becoming as life itself.[54]

In *After Life* (2010), Eugene Thacker argues that there are two central challenges when considering the term 'life' in our contemporary context: 'One of these challenges is to refuse a dichotomous concept of life, as caught between the poles of reductionism and mysticism, scientificity and religiosity, the empirical and romantic notions of life. [...] This opens onto a second challenge, and that is the pervasive anthropomorphism of the concept "life".'[55] In *The Waves*, I would like to suggest that Woolf is also considering the possibilities of a concept of life that is neither divided between a naïve realism and idealism, nor human-centred. That is not to say Woolf's conceptualisation of life is always consistent, however. This section will focus in the first instance on some of the occasions when we can see Woolf pointing to potential contradictions in a concept of life, and secondly when we witness her moving beyond this to experiment with and suggest notions of life as non-anthropocentric, immanent assemblages.

At the beginning of Bernard's long soliloquy which concludes *The Waves*, he conjures a 'life' that is possessed by him whilst at the same time acknowledging that it is beyond his grasp, that life cannot be captured by, or reduced to, the human: 'The illusion is upon me that something adheres for a moment, has roundness, weight, depth, is completed. This, for the moment, seems to be my life. If it were possible, I would hand it you entire. I would break it off as one breaks off a bunch of grapes. I would say, "Take it. This is my life"' (W 199). On the one hand Bernard presents an image of 'life' as unified and tangible, under the control of its human possessor, but on the other hand this vision is only a subjective perceptual 'illusion'. This passage illuminates an important problem *The Waves* raises and attempts to work through in its exploration of life, namely that in Western philosophy there is an internal split in the concept 'life' between the immanent life of a human (or nonhuman) agent, and the transcendent life as the force by which that agent is living. In Thacker's terms, this would be described as the difference between 'Life' and 'the living', which can be thought of as a problem that goes back to the roots of philosophical concerns – specifically, as Thacker points out, in terms of Aristotle's *De Anima* and the concept of *psukhē* (usually translated as 'soul' but more accurately understood as 'vital principle' or 'principle of life').[56] The contradiction inherent to Aristotle's *psukhē* is that on the one hand 'there is no thing called "life-in-itself" that is ever present apart from its formal, dynamic, and temporal instantiations in the variety of living beings', and on the other hand 'Aristotle does not dispense with the *archē*-of-life altogether. He seems to imply its necessary existence if one is to think something like "life" at all'.[57]

There is further evidence in Woolf's novel of this tension inherent in *psukhē* between Life and the living, transcendence and immanence. Life is described as a discrete entity apart from the human by Neville, at the same time as it is connected to him. It is therefore seen as an obstacle to self-progress: 'my life was unavailing' (W 18). When life is connected to the living, grammatical conventions often lead to it being possessed by a subject (and therefore by language itself); there are several other examples throughout the book when characters refer to 'my life'. These provide instances of the possessive life used by Neville (W 37), Louis (W 41), Susan (W 48), Rhoda (W 169), and Bernard (W 243), where, for example, 'my life' for Neville, Louis, and Susan signals temporal life tied to their experience as 'the living'. Intriguingly, it is Jinny who never refers in the novel to 'my life' in this way, perhaps supporting the view some critics have of her as most attuned to the nonhuman (as detailed below). But as we have already seen in the above quotations from Bernard, and in relation to quantum philosophy-physics, the 'my' in question cannot be easily joined to a distinct, fully individuated subject (the same way that Susan's 'I' is already more than a clearly-defined human individual); it is a multiplicitous 'my' – as Louis puts it, 'my many-folded life' (W 138).[58]

These examples are only hints in the text of the paradoxical, perhaps counterintuitive, notion of life founded on indeterminacy. But what moves *The Waves* beyond a concern with Life and the living as the irreconcilable conflict between transcendence and immanence is Woolf's exploration of life as a nonanthropocentric/nontheistic vital force. Although Bernard's thoughts suggest the elusiveness of 'life', it is never a question of sublimating it within a theological framework. Slightly later in the novel he again betrays an awareness of this illusory nature of life and the pretence of human agency over it as though it is an object to be captured and cultivated: 'Let us again pretend that life is a solid substance shaped like a globe, which we turn about in our fingers. Let us pretend that we can make out a plain and logical story, so that when one matter is despatched – love for instance – we go on, in an orderly manner, to the next' (W 210). In the sentences before this, Bernard claims that 'what one needs is nothing consecutive but a bark, a groan', and true to this his conceptualisation of life does not correspond to a wholeness which unfolds in an orderly progression as time passes; it is only pretending to be so. What is also interesting is the way in which this pretence that life is a tangible, solid object under control of human agency does open onto a materialist conceptualisation of 'life'. In other words, the pretence here is not so much about the materiality of life *per se* – that is, Woolf is not interested in giving up life to some transcendent sphere; rather, the pretence concerns the role of human control in this materiality, and precisely how capturable the material world is when taking into account the complicated web of 'circumstances' that Bernard is so aware of throughout the novel, and the 'different transitions' he makes depending on these circumstances (W 61, 65). This recalls Woolf's view in *A Room of One's Own* of 'the common life which is the real life' and of 'human beings not always in their relation to each other but in relation to reality' (RO 149), or, as Deleuze and Guattari put it in *Anti-Oedipus*, 'a bit of *relation to the outside*, a little real reality'.[59]

This question of the materiality of life therefore takes us back to issues that have been central throughout this book, starting with the ways in which Woolf's figuration taken from the material world of 'granite' and 'rainbow' complicates and undermines the binaries of fact/fiction, solid/intangible, materiality/theory and, in the context of this current discussion, we might add immanence/transcendence. Towards the end of *The Waves* 'life' for Bernard demonstrates both solidity and intangibility intermingling, as he returns for the final time to the image of the 'globe':

> The crystal, the globe of life as one calls it, far from being hard and cold to the touch, has walls of thinnest air. If I press them all will burst. Whatever sentence I extract whole and entire from this cauldron is only a string of six little fish that let themselves be caught while a million others leap and sizzle, making the cauldron bubble like boiling silver, and slip through my fingers. Faces recur, faces and faces – they press their beauty to the walls of my bubble – Neville, Susan, Louis, Jinny, Rhoda and a thousand others. How impossible to order them rightly; to detach one separately, or to give the effect of the whole – again like music. What a symphony, with its concord and its discord and its tunes on top and its complicated bass beneath, then grew up! (W 214)

Just as music is a key inspiration for Braidotti's 'transpositions', Woolf is here emphasising the musicality of the 'transversal transfer'[60] or, as she writes in the above quote, 'leap and sizzle' of qualitative multiplicities. Like 'a symphony with its concord and its discord', life is material but evasive; it is 'faces and faces' against 'walls of thinnest air'. And Woolf is also describing the transpositions of language here, where, as Braidotti puts it, 'words grow, split and multiply, sprouting new roots or side branches and resonating with all kinds of echoes and musical variations'.⁶¹ This again recalls 'Craftsmanship' where Woolf describes words as 'many-sided, flashing this way, then that' (*E6* 97), and also those aforementioned passages in *The Waves* where the relations between the friends are based on an ontological indeterminacy. But where Woolf's novel presents the meeting of quantum indeterminacy and 'some rapid unapprehended life' (*W* 203), it does so with an emphasis on the creative potential for locally determinate arrangements.

Things, assemblages, and walking haecceities

> What is an assemblage? It is a multiplicity which is made up of many heterogeneous terms and which establishes liaisons, relations between them, across ages, sexes and reigns – different natures. Thus, the assemblage's only unity is that of co-functioning: it is a symbiosis, a 'sympathy'.⁶²

In the first part of this chapter I highlighted some of the ways in which *The Waves* rejects a realism founded on humanist individualism in favour of a posthumanist, material and creative, array of intra-actions formed out of indeterminacy, and in the preceding section I suggested that Woolf's novel explores a nonanthropocentric/nontheistic conceptualisation of life. Crucial to this conceptualisation is the relationship between what we refer to as the human (and other organic forms of life), but also the agency of seemingly inanimate objects. In *Vibrant Matter*, Jane Bennett calls this 'thing-power', or 'the curious ability of inanimate things to animate, to act, to produce effects dramatic and subtle':⁶³ 'A primordial swerve says that the world is not determined, that an element of chanciness resides at the heart of things, but it also affirms that so-called inanimate things have a life, that deep within is an inexplicable vitality or energy, a moment of independence from and resistance to us and other bodies.'⁶⁴ This 'chanciness' and 'inexplicable' force is reminiscent of Niels Bohr's philosophy-physics, of an indeterminacy ingrained in the quantum materiality of life. It also shares similar aims with Braidotti's call for a 'vital politics of life itself, which means external non-human relations, life as *zoē*, or generative force. The "others" in question here are non-anthropomorphic and include planetary forces.'⁶⁵ Along with her aims to replace a focus on subjectivity with one on 'developing a vocabulary and syntax for, and thus a better discernment of, the active powers issuing from nonsubjects' and to create a political analysis that includes the 'contributions of nonhuman actants', Bennett, like Braidotti, is keen to dispel the onto-theological binary of life and matter.⁶⁶ She follows a Spinozan-Bergsonian-Deleuzian track to ultimately posit a 'vital materialism' which is thoroughly nonanthropocentric and nontheistic:

> What I am calling impersonal affect or material vibrancy is not a spiritual supplement of 'life force' added to the matter said to house it. Mine is not a vitalism in the traditional sense; I equate affect with materiality, rather than posit a separate force that can enter and animate a physical body.[67]

In *The Waves*, Bernard's denunciation of possessions might paradoxically be seen as an affirmation of the force of 'things'. Leaving possessions behind would really be a affirmative letting go of human power over them (and the illusion of human power over life), a reconceptualisation of life as intra-actions between an array of nonhuman as well as human agencies. As such, there would be a positive disavowal of 'life' as a possession and a move from a human subject-centred conceptualisation of life-as-object towards an affirmation of life as vibrant matter. In the following passage where he contemplates his impending marriage, Bernard denounces individual ownership of objects and of 'life':

> But I do not wish [...] to assume the burden of individual life. I, who have been since Monday, when she accepted me, charged in every nerve with a sense of identity, who could not see a tooth-brush in a glass without saying, '*My* tooth-brush,' now wish to unclasp my hands and let fall my possessions, and merely stand here in the street, taking no part, watching the omnibuses, without desire; without envy; with what would be boundless curiosity about human destiny if there were any longer an edge to my mind. But it has none. I have arrived; am accepted. I ask nothing. (W 92)

One striking aspect of this passage is that Bernard seems to move from a view of 'individual life', as life possessed by the living (human), to a more humble form of human agency. As Tamlyn Monson notes, 'Bernard experiences a feeling of claustrophobic horror at this phenomenon of individual life, which, he finds, is driven by agency exercised in response to "necessity".'[68] But although Bernard expresses the wish to consider 'human destiny' apart from his own involvement in that destiny, he realises that he cannot erase himself entirely – 'taking no part', 'without desire', 'without envy' – from a consideration of life. This impossibility has less to do with negation than with a very challenging of the subject-object relationship on which negation depends; what is more important is that there is no longer 'an edge to [his] mind', a clear border between his internal focus and external forces. Rather than a conscious relinquishing of possessions there is the realisation that he has already 'arrived' and is 'accepted' at this place where relations are not primarily between subject and object; the move from the 'individual life' to 'omnipresent, general life' (*W* 92), the 'general impulse' (*W* 93) into which he can 'sink down, deep, into what passes' (*W* 92).

Passages such as these in *The Waves* could then be an example of what Deleuze and Guattari describe as an 'assemblage' which includes 'semiotic flows, material flows, and social flows simultaneously'[69] and has 'has neither base nor superstructure, neither deep structure nor superficial structure, it flattens all of its dimensions and mutual insertions play themselves out'.[70] This more unassuming and shared notion of agency can also be understood as intra-acting with the 'vitality' and 'energy' of Bennett's materialist 'thing-power',[71] and Deleuze and Guattari's assemblages are crucial to Bennett's theory. Indeed, in his essay 'Literature and Life' Deleuze describes the entangled relations between writing and 'things': 'There are no straight lines, neither in things nor in language. Syntax is the set of necessary detours that are created in each case to reveal the life in things.'[72] In Woolf's novel we see the forming of a collective assemblage of life where instead of 'standing in the street, taking no part', Bernard asks:

> Am I not, as I walk, trembling with strange oscillations and vibrations of sympathy, which, unmoored as I am from a private being, bid me embrace these engrossed flocks; these starers and trippers; these errand-boys and furtive and fugitive girls who, ignoring their doom, look in at shop-windows? (*W* 93)

The inadequacy of a concept of 'life' that does not involve the human at all (as in Bernard's above description of wanting to watch with no desire) is replaced by the turn towards multiplicitous intra-actions with the life in things, the creation of assemblages which include nonhuman as well as human agents,[73] 'the growl of the traffic [which] might be any uproar – forest trees or the roar of wild beasts' at the same time as 'sensations, spontaneous and irrelevant, of curiosity, greed, desire' (*W* 93). Seen in light of Bennett's vital materialism, the shop-windows in the above quotation are as much a part of the assemblage here as the 'furtive and fugitive girls' who look in them, in a similar sense to Susan's naturalcultural entanglements, where her 'I' signalled a multiplicity of human and nonhuman elements.

Bernard shows further signs of creating assemblages with the nonhuman towards the end of the novel:

> 'Silence falls; silence falls,' said Bernard. 'But now listen, tick, tick; hoot, hoot; the world has hailed us back to it. I heard for one moment the howling winds of darkness as we passed beyond life. Then tick, tick (the clock); then hoot, hoot (the cars). We are landed; we are on shore; we are sitting, six of us,

at a table. It is the memory of my nose that recalls me. I rise; "Fight," I cry, "fight!" remembering the shape of my own nose and strike with this spoon upon this table pugnaciously.' (W 188)

Here the passing 'beyond life' does not lead to a transcendent escape from reality, but a subversion of a transcendent concept of life. Bernard is sonically attuned to the clock and the cars, which are materially intra-acting with the six friends at the table. It is these nonhuman and human entanglements that spark Bernard to rally and 'fight' in contrast to the nihilism expressed in the preceding lines by Susan, Rhoda, and Louis (it is Jinny who offers the most optimistic viewpoint here):

> 'In this silence,' said Susan, 'it seems as if no leaf would ever fall, or bird fly.'
> 'As if the miracle had happened,' said Jinny, 'and life were stayed here and now.'
> 'And,' said Rhoda, 'we had no more to live.'
> 'But listen,' said Louis, 'to the world moving through abysses of infinite space. It roars; the lighted strip of history is past and our Kings and Queens; we are gone; our civilisation; the Nile; and all life. Our separate drops are dissolved; we are extinct, lost in the abysses of time, in the darkness.' (W 187–8)

Bernard's desire to 'fight' is also in response to his own reflection that 'the earth is only a pebble flicked off accidentally from the face of the sun and that there is no life anywhere in the abysses of space' (W 187). In addition, it is important to note that even as these characters express their worries on transience, they are still involved in an assemblage (recalling Briggs' discussion of Woolf's 'mood waves') which, as Bennett puts it, 'are living, throbbing confederations that are able to function despite the persistent presence of energies that confound them from within'.[74] It is also significant that Bernard returns in the above passage to the table, a table that does not simply act as a meeting place for the thoughts of subjects, but is itself a vibrant, living object, materially and semiotically entangled here with the bodies of the friends.

In *The Waves* we can view Bernard's intra-actions with his environment – the human and the nonhuman – as creating a posthuman form of agency consisting of assemblages. According to Monaco, Bernard demonstrates this type of collective agency early on in the book when lying in bed he is 'afloat in the shallow light which is like a film of water drawn over my eyes by a wave. I hear through it far off, far away, faint and far, the chorus beginning' (W 20). For Monaco 'the child's hearing is like a net catching the sonic assemblages and inter-assemblages composing life [in my reading these assemblages *are* life] and connecting him to the wider world':

> These early sections have a heightened luminosity, due to the two-fold purity: of both the poetic form, and of the quality of the child's perception itself, which is unobstructed and untainted by habit, and whose senses penetrate, as we see above, in both a localised and a far-reaching way. The child's psyche is a membrane of becoming, which fuses its emotional life with the material world.[75]

Monaco also presents the example of Susan as a child, arguing that in the following passage 'her suffering is inseparable from the environment'[76] where, as Bernard describes, she 'trips and flings herself down on the roots under the trees, where the light seems to pant in and out, in and out. The branches heave up and down. There is agitation and trouble here. There is gloom.' As the passage continues: 'The roots make a skeleton on the ground, with dead leaves heaped in the angles. Susan has spread her anguish out' (W 9).

As we have seen, this relation between human and environment is highlighted through other characters in *The Waves*. Carrie Rohman argues that Jinny is the character most attuned to material entanglements with nature, recalling the kiss Jinny gives Louis at the beginning of the novel where she connects her own bodily movements with those of the natural world: 'What moved the leaves? What moves my heart, my legs? And I dashed in here [. . .] kissed you, with my heart jumping under my pink frock like the leaves, which go on moving, though there is nothing to move them' (W 8). This is evidence that 'Jinny's connection to nature is of the earth, not merely symbolic'.[77] Rohman reads *The Waves* alongside Grosz's writings on the connections between sexuality, animality, and art, and asks:

> how do we connect such inhuman forces to the novel's human characters? We do so by asking this question: how do Woolf's characters relate to the vibrational? How do the characters function *as* forces of creative rhythm, or *in relation to* forces of creative rhythm. And interestingly, it is Jinny who attracts one most in this respect. It is Jinny who seems most vibrational, and ultimately then, perhaps most creative or artistic, in the posthumanist sense. [. . .] Jinny is characterized by undulating movement and her connections to movement, by the bodily *as such* and her attraction to materiality, and by an awareness of and appreciation for [. . .] qualitative experiential states.[78]

As Rohman notes, this view of Jinny's 'becoming vibratory'[79] in the novel is at odds with those readings which have reduced her to the sexual (although Rohman's description of a vibratory Jinny does have its own erotic aesthetic).[80] Rohman offers examples where Jinny's sense of creation is bound up with 'animality, the floral, and even to birdsong', and it is particularly salient that she emphasises the connection between human and nonhuman in a similar sense to Haraway's 'naturecultures'. She focuses on the following passage as a key example of 'divergent natural and cultural arenas' intermingling:

> In one way or another we make this day, this Friday, some by going to the Law Courts; others to the city; others to the nursery; others by marching and forming fours. [. . .] The activity is endless. [. . .] Some take train for France; others ship for India. Some will never come into this room again. One may die tonight. Another will beget a child. From us every sort of building, policy, venture, picture, poem, child, factory, will spring. Life comes; life goes; we make life. So you say. (W 145)

Woolf reveals here that 'we don't make art, or literature. We don't live life or experience life. We make life. We create life. Could Jinny be recognizing the becoming-artistic of life itself in its inhuman manifestations?'[81] We could also return here to Woolf's declaration in 'Sketch of the Past' 'that the whole world is a work of art; that we are parts of the work'. When Woolf writes that 'we are the words; we are the music; we are the thing itself' (MB 85), it is not then an endorsement of an exclusively human subjectivity, but of the ways in which creation consists of the material intra-actions between human and nonhuman, that words and music do not exist in a higher realm apart from life as 'the thing itself', a 'thing' which we somehow feel is, as Suzanne Bellamy puts it, 'the core, the form, the life force'.[82]

In *The Waves*, rather than 'neat designs of life', the characters are attuned to 'the panorama of life' in all its complex entanglements (W 202). By the end of the novel Bernard's vision is one whereby nonhuman forces are emphasised and his own sense of a distinctly human subjectivity diminished:

> Lying in a ditch on a stormy day, when it has been raining, then enormous clouds come marching over the sky, tattered clouds, wisps of cloud. What delights me then is the confusion, the height, the indifference and the fury. Great clouds always changing, and movement; something sulphurous and sinister, bowled up, helter-skelter; towering, trailing, broken off, lost, and I forgotten, minute, in a ditch. Of story, of design I do not see a trace then. (W 200)

What 'delights' Bernard is precisely the 'confusion' and 'movement' of his environment – whether 'stormy' or 'sinister' – where the 'I' is 'forgotten'. If there is individuation here, then it is in the form of a Deleuzian assemblage – what he refers to as 'haecceity',[83] as the creation of a new event formed of aggregates of bodies, objects, and spaces: 'consist[ing] entirely of relations of movement and rest between molecules or particles, capacities to affect and be affected'.[84] In *Dialogues* Deleuze refers to Clarissa's walk through London at the beginning of *Mrs Dalloway* as providing an example of haecceity, and crucially its connection to the 'question of life': 'On her stroll Virginia Woolf's heroine penetrates like a blade through all things, and yet looks from the outside, with the impression that it is dangerous to live even a single day ("Never again will I say: I am this or that, he is this, he is that . . ."). But the stroll is itself a haecceity.' The proper name 'Mrs Dalloway' signifies an event: 'It is haecceities that are expressed [. . .] in proper names which do not designate people but mark events [. . .] HAECCEITY = EVENT. It is a question of life.'[85] Deleuze and Guattari expand the influence of Clarissa's walk in their consideration of literature in *What is Philosophy?*, pointing to this aspect of Woolf's writing as exemplary of 'affects' and 'percepts':

> Characters can only exist, and the author can only create them, because they do not perceive but have passed into the landscape and are themselves part of the compound of sensations. [. . .] It is Mrs Dalloway who perceives the town – but because she has passed into the town like 'a knife through everything' and becomes imperceptible herself. *Affects are precisely these nonhuman becomings of man*, just as percepts – including the town – are *nonhuman landscapes of nature*. [. . .] We are not in the world, we become with the world.

Woolf presents 'urban percepts' through Clarissa's walk,[86] which bring together nature with culture, the nonhuman with the human – a shared posthumanist worlding.

Woolf herself provides the perfect example of the event as haecceity in a diary entry from 27th February 1926, when she recounts walking through Russell Square the previous night:

> I have some restless searcher in me. Why is there not a discovery in life? Something one can lay hands on and say 'This is it'? What is it? And shall I die before I can find it? Then (as I was walking through Russell Square last night) I see mountains in the sky: the great clouds, and the moon which is risen over Persia; I have a great and astonishing sense of something there, which is 'it' [. . .] Is that what I meant to say? Not in the least. I was thinking about my own character; not about the universe. (*D3* 62)

This example is particularly revealing as at the very moment Woolf questions whether there is something determinate and fixed in life that she can find and grasp hold of, the 'it' of life transforms subject/object distinctions into the creation of an assemblage or haecceity, a becoming-cosmic. Indeed, Deleuze and Guattari return us to the cosmic materiality of Woolf's novel when they describe her attempt to 'saturate every atom' and 'eliminate all waste, deadness, superfluity' (*D3* 209), what she intended in *The Waves*, as a desire to 'eliminate all that is resemblance and analogy, but also "to put everything into it": eliminate everything that exceeds the moment, but put in everything that it includes'.[87] It is to transpose 'our current and lived perceptions' into 'the saturation that gives us the percept'.[88] But the entanglement of the human, nature, and the cosmic creates a moment which is 'not the instantaneous, it is the haecceity into which one slips and that slips into other haecceities by transparency [. . .] Such is the link between imperceptibility, indiscernibility, and impersonality'.[89]

In Woolf's short story 'A Simple Melody' (1985), written not long after *Mrs Dalloway*, we see another example of Woolf's writing on walking – this time in the countryside – as a 'haecceity' or Deleuzian 'event'. Here we read George Carslake's reflections on a landscape painting which leads him to describe precisely this becoming-imperceptible and becoming-impersonal, the saturation of every atom of air until 'walking thoughts were half sky', a phrase which perfectly captures Deleuze and Guattari's affirmation that 'walking is a haecceity':[90]

> to analyse this favourite theme of his – walking, different people walking to Norwich. He thought at once of the lark, of the sky, of the view. The walker's thoughts and emotions were largely made up of these outside influences. Walking thoughts were half sky; if you could submit them to chemical analysis you would find that they had some grains of colour in them, some gallons or quarts or pints of air attached to them. This at once made them airier, more impersonal. (*CSF* 206)

To be sure, these examples do not provide a straightforward distinction between individual and collective, but rather, as Deleuze and Guattari write in *A Thousand Plateaus*: 'haecceities, affects, subjectless individuations that constitute collective assemblages [. . .] Nothing subjectifies, but haecceities form according to compositions of nonsubjectified powers or affects.'[91] Thus, 'the proper name brings about an individuation by "haecceity", not at all by subjectivity [. . .] Virginia Woolf designates a state of reigns, ages and sexes.'[92]

Returning to *The Waves*, in the following passage Bernard, himself involved in many descriptions of walking in the final section of the novel, would then enter into composition with the 'undifferentiated chaos of life' which is not so much a homogenisation of difference, but the intra-acting, vital force of things including chiming bells, a 'girl on a bicycle', and even the apparently incidental 'corner of a curtain':

> while the fringe of my intelligence floating unattached caught those distant sensations which after a time the mind draws in and works upon; the chime of bells; general murmurs; vanishing figures; one girl on a bicycle who, as she rode, seemed to lift the corner of a curtain concealing the populous undifferentiated chaos of life which surged behind the outlines of my friends and the willow tree. (W 208)

Life may have 'surged behind the outlines' of Bernard's friends, but we need not think of it as either separate from the living (that is, transcendent) or reduced to mere background. If we think of this as an example of Deleuzian haecceity, then

> it should not be thought that a haecceity consists simply of a décor or backdrop that situates subjects, or of appendages that hold things and people to the ground. It is the entire assemblage in its individuated aggregate that is a haecceity; it is this assemblage that is defined by a longitude and a latitude, by speeds and affects, independently of forms and subjects, which belong to another plane [. . .] to become events, in assemblages that are inseparable from an hour, a season, an atmosphere, an air, a life.[93]

The final word in this quotation is crucial as 'a life' for Deleuze is a-subjective and pre-personal, as emphasised in his final essay 'Immanence: A Life' which I will consider in the next section. Following Deleuze, Bennett asks: 'can nonorganic bodies also have a life? Can materiality itself be vital?'[94] Her vital materialism is an attempt 'to articulate the elusive idea of a materiality that is *itself* heterogeneous, itself a differential of intensities, itself *a* life. In this strange, *vital* materialism, there is no point of pure stillness, no indivisible atom that is not itself aquiver with virtual force.'[95] This touches on one of the key challenges for Deleuzian philosophy, namely how to account for the concurrence of a flattening of hierarchical structures at the same time as the proliferation of heterogeneity – an issue which also speaks to my discussions of sexual difference and human-animal difference in previous chapters of this book. Turning to the concepts of univocity and specifically Deleuze's 'pure immanence' might be what ultimately brings together Barad's philosophy-physics, Bennett's vital materialism, and Woolf's *The Waves*, and might provide an ontology of life capable of creating such heterogeneity without hierarchy.

Pure immanence

> Absolute immanence is in itself: it is not in something, *to* something; it does not depend on an object or belong to a subject.[96]

Absolute or pure immanence takes us beyond the false dichotomy of the choice between life as heterogeneous hierarchy and homogeneous flatness. As Deleuze puts it in his final essay 'Immanence: A Life', 'we will say of pure immanence that it is A LIFE, and nothing else. It is not immanence to life, but the immanent that is in nothing is itself a life. A life is the immanence of immanence, absolute immanence: it is complete power, complete bliss.'[97] Or as Deleuze and Guattari write in *What is Philosophy?*: 'Immanence is immanent only to itself and consequently captures everything, absorbs All-One, and leaves nothing remaining to which it could be immanent.'[98] Thacker's *After Life* illustrates that to fully understand Deleuze's concept of pure immanence – 'immanence as not subordinate to transcendence'[99] – it is important to recognise the influence of Scholastic philosophers on his thinking. Scholasticism, Thacker notes, is never far away from Deleuze's philosophy, specifically in terms of his long-standing engagement with issues concerning the One, multiplicity, and pure immanence. There are direct references to Scholastic thinkers in his work, too, and perhaps the most notable example comes in a passage from *Difference and Repetition* where Deleuze considers Duns Scotus' conceptualisation of 'univocity':

> There has only ever been one ontological position: Being is univocal. There has only ever been one ontology, that of Duns Scotus, which gave being a single voice. We say Duns Scotus because he was the one who elevated univocal being to the highest point of subtlety, albeit at the price of abstraction [. . .] A single voice raises the clamour of being.[100]

Deleuze is wrestling here with a similar problem to Scotus: 'how to posit a univocity of being without flattening all distinctions within being'.[101] And Thacker poses his own further questions to challenge the idea of pure immanence: 'If immanence is pure immanence, immanent to nothing but itself, then how can immanence also be a ceaseless creation and invention of the new? How can creativity emerge out of what is already fully actual?'[102]

This goes to the heart of a common difficulty with Deleuze's thought and in order to answer it we need to turn first to Spinoza.[103] In *Expressionism in Philosophy: Spinoza* (1968), Deleuze engages a Spinozan ontology that is 'dominated by the notions of a *cause of itself, in itself* and *through itself*' – an 'immanent causality'.[104] Through his anti-Cartesian stance, Spinoza presents a theory of expression which 'supports univocity; and its whole import is to free univocal Being from a state of indifference or neutrality, to make it the object of a pure affirmation'.[105] Therefore, as Thacker rightly demonstrates, if one of the problems for Scholastic thinkers was that univocity signals 'all relation' (failing to account for differences or causation between individuated creatures) then Spinoza allows us to reimagine causality 'less in terms of a first cause or principle, and more in terms of a self-causality or auto-creation';[106] his emphasis on the generativity of univocity as affirmative becoming rather than neutral being (as in Scotus) allows Deleuze to think of univocity as creative.[107] In other words, causality becomes fundamentally immanent, and crucial to what Deleuze calls 'new immanent modes of existence'[108] is an ontology of life which necessarily features both the creation of variation or the primacy of difference in itself, and the collecting or assembling of that which varies or that which differs. Because univocity for the Scholastics was concerned with identity rather than difference, Thacker therefore emphasises that Deleuze's Scholasticism, via Spinoza, is heretical in a similar sense to his notorious formulation of the history of philosophy as a kind of 'buggery or (it comes to the same thing) immaculate conception [. . .] taking an author from behind and giving him a child that would be his own offspring, yet monstrous'.[109]

Taking up this concept of univocity as pure immanence, Deleuze in *Difference and Repetition* sees it as central to his ontology of difference, of difference as primary, and against identity and representation:

> In effect, the essential in univocity is not that Being is said in a single and same sense, but that it is said, in a single and same sense, *of* all its individuating differences or intrinsic modalities. Being is the same for all these modalities, but these modalities are not the same. It is 'equal' for all, but they themselves are not equal. It is said of all in a single sense, but they themselves do not have the same sense. The essence of univocal being is to include individuating differences, while these differences do not have the same essence and do not change the essence of being [. . .] Being is said in a single and same sense of everything of which it is said, but that of which it is said differs: it is said of difference itself.[110]

Monaco finds in *The Waves* this role of 'difference itself', a difference that '*is* life', rather than a difference following from identity and essence: '*The Waves* forms a differentiating substance and process, a univocity, simultaneously substantial and mobile [. . .] a unity that is not fixed, but dynamic and "living", and thus which implies community.' Life, then, is 'fundamentally communal', and this is the 'motivating concept of *The Waves*'.[111] Woolf's novel therefore attempts to articulate how matter, both organic and inorganic, combines to entangle the living with the force of life itself, providing 'a literary rendering of univocity'.[112] We might say then that Woolf demonstrates in the novel what Grosz describes, using similar terms to Thacker and emphasising the materiality of both 'life' and 'the living', as a materiality which 'is the secret heart of the living which unifies and affiliates life in all its forms [. . .] equally life is what returns to materiality a virtuality, a life of its own, nonorganic life.'[113]

Life as pure immanence is, therefore, the difference between 'a life' and 'the life'/'my life'. It is therefore intriguing that Jinny is the only character in *The Waves* to refer to 'a life' (and we will recall that she is the only character who never directly refers to 'my life' at any stage in the novel). This occurs when she is travelling north by train:

> 'I sit snug in my own corner going North,' said Jinny, 'in this roaring express which is yet so smooth that it flattens hedges, lengthens hills. We flash past signal-boxes; we make the earth rock slightly from side to side. The distance closes for ever in a point; and we for ever open the distance wide again. The telegraph poles bob up incessantly; one is felled, another rises. Now we roar and swing into a tunnel. The gentleman pulls up the window. I see reflections on the shining glass which lines the tunnel. I see him lower his paper. He smiles at my reflection in the tunnel. My body instantly of its own accord puts forth a frill under his gaze. My body lives *a life* of its own. Now the black window glass is green again. We are out of the tunnel. He reads his paper. But we have exchanged the approval of our bodies. There is then a great society of bodies, and mine is introduced; mine has come into the room where the gilt chairs are. Look – all the windows of the villas and their white-tented curtains dance; and the men sitting in the hedges in the cornfields with knotted blue handkerchiefs are aware too, as I am aware, of heat and rapture. One waves as we pass him. There are bowers and arbours in these villa gardens and young men in shirt-sleeves on ladders trimming roses. A man on a horse canters over the field. His horse plunges as we pass. And the rider turns to look at us. We roar again through blackness. And I lie back; I give myself up to rapture.' (*W* 49; my emphasis)

Jinny is here in the 'rapture' of 'a life' (recalling Orlando's 'rapture' of desire discussed in Chapter 3), the material entanglement of her body with a 'great society of bodies' both human (the gentleman at the window, the man on horse) and nonhuman (the window curtains which 'dance', the horse). Her body does not live 'a life of its own' in the sense that it is possessed and fixed in its individuation, but in the sense of Deleuze and Guattari's 'singularisation':

> A body is not defined by the form that determines it nor as a determinate substance or subject nor by the organs it possesses or the functions it fulfils. [. . .] *a body is defined only by a longitude and a latitude*: in other words the sum total of the material elements belonging to it under given relations of movement and rest, speed and slowness (longitude); the sum total of the intensive affects it is capable of at a given power or degree of potential (latitude). Nothing but affects and local movements, differential speeds.[114]

That is, Jinny's body is depersonalised in this moment of bodily affirmation, again in a similar sense to that discussed in relation to *Orlando* and desire. Although this paragraph ends with a seeming return to the possessive – 'Life is beginning. I now break into my hoard of life' (*W* 50) – there is a sense in which this 'my', like Susan's multiplicitous 'I', has been transformed by a 'hoard of life' that is always already intra-acting with the other human and nonhuman bodies mentioned above: 'The life of the individual gives way to an impersonal and yet singular life that releases a pure event freed from the accidents of internal and external life, that is, from the subjectivity and objectivity of what happens [. . .] It is a haecceity no longer of individuation but of singularisation.'[115]

This move from individuation to singularisation is encapsulated in *The Waves* by the multiplicity of Bernard: 'They do not understand that I have to effect different transitions; have to cover the entrances and exits of several different men who alternately act their parts as Bernard. I am abnormally aware of circumstances. [. . .] which of these people am I? It depends so much upon the room. When I say to myself, "Bernard", who comes?' (*TW* 61; 65) Bernard's heightened awareness of 'circumstances' – aligned with his rejection of individualism and letting go of possessions – shows that he is not partaking in a complete dispersal or flight from material reality (indeed he is hostile to the thought that his friends might think of him as 'evasive' or that he escapes their own world) (*W* 61); rather, there is a productive assembling: 'Once more, I who had thought myself immune, who had said, "Now I am rid of all that," find that the wave has tumbled me over, head over heels, scattering my possessions, leaving me to collect, to assemble, to heap together, summon my forces, rise and confront the enemy' (*W* 244). By scattering his possessions he now has to assemble something new, but this is not simply a re-piecing together of the old order of things. What he has to 'collect', 'assemble', and 'heap together' has no object; the verbs are left floating and intra-acting with his 'forces'. Accepting that he has been unable to become 'immune' to everyday life,[116] he realises the enemy is not so much life as it is death (*W* 247). The nonanthropocentric assembling of materiality (as immanent life) is his answer.

This is not the individual battle of the living against a death that would negate life, but rather the very struggle not to fall into an easy opposition between the immanence of the living and a transcendent teleology: 'we shouldn't enclose life in the single moment when individual life confronts universal death. *A* life is everywhere, in all the moments that a given living subject goes through and that are measured by given lived objects: an immanent life carrying with it the events or singularities that are merely actualised in subjects and objects.'[117] Where literature is concerned, Deleuze, as Lecercle notes, is interested in 'the expression of life, not the individual or personal life of a character or an author, but *a* life, in its non-human, a-subjective and pre-personal development or becoming'.[118] Indeed Deleuze is interested in a literature which is saturated, to return to Woolf's word, with life. It is therefore not incidental that Deleuze concludes his essay on 'Literature and Life' by turning to Woolf: 'To write is also to become something other than a writer. To those who ask what literature is, Virginia Woolf responds: To whom are you speaking of writing? The writer does not speak about it, but is concerned with something else.'[119] That something else for Woolf is life, and in *The Waves* it is about (re)generating and (re)conceptualising life as immanent, material assemblages. In the face of the enemy, death (and especially any notion of death as divine), Woolf's novel moves away from life as something tied inextricably to a subject or object ('the living') that comes and goes based on a transcendent force ('Life'). Instead, we discover material, non/human intra-actions as the creative immanence of 'the emerging monster to whom we are attached' (*W* 51), a life.

Notes

1. Banfield, *The Phantom Table*, p. 66. Contemporary theoretical considerations of tables include Sara Ahmed's *Queer Phenomenology*, where she draws attention to Woolf's writing table in *A Room of One's Own* as a site of feminist orientation: 'As Virginia Woolf shows us in *A Room of One's Own*, for women to claim a space to write is a political act. [. . .] For Virginia Woolf, the table appears with her writing on it, as a feminist message inscribed on paper: "I must ask you to imagine a room, like many thousands, with a window looking across people's hats and vans and motor-cars to other windows, and on the table inside the room a blank sheet of paper on which was written in large letters WOMEN AND FICTION and no more"' (*RO* 32). Ahmed, *Queer Phenomenology*, p. 61; see also p. 11.
2. Mackin, 'Private Worlds', p. 118.
3. This chapter is focused on some of the philosophical implications of quantum physics and it is therefore beyond its scope to go into detail on each scientific breakthrough of the new physics. For a contextual summary of these developments see Heisenberg, *Physics and Philosophy*, pp. 3–13. For Russell's own philosophical discussion of the developments in relativity and quantum mechanics see *Analysis of Matter*.
4. Coole and Frost, 'Introducing the New Materialisms', p. 11.
5. Banfield, *The Phantom Table*, p. 29.
6. Hintikka, 'Virginia Woolf and Our Knowledge', p. 14, fn.43. We also know now that Woolf studied Greek at King's College Ladies'

Department between 1897 and 1900. See Snaith and Kenyon-Jones, 'Tilting at Universities'.
7. Beer, *Virginia Woolf*, p. 114. For a specific discussion of Jeans see Beer, 'Wave, Atom, Dinosaur'. For an excellent discussion of the influence of Jeans' astronomy on *The Waves*, see Henry, *Virginia Woolf*, pp. 93–107.
8. Sun Yom, 'Bio-graphy and the Quantum Leap', p. 145.
9. Beer, *Virginia Woolf*, p. 113.
10. Beer, 'Wave, Atom, Dinosaur', p. 11.
11. Banfield, *The Phantom Table*, p. 30.
12. See for example Whitworth, *Einstein's Wake*, p. 162; Beer, *Virginia Woolf*, p. 113; Westling, 'Flesh of the World', p. 856.
13. The word 'atom' occurs too frequently in Woolf's writing to cite all instances here. For further examples see Whitworth, *Authors in Context*, pp. 178–80 and *Einstein's Wake*, pp. 166–9.
14. Brown, 'Relativity, Quantum Physics', p. 40.
15. Ibid., pp. 47–8.
16. Banfield, *The Phantom Table*, p. 108.
17. Brown, 'Relativity, Quantum Physics', p. 53.
18. Bohr, *Atomic Theory*, p. 119.
19. Brown, 'Relativity, Quantum Physics', p. 54.
20. Barad, *Meeting the Universe Halfway*, p. 26.
21. Coole and Frost, 'Introducing the New Materialisms', p. 9.
22. Heisenberg, *Physics and Philosophy*, p. 43.
23. See Zucker, 'Virginia Woolf's Uncertainty Principle', p. 151, and Froula, *Virginia Woolf*, p. 204.
24. Barad, *Meeting the Universe Halfway*, p. 129.
25. Ibid., p. 24. I am following Barad's preference for this term, because for Bohr 'physics and philosophy were one practice'.
26. Ibid., p. 135.
27. Ibid., p. 141.
28. Ibid., p. 33.
29. Ibid., p. 116. It is for this reason that one of the few literary references in Barad's book comes when she takes issue with the question posed by T. S. Eliot's Prufrock: 'Do I dare disturb the universe?': 'Disturbance is not the issue [. . .] There is no such exterior position where the contemplation of this possibility makes any sense [. . .] there is no inside, no outside' (396).
30. Ibid., p. 19. This is Barad's own elaboration of his insights, and she notes that Bohr himself was focused on experiments in lab, less concerned with larger ontological implications' (334). As the key aspects of the Copenhagen interpretation, complementarity and uncertainty 'constitute fundamentally different, indeed arguably incompatible, interpretive positions' (115). Barad notes that a commonly unreported fact is that 'Heisenberg acquiesced to Bohr's interpretation: it is complementarity that is at issue, not uncertainty' (20).
31. Ibid., p. 118. 'This can be contrasted with Schrödinger's notion of entanglement, which is explicitly epistemic (what is entangled is our knowledge of events)' (309).
32. Zucker, 'Virginia Woolf's Uncertainty Principle', p. 149, p. 147.
33. Sun Yom, 'Bio-graphy and the Quantum Leap', p. 146.

34. Westling, 'Flesh of the World', p. 868.
35. Brown, 'Relativity, Quantum Physics', p. 54.
36. Michael Whitworth also sees Bernard's doubting of the table's solidity as an ontological matter – terming it 'ontological insecurity' – and, whilst emphasising the influence of Russell here, like Gillian Beer he also points to the striking similarities between Eddington and Woolf. See Whitworth, *Einstein's Wake*, pp. 160–1.
37. Barad, *Meeting the Universe Halfway*, p. 149.
38. Deleuze and Guattari, *A Thousand Plateaus*, p. 278.
39. Barad, *Meeting the Universe Halfway*, p. 140.
40. Ibid., p. 377.
41. Ibid., p. 156.
42. Ibid., p. 338.
43. Ibid., p. 175.
44. Ibid., p. 136.
45. Ibid., p. 140.
46. Barad is sharing this notion of 'naturecultures' with Donna Haraway. In *When Species Meet*, Haraway notes an affinity between Barad and herself: They 'are in firm solidarity that this theory [of intra-action and agential realism] richly applies to animals entangled in relations of scientific practice'. Haraway, *When Species Meet*, p. 331, n.4.
47. As Erica Roebbelen has noted, 'the characters in *The Waves* express an increasingly diminished confidence in the human capacity to know throughout the novel'. See 'Manifestations of Twentieth-century Physics'. We could align this intra-acting of humans and nonhuman 'unknown quantities' with Johanna Garvey's sharp reading of *Mrs Dalloway* where London becomes a liquid cityscape, and human consciousness is inextricably part of it. See Garvey, 'Difference and Continuity'.
48. Barad, *Meeting the Universe Halfway*, p. 141.
49. Julia Kane has, however, argued that quantum physics is entangled with differing forms of mysticism. See her 'Varieties of Mystical Experience'.
50. Heisenberg, *Physics and Philosophy*, p. 43.
51. Briggs, 'Nuance, Metaphor', p. 110.
52. Ibid., p. 109.
53. Barad, *Meeting the Universe Halfway*, p. 93.
54. Grosz, *Becoming Undone*, p. 35.
55. Thacker, *After Life*, p. xv.
56. Ibid., p. 11.
57. Ibid., p. 14.
58. We might think here of Deleuze's concept of 'the fold' which disrupts simple interior/exterior relations and allows for possibilities of nonhuman subjectivity. See Deleuze, *The Fold*. Recent links between Woolf's writing and Deleuze's 'fold' have been made by Laci Mattison and Jessica Berman. See Mattison, 'Woolf's Un/Folding(s)' and Berman, 'Ethical Folds'.
59. Deleuze and Guattari, *Anti-Oedipus*, p. 367.
60. Braidotti, *Transpositions*, p. 5.
61. Ibid., p. 175.
62. Deleuze and Parnet, *Dialogues*, p. 52.
63. Bennett, *Vibrant Matter*, p. 6. Bennett's 'thing-power' therefore adds to

the growing interest in contemporary theory on the distinction between 'objects' and 'things'. As Bill Brown has put it in relation to what he coined as 'thing theory', which is concerned with 'objects asserting themselves as things', this marks 'a changed relation to the human subject and thus the story of how the thing really names less an object than a particular subject-object relation'. Brown, 'Thing Theory', p. 4. Woolf's short story 'Solid Objects' was a key consideration in Brown's theory of things. See Brown, 'The Secret Life of Things'. For a discussion of the relation between objects and things also see Ahmed, *Queer Phenomenology*, pp. 44–51.

64. Bennett, *Vibrant Matter*, p. 18.
65. Braidotti, 'On Putting the Active Back', p. 48. *Zoē* for Braidotti is affirmative, it is life as inhuman, generative, vital force. This is not to be confused with Giorgio Agamben's *zoē* or 'bare life' which, Braidotti argues, is linked with a philosophy of finitude and a politics of loss and melancholia. See Braidotti, 'Bio-Power'. See also Agamben, *Homo Sacer*, pp. 1–11; Braidotti, *Transpositions*, pp. 36–43; pp. 129–38; pp. 232–6; Esposito, *Bíos*.
66. Bennett, *Vibrant Matter*, p. ix; p. x. Bennett is utilising Bruno Latour's term 'actant' from Actor-Network Theory. An actant is 'something that acts or to which activity is granted by others. It implies no special motivation of human individual actors, nor of humans in general.' Latour, 'On Actor-Network Theory'. For more on ANT see Latour, *Reassembling the Social*.
67. Bennett is influenced here by Deleuze and Guattari's term 'material vitalism' in *A Thousand Plateaus*, p. 454. For a discussion of the influence of the vitalisms of Hans Driesch's 'Entelechy' and Bergson's 'élan vital' on her thought see Bennett, *Vibrant Matter*, pp. 62–81. Bennett explains how 'Driesch and Bergson, in their attempts to give philosophical voice to the vitality of things, came very close to articulating a vital materialism. But they stopped short: they could not imagine a materialism adequate to the vitality they discerned in natural processes. (Instead, they dreamed of a not-quite-material life force)' (63).
68. Monson, '"A Trick of the Mind"', p. 181.
69. Deleuze and Guattari, *A Thousand Plateaus*, p. 25.
70. Ibid., p. 95.
71. Bennett, *Vibrant Matter*, p. 18.
72. Deleuze, *Critical and Clinical*, p. 2.
73. This intermingling of human and nonhuman is also prominent in *Between the Acts*, as several eco-critical readings have suggested. For example see Andrés, '"O Let's Keep Together!"'; Sultzbach, 'The Fertile Potential'; and Westling, 'Flesh of the World'.
74. Bennett, *Vibrant Matter*, p. 23.
75. Monaco, *Machinic Modernism*, p. 162.
76. Ibid., p. 162.
77. Rohman, '"We Make Life"', p. 16.
78. Ibid., p. 19. Rohman also argues, using Grosz's incorporation of Deleuze's conceptualisation of the refrain in *Chaos, Territory, Art*, that this is evident in the interludes: 'These repetitions mark the most overt "natural"

material in the text. The interludes attest to the inhuman rhythms, the cosmological forces that in one sense stand outside of narrowly human or conventionally humanist preoccupations' (14). This corresponds with Beatrice Monaco's view: 'by way of the interludes [*The Waves*] contains the implication that there is much that is out of reach of human intelligence and perception'. Monaco, *Machinic Modernism*, p. 160. Rohman rightly argues however that this is not to say Woolf's text presents a 'final disconnect' between the natural world and the human world but rather opens up a posthumanist reading 'that need not be trapped by views of nature as either "sympathetic" and sentimentally human or hostile and violently anti-human'. Rohman, '"We Make Life"', p. 14. Deleuze and Guattari themselves describe the interludes: 'each chapter of Woolf's novel is preceded by a meditation on an aspect of the waves, on one of their hours, on one of their becomings'. See *A Thousand Plateaus*, p. 278.
79. Rohman, '"We Make Life"', p. 17.
80. See for example Jane Marcus' provocative labelling of Jinny as a prostitute in 'Britannia Rules *The Waves*', p. 70.
81. Rohman, '"We Make Life"', p. 20
82. Bellamy, 'The Pattern', p. 22.
83. 'Haecceity' was commonly used in scholastic philosophy, in particular by Duns Scotus, to refer to the individuating principle or 'thisness' of beings. Deleuze's own distinct use of this term is to designate 'an individuation which is not that of an object, nor of a person, but rather of an event (wind, river, day or even hour of day)'. Deleuze and Parnet, *Dialogues*, p. 118, n.9.
84. Deleuze and Guattari, *A Thousand Plateaus*, p. 288.
85. Deleuze and Parnet, *Dialogues*, pp. 68–9. The precise quotation from *Mrs Dalloway* Deleuze paraphrases here is: 'She would not say of anyone in the world now that they were this or were that. She felt very young; at the same time unspeakably aged. She sliced like a knife through everything; at the same time was outside, looking on. [. . .] she always had the feeling that it was very, very dangerous to live even one day. [. . .] She would not say of Peter, she would not say of herself, I am this, I am that' (*MD* 7). Deleuze and Guattari also make this link, and quote this passage correctly, in *A Thousand Plateaus*, p. 290. Interestingly in both instances Deleuze focuses on Clarrisa's walk rather than Peter Walsh's, and my own examples below also include those of the female walker as well as the male, therefore offering a new perspective on the relationship between 'women, walking and writing' discussed by Bowlby in an essay of that title. See Bowlby, *Feminist Destinations*, pp. 191–219.
86. Deleuze and Guattari, *What is Philosophy?*, p. 169.
87. Deleuze and Guattari, *A Thousand Plateaus*, p. 309.
88. Deleuze and Guattari, *What is Philosophy?*, p. 172.
89. Deleuze and Guattari, *A Thousand Plateaus*, p. 309. The 'impersonal' returns us to Banfield's reading of 'Russell and Woolf alike' choosing 'an ethics of the impersonal'. Banfield, *The Phantom Table*, p. 45.
90. Deleuze and Guattari, *A Thousand Plateaus*, p. 290.
91. Ibid., p. 294.
92. Deleuze and Parnet, *Dialogues*, p. 89.

93. Deleuze and Guattari, *A Thousand Plateaus*, p. 289.
94. Bennett, *Vibrant Matter*, p. 53.
95. Ibid., p. 57.
96. Deleuze, *Pure Immanence*, p. 26.
97. Ibid., p. 27.
98. Deleuze and Guattari, *What is Philosophy?*, p. 45.
99. Thacker, *After Life*, p. 170.
100. Deleuze, *Difference and Repetition*, p. 44. This is the passage where Badiou takes the title of his scathing book on Deleuze. See Badiou, *Deleuze*. For an excellent and balanced recent survey of the relationship between the philosophies of Deleuze and Badiou in relation to literature, see Lecercle, *Badiou and Deleuze*.
101. Thacker, *After Life*, p. 137.
102. Ibid., p. 213.
103. For an insightful recent discussion of Deleuze and Spinoza see Bell, 'Between Realism and Anti-realism'.
104. Deleuze, *Expressionism in Philosophy*, p. 162, p. 233.
105. Ibid., p. 333.
106. Thacker, *After Life*, p. 138.
107. Ibid., p. 144.
108. Deleuze and Guattari, *What is Philosophy?*, p. 113.
109. See Thacker, *After Life*, p. 141; Deleuze, *Negotiations*, p. 6.
110. Deleuze, *Difference and Repetition*, p. 45.
111. Monaco, *Machinic Modernism*, p. 175.
112. Ibid., p. 168.
113. Grosz, *Becoming Undone*, p. 36.
114. Deleuze and Guattari, *A Thousand Plateaus*, p. 287.
115. Deleuze, *Pure Immanence*, p. 28.
116. For an incisive discussion of 'everyday life' in *The Waves* see Randall, *Modernism*, pp. 167–84.
117. Deleuze, *Pure Immanence*, p. 29.
118. Lecercle, *Badiou and Deleuze*, p. 203.
119. Deleuze, *Critical and Clinical*, p. 6.

Bibliography

Abel, Elizabeth. *Virginia Woolf and the Fictions of Psychoanalysis*. Chicago: University of Chicago Press, 1989.
Adams, Maureen. *Shaggy Muses: The Dogs Who Inspired Virginia Woolf, Emily Dickinson, Elizabeth Barrett Browning, Edith Wharton and Emily Brontë*. New York: Ballantine Books, 2007.
Agamben, Giorgio. *Homo Sacer: Sovereign Power and Bare Life*, trans. Daniel Heller-Roazen. Stanford: Stanford University Press, 1998.
—. *The Open: Man and Animal*, trans. Kevin Attell. Stanford: Stanford University Press, 2004.
Ahmed, Sara. *Queer Phenomenology: Orientations, Objects, Others*. Durham NC: Duke University Press, 2006.
Albright, Daniel. *Quantum Poetics: Yeats, Pound, Eliot, and the Science of Modernism*. Cambridge: Cambridge University Press, 1997.
Allen, Judith. *Virginia Woolf and the Politics of Language*. Edinburgh: Edinburgh University Press, 2010.
—. '"But . . . I had said 'but' too often." Why "but"?' *Contradictory Woolf: Selected Papers from the Twenty-first Annual International Conference on Virginia Woolf*, ed. Derek Ryan and Stella Bolaki. Clemson: Clemson University Digital Press, 2012, 1–10.
Anaxagoras. *Anaxagoras of Clazomenae: Fragments and Testimonia*, ed. Patricia Curd. Toronto: University of Toronto Press, 2007.
Andrés, Isabel. '"O Let's Keep Together!" The Blurring of Individual Consciousness in Virginia Woolf's *Between the Acts*', *Consciousness, Literature and the Arts* 7:3 (2006).
Ardoin, Paul, S. E. Gontarski, and Laci Mattison (eds). *Understanding Bergson, Understanding Modernism*, London: Continuum, 2013.
Badiou, Alain. *Deleuze: The Clamour of Being*, trans. Louise Burchill. Minneapolis: University of Minnesota Press, 1999.
Baker, Steve. *The Postmodern Animal*. London: Reaktion Books, 2000.
Balcombe, Jonathan. *Second Nature: The Inner Lives of Animals*. New York: Palgrave Macmillan, 2010.
Banfield, Ann. *The Phantom Table: Woolf, Fry, Russell and the Epistemology of Modernism*. Cambridge: Cambridge University Press, 2000.
Barad, Karen. *Meeting the Universe Halfway: Quantum Physics and the*

Entanglement of Matter and Meaning. Durham NC: Duke University Press, 2007.
Barrett, Eileen and Patricia Cramer (eds). *Virginia Woolf: Lesbian Readings*. New York: New York University Press, 1997.
Barrett, Michèle. 'Introduction', *Virginia Woolf: Women & Writing*, ed. Michèle Barrett. London: The Women's Press, 1979.
—. *Women's Oppression Today: The Marxist/Feminist Encounter*. London: Verso, 1980.
—. *The Politics of Truth: From Marx to Foucault*. Cambridge: Polity Press, 1992.
—. *Imagination in Theory: Essays on Writing and Culture*. Cambridge: Polity Press, 1999.
Baugh, Bruce. 'Making the Difference: Deleuze's Difference and Derrida's Différance', *Social Semiotics* 7:2 (1997): 127–46.
Bazin, Nancy Topping. *Virginia Woolf and the Androgynous Vision*. New Brunswick NJ: Rutgers University Press, 1973.
Bazin, Nancy Topping and Alma Freeman. 'The Androgynous Vision', *Women's Studies* 2:2 (1974): 185–216.
Beames, Thomas. *The Rookeries of London: Past, Present and Prospective*, 2nd edn. London: Thomas Bosworth, 1852.
Beer, Gillian. *Virginia Woolf: The Common Ground*. Edinburgh: Edinburgh University Press, 1996.
—. 'Wave, Atom, Dinosaur: Woolf's Science', *The English Literary Society of Japan*. Tokyo: Kentkyusha Ltd, 2000.
Bell, Jeffrey. 'Between Realism and Anti-realism: Deleuze and the Spinozist Tradition in Philosophy', *Deleuze Studies* 5:1 (2011): 1–17.
Bell, Quentin. *Virginia Woolf: A Biography*. London: Hogarth, 1972.
Bellamy, Suzanne. 'The Pattern Behind the Words', *Virginia Woolf: Lesbian Readings*, ed. Eileen Barrett and Patricia Cramer. New York: New York University Press, 1997, 21–36.
Benjamin, Walter. 'Theses on the Philosophy of History', *Illuminations*, ed. Hannah Arendt. London: Pimlico, [1955] 1999.
Bennett, Jane. *Vibrant Matter: A Political Ecology of Things*. Durham NC: Duke University Press, 2010.
Berman, Jessica. *Modernist Fiction, Cosmopolitanism and the Politics of Community*. Cambridge: Cambridge University Press, 2001.
—. 'Ethical Folds: Ethics, Aesthetics, Woolf', *Modern Fiction Studies* 50:1 (2004): 151–72.
—. *Modernist Commitments: Ethics, Politics, and Transnational Modernism*. New York: Columbia University Press, 2011.
Black, Naomi. *Virginia Woolf as Feminist*. New York: Cornell University Press, 2004.
Blair, Kirstie. 'Gypsies and Lesbian Desire: Vita Sackville-West, Violet Trefusis, and Virginia Woolf', *Twentieth-Century Literature* 50:2 (2004): 141–66.
Bohr, Niels. *Atomic Theory and the Description of Nature*. Cambridge: Cambridge University Press, 1934.
Booth, Alison. 'The Scent of a Narrative: Rank Discourse in *Flush* and *Written on the Body*', *Narrative* 8:1 (2000): 3–22.
Bowlby, Rachel. *Feminist Destinations and Further Essays on Virginia Woolf*. Edinburgh: Edinburgh University Press, 1997.

Bradshaw, David. '"Great Avenues of Civilisation": The Victoria Embankment and Piccadilly Circus Underground Station in the Novels of Virginia Woolf and Chelsea Embankment in *Howards End*', *Transits: The Nomadic Geographies of Anglo-American Modernism*, ed. Giovanni Cianci, Caroline Patey, and Sara Sullam. Oxford: Peter Lang, 2010, 183–204.
Braidotti, Rosi. *Patterns of Dissonance: A Study of Women in Contemporary Philosophy*, trans. Elizabeth Guild. New York: Routledge, 1991.
—. *Nomadic Subjects: Embodiment and Sexual Difference in Contemporary Feminist Theory*. New York: Columbia University Press, 1994.
—. *Metamorphoses: Towards a Materialist Theory of Becoming*. Cambridge: Polity Press, 2002.
—. *Transpositions: On Nomadic Ethics*. Cambridge: Polity Press, 2006.
—. 'Posthuman, All Too Human: Towards a New Process Ontology', *Theory Culture Society* 23 (2006): 197–208.
—. 'Bio-Power and Necro-Politics: Reflections on an Ethics of Sustainability', *Springerin* 2:7 (2007).
—. 'On Putting the Active Back into Activism', *New Formations* 68 (2009): 42–57.
—. 'The Politics of "Life Itself" and New Ways of Dying', *New Materialisms: Ontology, Agency, and Politics*, ed. Diana Coole and Samantha Frost. Durham NC: Duke University Press, 2010, 201–18.
—. *Nomadic Subjects: Embodiment and Sexual Difference in Contemporary Feminist Theory*, 2nd edn. New York: Columbia University Press, [1994] 2011.
Braidotti, Rosi and Judith Butler. 'Feminism by Any Other Name', *Feminism Meets Queer Theory*, ed. Elizabeth Weed and Naomi Schor. Bloomington and Indianapolis: Indiana University Press, 1997, 31–67.
Briggs, John. 'Nuance, Metaphor and the Rhythm of the Mood Wave in Virginia Woolf', *Virginia Woolf Miscellanies: Proceedings of the First Annual Conference on Virginia Woolf*, ed. Mark Hussey and Vara Neverow-Turk. New York: Pace University Press, 1992, 107–18.
Briggs, Julia (ed.). *Night and Day*, by Virginia Woolf. London: Penguin, 1992.
—. *Reading Virginia Woolf*. Edinburgh: Edinburgh University Press, 2006.
Brown, Bill. 'The Secret Life of Things: Virginia Woolf and the Matter of Modernism', *Modernism/Modernity* 6:2 (1999): 1–28.
—. 'Thing Theory', *Critical Inquiry* 28:1 (2001): 1–22.
Brown, Lori. 'Becoming-Animal in the Flesh: Expanding the Ethical Reach of Deleuze and Guattari's Tenth Plateau', *PhaenEx* 2:2 (2007): 260–78.
Brown, Paul Tolliver. 'Relativity, Quantum Physics, and Consciousness in Virginia Woolf's *To the Lighthouse*', *Journal of Modern Literature* 32:3 (2009): 39–62.
Browning, Elizabeth Barrett. 'To Flush, My Dog', *Sonnets from the Portuguese and Other Poems*, ed. Stanley Appelbaum. New York: Dover, [1843] 1992, 12–15.
—. 'Flush or Faunus', *Selected Poems*, ed. Marjorie Stone and Beverly Taylor. Ontario: Broadview, [1850] 2009, 188.
Bruns, Gerald L. 'Becoming-Animal (Some Simple Ways)', *New Literary History* 38:4 (2007): 703–20.
Bryden, Mary. *Gilles Deleuze: Travels in Literature*. Basingstoke: Palgrave, 2007.

Buchanan, Ian and Claire Colebrook (eds). *Deleuze and Feminist Theory*. Edinburgh: Edinburgh University Press, 2000.

Burns, Christy L. 'Re-dressing Feminist Identities: Tensions Between Essential and Constructed Selves in Virginia Woolf's Orlando', *Twentieth Century Literature* 40:3 (1994): 342–64.

Butler, Judith. *Subjects of Desire: Hegelian Reflections in Twentieth-Century France*. New York: Columbia University Press, [1987] 1999.

—. *Gender Trouble: Feminism and the Subversion of Identity*, 2nd edn. London: Routledge, [1990] 1999.

—. *Bodies That Matter: On the Discursive Limits of "Sex"*. London: Routledge, 1993.

—. 'Gender as Performance: An Interview with Judith Butler', Interview by Peter Osborne and Lynne Segal, London, 1993, <http://www.theory.org.uk/but-int1.htm> (accessed 9 October 2012).

—. *Undoing Gender*. London: Routledge, 2004.

Calarco, Matthew. *Zoographies: The Question of the Animal from Heidegger to Derrida*. New York: Columbia University Press, 2008.

Caughie, Pamela L. *Virginia Woolf and Postmodernism: Literature in Quest and Question of Itself*. Urbana and Chicago: University of Illinois Press, 1991.

—— (ed.). *Virginia Woolf in the Age of Mechanical Reproduction*. New York: Garland, 2000.

—. 'Poststructuralist and Postmodernist Approaches to Virginia Woolf', *Palgrave Advances in Virginia Woolf Studies*, ed. Anna Snaith. Basingstoke: Palgrave Macmillan, 2007, 143–68.

—. 'Time's Exception', *Modernism and Theory: A Critical Debate*. New York: Routledge, 2009, 99–111.

Cheah, Pheng. 'Non-Dialectical Materialism', *New Materialisms: Ontology, Agency, and Politics*, ed. Diana Coole and Samantha Frost. Durham NC: Duke University Press, 2010, 70–91.

Chen, Guo-Neng and Rodney Grapes. *Granite Genesis: In-situ Melting and Crustal Evolution*. Dordrecht: Springer, 2007.

Cianci, Giovanni, Caroline Patey, and Sara Sullam (eds). *Transits: The Nomadic Geographies of Anglo-American Modernism*. Oxford: Peter Lang, 2010.

Coffman, Chris. 'Woolf's *Orlando* and the Resonances of Trans Studies', *Genders* 51 (2010).

Cohen, Jeffrey J. and Todd R. Ramlow. 'Pink Vectors of Deleuze: Queer Theory and Inhumanism', *Rhizomes* 11/12 (2005/2006).

Colebrook, Claire. 'Introduction', *Deleuze and Feminist Theory*, ed. Ian Buchanan and Claire Colebrook. Edinburgh: Edinburgh University Press, 2000, 1–17.

—. 'How Queer Can You Go?: Theory, Normality and Normativity', *Queering the Non-Human*, ed. Noreen Giffney and Myra Hird. London: Ashgate, 2008, 17–34.

—. 'Queer Vitalism', *New Formations* 68 (2009): 77–92.

—. 'Extinct Theory', *Theory After 'Theory'*, ed. Jane Elliott and Derek Attridge. New York: Routledge, 2011, 62–72.

—. 'Woolf and "Theory"', *Virginia Woolf in Context*, ed. Bryony Randall and Jane Goldman. Cambridge: Cambridge University Press, 2012.

Colombat, André Pierre. 'Deleuze and Signs', *Deleuze and Literature*, ed. Ian Buchanan and John Marks. Edinburgh: Edinburgh University Press, 2000, 14–33.
Conley, Verena Andermatt. 'Thirty-six Thousand Forms of Love: The Queering of Deleuze and Guattari', *Deleuze and Queer Theory*, ed. Chrysanthi Nigianni and Merl Storr. Edinburgh: Edinburgh University Press, 24–36.
Coole, Diana and Samantha Frost (eds). *New Materialisms: Ontology, Agency, and Politics*. Durham NC: Duke University Press, 2010.
—. 'Introducing the New Materialisms', *New Materialisms: Ontology, Agency, and Politics*, ed. Diana Coole and Samantha Frost. Durham NC: Duke University Press, 2010, 1–43.
Cooley, Elizabeth. 'Revolutionizing Biography: *Orlando*, *Roger Fry*, and the Tradition', *Virginia Woolf: Critical Assessments vol. II*. East Sussex: Helm Information, 1994, 398–407.
Crawford, T. Hugh. 'The Paterson Plateau: Deleuze, Guattari and William Carlos Williams', *Deleuze and Literature*, ed. Ian Buchanan and John Marks. Edinburgh: Edinburgh University Press, 2000, 57–79.
Czarnecki, Kristin and Carrie Rohman (eds). *Virginia Woolf and the Natural World: Selected Papers from the Twentieth International Conference on Virginia Woolf*. Clemson: Clemson University Digital Press, 2011.
Darwin, Charles. *Journal of Researches into the Natural History and Geology of the Countries Visited during the Voyage of H.M.S. Beagle*. Cambridge: Cambridge University Press, [1845] 2011.
Daston, Lorraine and Gregg Mitman (eds). *Thinking with Animals: New Perspectives on Anthropomorphism*. New York: Columbia University Press, 2005.
Dawkins, Richard. *Unweaving the Rainbow: Science, Delusion, and the Appetite for Wonder*. London, Allen Lane, 1998.
Deleuze, Gilles. *Nietzsche and Philosophy*, trans. Hugh Tomlinson. London: Continuum, [1962] 2006.
—. *Proust and Signs*, trans. Richard Howard. London: Continuum, [1964] 2008.
—. *Bergsonism*, trans. Hugh Tomlinson and Barbara Habberjam. New York: Zone Books, [1966] 1991.
—. *Difference and Repetition*, trans. Paul Patton. London: Continuum, [1968] 2004.
—. *Expressionism in Philosophy: Spinoza*, trans. Martin Joughin. New York: Zone, [1968] 1992.
—. *Francis Bacon: The Logic of Sensation*, trans. Daniel W. Smith. London: Continuum, [1981] 2005.
—. *The Fold*, trans. Tom Conley. London: Continuum, [1988] 2006.
—. *Negotiations: 1972–1990*, trans. Martin Joughin. New York: Columbia University Press, [1990] 1995.
—. *Essays Critical and Clinical*, trans. Daniel W. Smith and Michael A. Greco. Minneapolis: University of Minnesota Press, [1993] 1997.
—. *Pure Immanence: Essays on a Life*, trans. Anne Boyman. Massachusetts: Zone Books, 2001.
—. *Desert Islands: and Other Texts, 1953–1974*, trans. Ames Hodges and Mike Taormina. Los Angeles: Semiotext(e), [2002] 2004.

Deleuze, Gilles and Félix Guattari. *Anti-Oedipus: Capitalism and Schizophrenia*, trans. Robert Hurley, Mark Seem, and Helen R. Lane. London: Continuum, [1972] 2004.
—. *Kafka: Toward a Minor Literature*, trans. Dana Polan. Minneapolis: University of Minnesota Press, [1975] 1986.
—. *A Thousand Plateaus: Capitalism and Schizophrenia*, trans. Brian Massumi. London: Continuum, [1980] 2004.
—. *What is Philosophy?*, trans. Graham Burchell and Hugh Tomlinson. London: Verso, [1991] 1994.
Deleuze, Gilles and Claire Parnet. *Dialogues II*, trans. Hugh Tomlinson and Barbara Habberjam. London: Continuum, [1977] 2006.
—. *From A to Z*, dir. Pierre-André Boutang, trans. Charles J. Stivale. Los Angeles : Semiotext(e), DVD, [1996] 2012.
Delpech-Ramey, Joshua. 'Deleuze, Guattari, and the "Politics of Sorcery"', *SubStance* 39:1 (2010): 8–23.
Delsandro, Erica. '"Myself – it was impossible": Queering History in *Between the Acts*', *Woolf Studies Annual* 13 (2007): 87–109.
Derrida, Jacques. *Writing and Difference*, trans. Alan Bass. London: Routledge, [1967] 2001.
—. 'I'll have to wander all alone', trans. David Kammerman, <http://www.usc.edu/dept/comp-lit/tympanum/1/derrida.html> (accessed 9 October 2012).
—. *The Animal That Therefore I Am*, ed. Marie-Louise Mallet, trans. David Wills. New York: Fordham University Press, 2008.
—. *The Beast and the Sovereign, Volume 1*, ed. Geoffrey Bennington and Peggy Kamuf, trans. Geoffrey Bennington. Chicago: University of Chicago Press, 2009.
DeSalvo, Louise A. 'Lighting the Cave: The Relationship between Vita Sackville-West and Virginia Woolf', *Signs* 8.2 (1982): 195–214.
DiBattista, Maria. *Virginia Woolf's Major Novels: The Fables of Anon*. New Haven: Yale University Press, 1980.
Dickson, Jay. 'Review: *Virginia Woolf's Nose: Essays on Biography* by Hermoine Lee; *Bombay to Bloomsbury: A Biography of the Strachey Family* by Barbara Caine', *Woolf Studies Annual* 13 (2007): 225–9.
Doyle, Laura. '"These Emotions of the Body": Intercorporeal Narrative in *To The Lighthouse*', *Twentieth Century Literature* 40:1 (1994): 42–71.
Driscoll, Catherine. 'The Woman in Process: Deleuze, Kristeva and Feminism', *Deleuze and Feminist Theory*, ed. Ian Buchanan and Claire Colebrook. Edinburgh: Edinburgh University Press, 2000, 64–85.
Dubino, Jeanne. 'Evolution, History, and Flush; or, The Origin of Spaniels', *Virginia Woolf and the Natural World: Selected Papers from the Twentieth International Conference on Virginia Woolf*, ed. Kristin Czarnecki and Carrie Rohman. Clemson: Clemson University Digital Press, 2011, 143–50.
—. 'The Bispecies Environment, Coevolution, and *Flush*', *Contradictory Woolf: Selected Papers from the Twenty-first Annual International Conference on Virginia Woolf*, ed. Derek Ryan and Stella Bolaki, Clemson: Clemson University Digital Press, 2012, 150–7.
Eberly, David. 'Housebroken: The Domesticated Relations of *Flush*', *Texts and Contexts: Proceedings of the Fifth Annual Conference on Virginia Woolf*, ed.

Beth Rigel Daugherty and Eileen Barrett. New York: Pace University Press, 1996, 21–5.
Edwards, Jason. 'The Materialism of Historical Materialism', *New Materialisms: Ontology, Agency, and Politics*, ed. Diana Coole and Samantha Frost. Durham NC: Duke University Press, 2010, 281–98.
Elliott, Jane and Derek Attridge (eds). *Theory After 'Theory'*, New York: Routledge, 2011.
—. 'Introduction: Theory's Nine Lives', *Theory After 'Theory'*, ed. Jane Elliott and Derek Attridge. New York: Routledge, 2011, 1–15.
Esposito, Roberto. *Bíos: Biopolitics and Philosophy*, trans. Timothy Campbell. Minneapolis: University of Minnesota Press, [2004] 2008.
Farwell, Marilyn R. 'Virginia Woolf and Androgyny', *Contemporary Literature* 16:4 (1975): 433–51.
Ferrer, Daniel. *Virginia Woolf and the Madness of Language*, trans. Geoffrey Bennington and Rachel Bowlby. London: Routledge, 1990.
Forster, E. M. *Howards End*. New York: Penguin, [1910] 2000.
French, Sabine. 'Peeling the Gypsy', *Virginia Woolf Miscellany* 67 (2005): 8–11.
Friedman, Susan Stanford. 'Theory', *Modernism and Theory: A Critical Debate*, ed. Stephen Ross. New York: Routledge, 2009, 237–45.
Froula, Christine. *Virginia Woolf and the Bloomsbury Avant-Garde*. New York: Columbia University Press, 2005.
Gad, Osnat. *Wedding Rings*. New York: Stewart, Tabori & Chang, 2004.
Garber, Marjorie. *Dog Love*. New York: Simon & Schuster, 1996.
Garvey, Johanna X. K. 'Difference and Continuity: The Voices of *Mrs Dalloway*', *College English* 53:1 (1991): 59–76.
Giffney, Noreen and Myra J. Hird (eds). *Queering the Non/Human*. Aldershot: Ashgate, 2008.
Giffney, Noreen and Myra J. Hird. 'Introduction: Queering the Non/Human', *Queering the Non/Human*. Aldershot: Ashgate, 2008.
Gillies, Mary Ann. *Henri Bergson and British Modernism*. London: McGill-Queen's University Press, 1996.
Goldman, Jane. *The Feminist Aesthetics of Virginia Woolf: Modernism, Post-Impressionism, and the Politics of the Visual*. Cambridge: Cambridge University Press, 1998.
—. *The Cambridge Introduction to Virginia Woolf*. Cambridge: Cambridge University Press, 2006.
—. '"Ce chien est à moi": Virginia Woolf and the Signifying Dog', *Woolf Studies Annual* 13 (2007), 49–86.
—. 'Avant-garde', *Modernism and Theory: A Critical Debate*, ed. Stephen Ross. New York: Routledge, 2009, 225–36.
—. '"When Dogs Will Become Men": Melancholia, Canine Allegories, and Theriocephalous Figures in Woolf's Urban Contact Zones', *Woolf and the City: Selected Papers from the Nineteenth Annual International Conference on Virginia Woolf*, ed. Elizabeth F. Evans and Sarah E. Cornish. Clemson: Clemson University Digital Press, 2010, 180–8.
—. 'The Dogs That Therefore Woolf Follows: Some Canine Sources for *A Room of One's Own* in Nature and Art', *Virginia Woolf and the Natural World: Selected Papers from the Twentieth Annual International Conference*

on Virginia Woolf, ed. Kristin Czarnecki and Carrie Rohman. Clemson: Clemson University Digital Press, 2011, 125–32.

Goulimari, Pelagia. 'A Minoritarian Feminism? Things to Do with Deleuze and Guattari', *Hypatia* 14:2 (1999): 97–120.

Griffiths, Jacqui. 'Almost Human: Indeterminate Children and Dogs in *Flush* and *The Sound and the Fury*', *The Yearbook of English Studies* 32 (2002): 163–76.

Grosz, Elizabeth. *Volatile Bodies: Toward a Corporeal Feminism*. Bloomington and Indianapolis: Indiana University Press, 1994.

—. *Chaos, Territory, Art: Deleuze and the Framing of the Earth*. New York: Columbia University Press, 2008.

—. *Becoming Undone: Darwinian Reflections on Life, Politics, and Art*. Durham NC: Duke University Press, 2011.

Grubar, Ruth. *Virginia Woolf: The Will to Create as a Woman*. New York: Carroll and Graf, [1935] 2005.

Guiguet, Jean. *Virginia Woolf and Her Works*, trans. Jean Stewart. London: Hogarth Press, 1965.

Hafley, James. *The Glass Roof: Virginia Woolf as Novelist*. New York: Russell & Russell, 1963.

Hägglund, Martin. 'The Arche-Materiality of Time: Deconstruction, Evolution and Speculative Materialism', *Theory After 'Theory'*, ed. Jane Elliott and Derek Attridge. New York: Routledge, 2011, 265–77.

Hankins, Leslie K. 'Switching Sex and Redirecting Desire: the Surrealist Film, *Entr'acte*, and Woolf's *Orlando*', *Virginia Woolf Miscellany* 67 (2005): 25–7.

Haraway, Donna. *The Companion Species Manifesto: Dogs, People and Significant Otherness*. Chicago: Chicago University Press, 2003.

—. *When Species Meet*. Minneapolis: University of Minnesota Press, 2008.

Hargreaves, Tracey. *Virginia Woolf and Twentieth Century Narratives of Androgyny*. PhD thesis submitted to University of London, 1994.

Harris, Daniel A. 'Androgyny: The Sexist Myth in Disguise', *Women's Studies* 2:2 (1974): 171–84.

Heilbrun, Carolyn. *Toward a Recognition of Androgyny*. New York: W. W. Norton and Co., [1964] 1982.

Heisenberg, Werner. *Physics and Philosophy*. London: Penguin, [1958] 2000.

Helt, Brenda S. 'Passionate Debates on "Odious Subjects": Bisexuality and Woolf's Opposition to Theories of Androgyny and Sexual Identity', *Twentieth Century Literature* 56:2 (2010): 131–67.

Henke, Suzette. 'Virginia Woolf's The Waves: A Phenomenological Reading', *Neophilologus* 73:3 (1989): 461–72.

Henry, Holly. *Virginia Woolf and the Discourse of Science: The Aesthetics of Astronomy*. Cambridge: Cambridge University Press, 2003.

Hinnov, Emily M. '"To give the moment whole": The Nature of Time and Cosmic (Comm)unity in Virginia Woolf's *The Waves*', *Virginia Woolf and the Natural World: Selected Papers from the Twentieth International Conference on Virginia Woolf*, ed. Kristin Czarnecki and Carrie Rohman. Clemson: Clemson University Digital Press, 2011, 214–20.

Hintikka, Jaakko. 'Virginia Woolf and Our Knowledge of the External World', *The Journal of Aesthetics and Art Criticism* 38:1 (1979): 5–14.

Howie, Gillian. 'Becoming-Woman: A Flight into Abstraction', *Deleuze Studies* 2: Issue Supplement (2008): 83–106.
Hseih, Lili. 'The Other Side of the Picture: The Politics of Affect in Virginia Woolf's *Three Guineas*', *Journal of Narrative Theory* 36:1 (2006): 20–54.
Hughes, John. *Lines of Flight: Reading Deleuze with Hardy, Gissing, Conrad, Woolf*. Sheffield: Sheffield Academic Press, 1997.
Hussey, Mark. *Virginia Woolf and the Singing of the Real World: The Philosophy of Virginia Woolf's Fiction*. Columbus: Ohio State University Press, 1986.
—. '"Hiding Behind the Curtain": Reading (Woolf) Like a Man', *Virginia Woolf: Texts and Contexts: Selected Papers from the Fifth Annual Conference on Virginia Woolf*, ed. Beth Rigel Daugherty and Eileen Barrett. New York: Pace University Press, 1996, 1–15.
—. 'Virginia Woolf: After Lives', *Virginia Woolf in Context*, ed. Bryony Randall and Jane Goldman. Cambridge: Cambridge University Press, 2012.
—(ed.). *Virginia Woolf: Major Authors on CD-ROM*. Woodbridge CT: Primary Sources Media, 1997.
Ittner, Jutta. 'Part Spaniel, Part Canine Puzzle: Anthropomorphism in Woolf's *Flush* and Auster's *Timbuktu*', *Mosaic* 39:4 (2006): 181–96.
Jacobus, Mary. 'The Difference of View', *Women Writing and Writing About Women*, ed. Mary Jacobus. London: Harper & Row, 1979, 10–21.
Jameson, Fredric. 'Afterword', *Modernism and Theory: A Critical Debate*, ed. Stephen Ross. New York: Routledge, 2009, 247–51.
Jardine, Alice. 'Woman in Limbo: Deleuze and His Br(others)', *SubStance* 44/45 (1984): 46–60.
Jouve, Nicole Ward. 'Virginia Woolf and Psychoanalysis', *The Cambridge Companion to Virginia Woolf*, ed. Sue Roe and Susan Sellers. Cambridge: Cambridge University Press, 2000, 245–72.
Kaivola, Karen. 'Virginia Woolf, Vita Sackville-West, and the Question of Sexual Identity', *Woolf Studies Annual* 4 (1998): 18–40.
Kamuf, Peggy. 'Penelope at Work: Interruptions in *A Room of One's Own*', *Novel* 16 (1982): 5–18.
Kane, Julie. 'Varieties of Mystical Experience in the Writings of Virginia Woolf', *Twentieth Century Literature* 41:4 (1995): 328–49.
Keats, John. 'Lamia', *The Complete Poems of John Keats*. London: Wordsworth, [1820] 2001.
Kirby, Vicki. *Quantum Anthropologies: Life at Large*. Durham NC: Duke University Press, 2011.
Kohn, Robert E. 'Erotic Daydreams in Virginia Woolf's *Orlando*', *Explicator* 68:3 (2010): 185–8.
Kore-Schröder, Leena. 'Reflections in a Motor Car: Virginia Woolf's Phenomenological Relations of Time and Space', *Locating Woolf: The Politics of Space and Place*, ed. Anna Snaith and Michael Whitworth. Basingstoke: Palgrave Macmillan, 2007, 131–47.
Knopp, Sherron E. '"If I Saw You Would You Kiss Me?": Sapphism and the Subversiveness of Virginia Woolf's *Orlando*', *PMLA* 103:1 (1988): 24–34.
Kristeva, Julia. 'Women's Time', *Feminisms: An Anthology of Literary Theory and Criticism*, 2nd edn, ed. Robyn R. Warhol and Diane Price Herndl. New Brunswick NJ: Rutgers University Press, 1997 [1981], 860–79.

Kumar, Shiv. *Bergson and the Stream of Consciousness Novel*. London: Blackie & Son, 1962.
Lackey, Michael. 'Modernist Anti-Philosophicalism and Virginia Woolf's Critique of Philosophy', *Journal of Modern Literature* 29:4 (2006): 76–98.
Landefeld, Ronnelle Rae. 'Becoming Light: Releasing Woolf from the Modernists Through the Theories of Giles Deleuze and Félix Guattari', MA thesis submitted to the Virginia Polytechnic Institute and State University, 2005.
Latour, Bruno. *We Have Never Been Modern*, trans. Catherine Porter. Cambridge MA: Harvard University Press, 1993.
—. 'On Actor-Network Theory: A Few Clarifications', *Soziale Welt* 47:4 (1996): 369–81.
—. *Reassembling the Social: An Introductuion to Actor-Network Theory*. Oxford: Oxford University Press, 2005.
Lawlor, Leonard. 'Following the Rats: Becoming-Animal in Deleuze and Guattari', *SubStance* 37:3 (2008):169–87.
Lawrence, D. H. *The Rainbow*, ed. Kate Flint. Oxford: Oxford University Press, [1915] 1998.
—. *Kangaroo*, ed. Bruce Steele. Cambridge: Cambridge University Press, [1923] 2002.
Leaska, Mitchell A. 'Virginia Woolf, the Pargeter: A Reading of *The Years*', *Bulletin of the New York Public Library* 80 (Winter 1977): 172–210.
—. 'Introduction', *The Pargiters: The Novel-Essay Portion of* The Years. London: The Hogarth Press, 1978.
Lecercle, Jean-Jacques. *Deleuze and Language*. Basingstoke: Palgrave Macmillan, 2002.
—. *Badiou and Deleuze Read Literature*. Edinburgh: Edinburgh University Press, 2010.
Lee, Raymond L. and Alistair B. Fraser. *The Rainbow Bridge: Rainbows in Art, Myth, and Science*. University Park PA: Pennsylvania State University Press, 2001.
Lewis, Thomas. S. W. 'Combining "The Advantages of Fact and Fiction": Virginia Woolf's Biographies of Vita Sackville-West, Flush, and Roger Fry', *Virginia Woolf: Critical Assessments vol. II*. Hastings: Helm Information, 1994, 376–97.
Llewelyn, John. 'Where to Cut: Boucherie and Delikatessen', *Research in Phenomenology* 40:2 (2010): 161–87.
Lorraine, Tamsin. 'Feminist Lines of Flight from the Majoritarian Subject', *Deleuze Studies* 2: Issue Supplement (2008): 60–82.
Love, Jean O. *Worlds in Consciousness*. London: University of California Press, 1970.
MacCormack, Patricia. 'Necrosexuality', *Queering the Non-Human*, ed. Noreen Giffney and Myra Hird. London: Ashgate, 2008, 339–62.
McHugh, Susan. 'Queer (and) Animal Theories', *GLQ: A Journal of Lesbian and Gay Studies* 15 (2009): 153–69.
—. *Animal Stories: Narrating Across Species Lines*. Minneapolis: University of Minnesota Press, 2011.
Mackin, Timothy. 'Private Worlds, Public Minds: Woolf, Russell and Photographic Vision', *Journal of Modern Literature* 33:3 (2010): 112–30.

McLaurin, Allen. *Virginia Woolf: the Echoes Enslaved*. Cambridge: Cambridge University Press, 1973.
McQuade, Molly. 'Woolf's Verb Impersonators (and Other Deviants)', *Virginia Woolf Miscellany* 70 (2006): 6.
Mao, Douglas. *Solid Objects: Modernism and the Test of Production*. Princeton: Princeton University Press, 1998.
Marcus, Jane. 'Art and Anger', *Feminist Studies* 4:1 (February 1978): 69–98.
—. 'Thinking Back Through Our Mothers', *New Feminist Essays on Virginia Woolf*, ed. Jane Marcus. Lincoln: University of Nebraska Press, 1981, 1–30.
—. 'Storming the Toolshed', *Feminisms: An Anthology of Literary Theory and Criticism*, 2nd edn, ed. Robyn R. Warhol and Diane Price Herndl. New Brunswick NJ: Rutgers University Press, [1982] 1997, 263–78.
—. 'Quentin's Bogey', *Critical Inquiry* 11:3 (1985): 486–97.
—. 'Britannia Rules *The Waves*', *Hearts of Darkness: White Women Write Race*. New Brunswick NJ: Rutgers University Press, 2004, 59–85.
—. '"A Very Fine Negress"', *Hearts of Darkness: White Women Write Race*. New Brunswick NJ: Rutgers University Press, 2004, 24–58.
Marcus, Laura. *Virginia Woolf*, 2nd edn. Devon: Northcote House, [1997] 2004.
Masschelein, Anneleen. '"Rip the veil of the old vision across, and walk through the rent": Reading D. H. Lawrence with Deleuze and Guattari', *Modernism and Theory: A Critical Debate*, ed. Stephen Ross. New York: Routledge, 2009, 23–39.
Mattison, Laci. 'The Metaphysics of Flowers in The Waves: Virginia Woolf's "Seven-Sided Flower" and Henri Bergson's Intuition', *Virginia Woolf and the Natural World: Selected Papers from the Twentieth International Conference on Virginia Woolf*, ed. Kristin Czarnecki and Carrie Rohman. Clemson: Clemson University Digital Press, 2011, 71–7.
—. 'Woolf's Un/Folding(s): The Artist and the Event of the Neo-Baroque', *Contradictory Woolf: Selected Papers from the Twenty-first Annual International Conference on Virginia Woolf*, ed. Derek Ryan and Stella Bolaki, Clemson: Clemson University Digital Press, 2012, 96–100.
—. 'Virginia Woolf's *Heart of Darkness* and Deleuzo-Guattarian De/territorialization: Fear, Desire and the Aesthetics of Becoming', Conference paper presented at 'Interdisciplinary/Multidisciplinary Woolf: the Twenty-second Annual International Conference on Virginia Woolf', 2012.
Meese, Elizabeth. 'When Virginia Looked at Vita, What Did She See; or, Lesbian: Feminist: Woman – What's the Differ(e/a)nce?', *Feminisms: An Anthology of Literary Theory and Criticism*, 2nd edn, ed. Robyn R. Warhol and Diane Price Herndl. New Brunswick NJ: Rutgers University Press, [1992] 1997, 467–81.
Meisel, Perry. *The Absent Father: Virginia Woolf and Walter Pater*. New Haven: Yale University Press, 1980.
Miles, Kathryn. '"That perpetual marriage of granite and rainbow": Searching for "The New Biography" in Virginia Woolf's *Orlando*', *Virginia Woolf and Communities: Selected Papers from the Eight Annual Conference on Virginia Woolf*, ed. Jeanette McVicker and Laura Davis. New York: Pace University Press, 1999, 212–18.
Minow-Pinkney, Makiko. *Virginia Woolf and The Problem of the Subject*. Brighton: The Harvester Press, 1987.

—. 'Virginia Woolf and the Age of Motor Cars', *Virginia Woolf in the Age of Mechanical Reproduction*, ed. Pamela L. Caughie. New York: Garland, 2000, 159–82.
—. 'Psychoanalytic Approaches', *Palgrave Advances in Virginia Woolf Studies*, ed. Anna Snaith. Basingstoke: Palgrave Macmillan, 2007, 60–82.
Moi, Toril. *Sexual/Textual Politics: Feminist Literary Theory*, 2nd edn. London: Routledge, [1985] 1995.
—. '"I Am Not a Feminist, But ...": How Feminism Became the F-Word', *PMLA* 121 (2006): 1735–41.
Monaco, Beatrice. *Machinic Modernism: The Deleuzian Literary Machines of Woolf, Lawrence and Joyce*. Basingstoke: Palgrave Macmillan, 2008.
Monk, Ray. 'This Fictitious Life: Virginia Woolf on Biography and Reality', *Philosophy and Literature* 31:1 (2007): 1–40.
Monson, Tamlyn. '"A Trick of the Mind": Alterity, Ontology, and Representation in Virginia Woolf's *The Waves*', *Modern Fiction Studies* 50:1 (2004): 173–96.
Moore, Madeline (ed.). 'Orlando: An Edition of the Manuscript', *Twentieth Century Literature* 25:3/4 (1979): 303–55.
Moore, Thomas Sturge. *Albert Dürer*. London: Duckworth, 1905.
Morris, Pam. 'Virginia Woolf's Metonymic Realism in *Mrs Dalloway*', English Literature Visiting Speaker Series, University of Glasgow, 2008.
—. 'Woolf and Realism', *Virginia Woolf in Context*, ed. Bryony Randall and Jane Goldman. Cambridge: Cambridge University Press, 2012.
'Myths and Legends of Cornwall', *Cornwall in Focus*. 2010, <http://www.corn wallinfocus.co.uk/history/legends.php> (accessed 9 October 2012).
Naremore, James. *The World Without a Self*. New Haven: Yale University Press, 1973.
Nicolson, Nigel. *Portrait of a Marriage: Vita Sackville-West and Harold Nicolson*. London: Orion, [1973] 1992.
Nigianni, Chrysanthi and Merl Storr (eds). *Deleuze and Queer Theory*. Edinburgh: Edinburgh University Press, 2009.
Osborne, Peter. 'Philosophy After Theory: Transdisciplinarity and the New', *Theory After 'Theory'*, ed. Jane Elliott and Derek Attridge. New York: Routledge, 2011, 19–33.
Parkes, Adam. 'Lesbianism, History, and Censorship: The Well of Loneliness and the SUPPRESSED RANDINESS of Virginia Woolf's *Orlando*', *Twentieth Century Literature* 40:4 (1994): 434–60.
Patton, Paul and John Protevi (eds). *Between Deleuze and Derrida*. London: Continuum, 2003.
—. 'Introduction', *Between Deleuze and Derrida*, ed. Paul Patton and John Protevi. London: Continuum, 2003, 1–14.
Peach, Linden. 'Editing Flush and Woolf's Editing in Flush', *Woolf Editing/Editing Woolf: Selected Papers from the Eighteenth Annual Conference on Virginia Woolf*, ed. Eleanor McNees and Sara Veglahn. Clemson: Clemson University Digital Press, 2009, 201–5.
Pearce, John M. *Animal Learning and Cognition: An Introduction*, 3rd edn. New York: Psychology Press, 2008.
Phillips, Kathy J. *Virginia Woolf Against Empire*. Knoxville: University of Tennessee Press, 1994.

Pisters, Patricia. *The Matrix of Visual Culture: Working with Deleuze in Film Theory*. Stanford: Stanford University Press, 2003.
Pitcher, Wallace S. *The Nature and Origin of Granite*. London: Blackie Academic & Professional, 1993.
Pollentier, Caroline. 'Imagining Flânerie Beyond Anthropocentrism: Virginia Woolf, the London Archipelago, and City Tortoises', *Woolf and the City: Selected Papers from the Nineteenth Annual International Conference on Virginia Woolf*, ed. Elizabeth F. Evans and Sarah E. Cornish. Clemson: Clemson University Digital Press, 2010, 20–30.
Potts, Gina. 'Woolf and the War Machine', *The Theme of Peace and War in Virginia Woolf's Writings: Essays on her Political Philosophy*, ed. Jane Wood. Lewiston: Edwin Mellen, 2010.
Raitt, Suzanne. *Vita and Virginia: The Work and Friendship of Vita Sackville-West and Virginia Woolf*. Oxford: Oxford University Press, 1993.
Ramsey, Tamara Ann. 'Producing Queer Affiliations: Feminist, Lesbian, Aesthetic, and Queer Reading Practices', *Virginia Woolf and Her Influences: Selected Papers from the Seventh Annual Conference on Virginia Woolf*, ed. Laura Davis and Jeanette McVicker. New York: Pace University Press, 1998, 275–81.
Randall, Bryony. *Modernism, Daily Time and Everyday Life*. Cambridge: Cambridge University Press, 2007.
Randall, Bryony and Jane Goldman (eds). *Virginia Woolf in Context*. Cambridge: Cambridge University Press, 2012.
Roebbelen, Erica. 'Manifestations of Twentieth-century Physics in Virginia Woolf's *The Waves*: Undermining the Ideological Foundations of the British Imperial Project', *Erudito* 1 (2010).
Rohman, Carrie. 'On Singularity and the Symbolic: The Threshold of the Human in Calvino's *Mr. Palomar*', *Criticism* 51:1 (2009): 63–78.
—. '"We Make Life": Vibration, Aesthetics, and the Inhuman in *The Waves*', *Virginia Woolf and the Natural World: Selected Papers from the Twentieth International Conference on Virginia Woolf*, ed. Kristin Czarnecki and Carrie Rohman. Clemson: Clemson University Digital Press, 2011, 12–23.
Rosenthal, Michael. *Virginia Woolf*. New York: Columbia University Press, 1979.
Ross, Stephen (ed.). *Modernism and Theory: A Critical Debate*. New York: Routledge, 2009.
—. 'Introduction: The Missing Link', *Modernism and Theory: A Critical Debate*, ed. Stephen Ross. New York: Routledge, 2009, 1–17.
Russell, Bertrand. *Analysis of Matter*. London: Routledge, [1927] 1992.
Ryan, Derek and Stella Bolaki (eds). *Contradictory Woolf: Selected Papers from the Twenty-first Annual International Conference on Virginia Woolf*. Clemson: Clemson University Digital Press, 2012.
Sackville-West, Vita. *The Letters of Vita Sackville-West to Virginia Woolf*, ed. Louise DeSalvo and Mitchell A. Leaska. New York: Morrow, 1985.
Scott, Bonnie Kime. *In the Hollow of the Wave: Virginia Woolf and Modernist Uses of Nature*. Charlottesville: University of Virginia Press, 2012.
Secor, Cynthia. 'Androgyny: an Early Reappraisal', *Women's Studies* 2:2 (1974): 161–70.
Sedgwick, Eve Kosofsky. *Tendencies*. London: Routledge, 1994.

Showalter, Elaine. *A Literature of Their Own: From Charlotte Brontë to Doris Lessing*. London: Virago, [1977] 1982.

Silver, Brenda R. 'The Authority of Anger: *Three Guineas* as Case Study', *Signs* 16:2 (1991): 340–70.

—. 'Editing Mrs. Ramsay: or, "8 Qualities of Mrs. Ramsay That Could be Annoying to Others"', *Woolf Editing/Editing Woolf: Selected Papers from the Eighteenth Annual Conference on Virginia Woolf*, ed. Eleanor McNees and Sara Veglahn. Clemson: Clemson University Digital Press 2009, 1–10.

Sim, Lorraine. 'Virginia Woolf Tracing Patterns through Plato's Forms', *Journal of Modern Literature* 28:2 (2005): 38–48.

—. *Virginia Woolf: The Patterns of Ordinary Experience*. Surrey: Ashgate, 2010.

Simpson, Kathryn. 'Queer Fish: Woolf's Writing of Desire between Women in *The Voyage Out* and *Mrs Dalloway*', *Woolf Studies Annual* 9 (2003): 55–82.

—. 'Pearl-diving: Inscriptions of Desire and Creativity in H.D. and Woolf', *Journal of Modern Literature* 27:4 (2004): 37–58.

Skeet, Jason. 'Woolf plus Deleuze: Cinema, Literature and Time Travel', *Rhizomes* 16 (2008).

Smith, Craig. 'Across the Widest Gulf: Nonhuman Subjectivity in Virginia Woolf's *Flush*', *Twentieth Century Literature* 48:3 (2002): 348–61.

Smith, Daniel W. 'Introduction', *Essays Critical and Clinical*, trans. Daniel W. Smith and Michael A. Greco. Minneapolis: University of Minnesota Press, [1993] 1997, xi–lvi.

—. 'The Inverse Side of the Structure: Žižek on Deleuze on Lacan', *Criticism* 46:4 (2004): 635–50.

Snaith, Anna. *Virginia Woolf: Public and Private Negotiations*. Basingstoke: Palgrave Macmillan, 2000.

—. 'Of Fanciers, Footnotes, and Fascism: Virginia Woolf's *Flush*', *Modern Fiction Studies* 48:3 (2002): 614–36.

— (ed.). *Palgrave Advances in Virginia Woolf Studies*. Basingstoke: Palgrave Macmillan, 2007.

Snaith, Anna and Christine Kenyon-Jones. 'Tilting at Universities: Virginia Woolf at King's College London', *Woolf Studies Annual* 16 (2010): 1–44.

Snaith, Anna and Michael Whitworth (eds). *Locating Woolf: The Politics of Space and Place*. Basingstoke: Palgrave Macmillan, 2007.

Sparks, Elisa Kay. '"Everything tended to set itself in a garden": Virginia Woolf's Literary and Quotidian Flowers: A Bar-Graphical Approach', *Virginia Woolf and the Natural World: Selected Papers from the Twentieth Annual International Conference on Virginia Woolf*, ed. Kristin Czarnecki and Carrie Rohman. Clemson: Clemson University Digital Press, 2011, 42–60.

Spiropoulou, Angeliki. *Virginia Woolf, Modernity and History: Constellations with Walter Benjamin*. Basingstoke: Palgrave Macmillan, 2010.

Spivak, Gayatri Chakravorty. 'Unmaking and Making in *To the Lighthouse*', *Other Worlds: Essays in Cultural Politics*. London: Routledge, [1980] 1988.

Sproles, Karyn Z. *Desiring Women: A Partnership of Virginia Woolf and Vita Sackville-West*. Toronto: University of Toronto Press, 2006.

Squier, Susan Merrill. *Virginia Woolf and London: The Sexual Politics of the City*. Chapel Hill: University of North Carolina Press, 1985.

Sultzbach, Kelly. 'The Fertile Potential of Virginia Woolf's Environmental

Ethic', *Woolf and the Art of Exploration: Selected Papers from the Fifteenth Annual Conference on Virginia Woolf*, ed. H. H. Southworth and E. Kay. Clemson: Clemson University Digital Press, 2006, 71–8.
Sun Yom, Sue. 'Bio-graphy and the Quantum Leap: Waves, Particles, and Light as a Theory of Writing the Human Life', *Texts and Contexts: Proceedings of the Fifth Annual Conference on Virginia Woolf*, ed. Beth Rigel Daugherty and Eileen Barrett. New York: Pace University Press, 1996: 145–50.
Swanson, Diana L. 'Lesbian Approaches', *Palgrave Advances in Virginia Woolf Studies*, ed. Anna Snaith. Basingstoke: Palgrave Macmillan, 2007, 184–208.
Thacker, Andrew. *Moving Through Modernity: Space and Geography in Modernism*. Manchester: Manchester University Press, 2003.
Thacker, Eugene. *After Life*. Chicago: University of Chicago Press, 2010.
'The Secret Life of the Dog', *Horizon*. First broadcast on the BBC, 6th January 2010.
Thompson, Hilary. 'Time and its Countermeasures: Modern Messianisms in Woolf, Benjamin, and Agamben', *Modernism and Theory: A Critical Debate*, ed. Stephen Ross. New York: Routledge, 2009, 86–98.
'Transformative Thresholds: Braidotti, Butler & the Ethics of Relation', *Mute: Culture and Politics After The Net*. 2006, <http://www.metamute.org/en/node/8508> (accessed 9 October 2012).
Vanita, Ruth. '"Love Unspeakable:" The Uses of Allusion in *Flush*', *Themes and Variations: Proceedings of the Second Annual Conference on Virginia Woolf*, ed. Vera Neverow-Turk and Mark Hussey. New York: Pace University Press, 1993, 248–57.
Weed, Elizabeth and Naomi Schor (eds). *Feminism Meets Queer Theory*. Bloomington and Indianapolis: Indiana University Press, 1997.
Westling, Louise Hutchings. 'Virginia Woolf and the Flesh of the World', *New Literary History* 30:4 (1999), 855–75.
Whitworth, Michael H. *Einstein's Wake: Relativity, Metaphor, and Modernist Literature*. Oxford: Oxford University Press, 2001.
—. *Authors in Context: Virginia Woolf*. Oxford: Oxford University Press, 2005.
—. 'Woolf, Context, and Contradiction', *Contradictory Woolf: Selected Papers from the Twenty-first Annual International Conference on Virginia Woolf*, ed. Derek Ryan and Stella Bolaki, Clemson: Clemson University Digital Press, 2012, 11–22.
Wolfe, Cary. *Critical Environments: Postmodern Theory and the Pragmatics of the "Outside"*. Minneapolis: University of Minnesota Press, 1998.
Wood, Jane (ed.). *The Theme of Peace and War in Virginia Woolf's Writings: Essays on her Political Philosophy*. Lewiston: Edwin Mellen, 2010.
Woolf, Virginia. 'Impressions at Bayreuth', *The Essays of Virginia Woolf, vol. 1.*, ed. Andrew McNeillie. London: The Hogarth Press, [1909] 1986, 288–93.
—. *The Voyage Out*. London: Vintage, [1915] 2004.
—. 'Coleridge as Critic', *The Essays of Virginia Woolf, vol. 2*, ed. Andrew McNeillie. London: The Hogarth Press, [1918] 1987, 221–5.
—. 'Women Novelists', *The Essays of Virginia Woolf, vol. 2*, ed. Andrew McNeillie. London: The Hogarth Press, [1918] 1987, 314–17.
—. *Night and Day*. London: Vintage, [1919] 2005.
—. 'Herman Melville', *The Essays of Virginia Woolf, vol. 3*, ed. Andrew McNeillie. London: The Hogarth Press, [1919] 1988, 77–83.

—. 'Monday or Tuesday', *The Complete Shorter Fiction of Virginia Woolf*, 2nd edn, ed. Susan Dick. London: Harcourt, [1920] 1989, 137.
—. 'Freudian Fiction', *The Essays of Virginia Woolf, vol. 2*, ed. Andrew McNeillie. London: The Hogarth Press, [1920] 1987, 195–7.
—. *Jacob's Room*. London: Vintage, [1922] 2004.
—. *Mrs Dalloway*, ed. David Bradshaw. Oxford: Oxford University Press, [1925] 2000.
—. 'Outlines', *The Common Reader, vol. 1*, ed. Andrew McNeillie. London: Vintage, [1925] 2003, 183–205.
—. 'How it Strikes a Contemporary', *The Common Reader, vol. 1*, ed. Andrew McNeillie. London: Vintage, [1925] 2003, 231–41.
—. 'On Not Knowing Greek', *The Common Reader, vol. 1*, ed. Andrew McNeillie. London: Vintage, [1925] 2003, 23–38.
—. 'The Duchess of Newcastle', *The Common Reader, vol. 1*, ed. Andrew McNeillie. London: Vintage, [1925] 2003, 69–77.
—. 'Life and the Novelist', *The Essays of Virginia Woolf, vol. 4.*, ed. Andrew McNeillie. London: The Hogarth Press, [1926] 1994, 400–6.
—. *To the Lighthouse*. London: Penguin, [1927] 1964.
—. 'Poetry, Fiction and the Future', *The Essays of Virginia Woolf, vol. 4.*, ed. Andrew McNeillie. London: The Hogarth Press, [1927] 1994, 428–41.
—. 'The New Biography', *The Essays of Virginia Woolf, vol. 4*, ed. Andrew McNeillie. London: The Hogarth Press, [1927] 1994, 473–80.
—. 'The Novels of E. M. Forster', *The Essays of Virginia Woolf, vol. 4.*, ed. Andrew McNeillie. London: The Hogarth Press, [1927] 1994, 491–502.
—. *Orlando: A Biography*. London: Vintage, [1928] 2004.
—. 'The Sun and the Fish', *The Essays of Virginia Woolf, vol. 4.*, ed. Andrew McNeillie. London: The Hogarth Press, [1928] 1994: 519–24.
—. *A Room of One's Own* and *Three Guineas*. Oxford: Oxford University Press, [1929; 1938] 1998.
—. *The Waves*, ed. Gillian Beer. Oxford: Oxford University Press, [1931] 1998.
—. '"This is the House of Commons."' *The Essays of Virginia Woolf, vol. 5*, ed. Stuart N. Clarke. London: The Hogarth Press, [1932] 2009, 323–30.
—. *Flush: A Biography*, ed. Kate Flint. Oxford: Oxford University Press, [1933] 1998.
—. *The Years*. London: Vintage, [1937] 2004.
—. 'Craftsmanship', *The Essays of Virginia Woolf, vol. 6*, ed. Stuart N. Clarke. London: The Hogarth Press, [1937] 2011, 91–102.
—. *Between the Acts*, ed. Frank Kermode. Oxford: Oxford University Press, [1941] 1998.
—. 'Professions for Women', *The Essays of Virginia Woolf, vol. 6*, ed. Stuart N. Clarke. London: The Hogarth Press, [1942] 2011, 479–86.
—. 'Evening Over Sussex: Reflections in a Motor Car', *The Essays of Virginia Woolf, vol. 6.*, ed. Stuart N. Clarke. London: The Hogarth Press, [1942] 2011, 453–6.
—. *The Letters of Virginia Woolf*, 6 vols, ed. Nigel Nicolson and Joanne Trautmann. New York: Harcourt Brace Jovanovich, 1975–80.
—. *Moments of Being*, ed. Jeanne Schulkind. London: Pimlico, [1976] 2002.
—. 'Sketch of the Past', *Moments of Being*, ed. Jeanne Schulkind. London: Pimlico, [1976] 2002, 78–160.

—. 'Old Bloomsbury', *Moments of Being*, ed. Jeanne Schulkind. London: Pimlico, [1976] 2002, 43–61.
—. *The Diary of Virginia Woolf*, 5 vols, ed. Anne Olivier Bell. New York: Harcourt Brace Jovanovich, 1977–84.
—. *The Pargiters: The Novel-Essay Portion of* The Years, ed. Mictchell A. Leaska. London: The Hogarth Press, 1978.
—. 'A Simple Melody', *The Complete Shorter Fiction of Virginia Woolf*, 2nd edn, ed. Susan Dick. San Diego: Harcourt, [1982] 1989, 201–7.
—. 'The Widow and the Parrot: A True Story', *The Complete Shorter Fiction of Virginia Woolf*, 2nd edn, ed. Susan Dick. San Diego: Harcourt, [1982] 1989, 162–9.
—. 'Nineteen Letters to Eleven Recipients', ed. Joanne Trautmann Banks. *Modern Fiction Studies* 30 (1984): 175–202.
—. *The Complete Shorter Fiction of Virginia Woolf*, 2nd edn, ed. Susan Dick. San Diego: Harcourt, [1985] 1989.
—. 'The Dog', *The Complete Shorter Fiction of Virginia Woolf*, 2nd edn, ed. Susan Dick. San Diego: Harcourt, [1985] 1989, 334–5.
—. *The Essays of Virginia Woolf*, 6 vols, ed. Andrew McNeillie (vols 1–4) and Stuart N. Clarke (vols 5–6). London: The Hogarth Press, 1986–2011.
—. *A Passionate Apprentice. The Early Journals: 1897–1909*, ed. Mitchell A. Leaska. San Diego: Harvest/Harcourt Brace Jovanovich, 1990.
—. *Women and Fiction: The Manuscript Versions of* A Room of One's Own, ed. S. P. Rosenbaum. Oxford: Blackwell, 1992.
Wright, Terence R. *D. H. Lawrence and the Bible*. Cambridge: Cambridge University Press, 2000.
Wylie, Dan. 'The Anthropomorphic Ethic: Fiction and the Animal Mind in Virginia Woolf's *Flush* and Barbara Gowdy's *The White Bone*', *Isle: Interdisciplinary Studies in Literature and Environment* 9:2 (2002): 115–31.
Xenophanes. *Xenophanes of Colophon: Fragments*, ed. James H. Lesher. Toronto: University of Toronto Press, 2001.
Young, Davis A. *Mind Over Magma: The Story of Igneous Petrology*. Princeton: Princeton University Press, 2003.
Zamith, Maria Cândida and Flora, Luísa (eds). *Virginia Woolf: Three Centenary Celebrations*. Porto: Universidade do Porto, 2007.
Zucker, Marilyn Slutzky. 'Virginia Woolf's Uncertainty Principle of Language', *Virginia Woolf : Three Centenary Celebrations*, ed. Maria Cândida Zamith and Luísa Flora. Porto: Universidade do Porto, 2007, 145–54.
Zwerdling, Alex. *Virginia Woolf and the Real World*. Berkeley: University of California Press, 1986.

Index

affects/percepts, 190–2
Agamben, Giorgio, 134–5, 200n
Ahmed, Sara, 114, 197n, 200n
androgyny, 58–77, 95, 116
animals/animality, 9, 12, 132–64, 165n, 166n, 188, 199n
anthropocentrism, 12–13, 133–8, 153–4, 166n, 177, 181–5
anthropomorphism, 134–6, 140–1, 146, 153, 164n, 166n, 181, 184
Aristotle, 46, 181–2

Bacon, Francis, 162, 169n
Badiou, Alain, 137, 202n
Banfield, Ann, 22n, 54n, 171–3
Barad, Karen, 171, 174–6, 180, 192, 198n, 199n
Barrett, Michèle, 11–12, 23n
Barrett Browning, Elizabeth, 132, 134, 137, 144, 169n
becoming-
  animal, 17, 152–60, 168n, 169n
  imperceptible, 89, 95, 190–1
  woman, 9, 61, 71–7
Beer, Gillian, 22n, 31, 172, 198n
Bennett, Jane, 12, 136, 184–7, 192, 199n, 200n
Bergson, Henri, 5, 15–16, 21n, 22n, 23n, 77, 121, 131n, 184, 200n
Berman, Jessica, 16, 22n, 119, 199n
Between the Acts, 18, 32, 56n, 130n, 180, 200n
bios/zoē, 102, 184, 200n
Bohr, Niels, 171–5, 198n
Bowlby, Rachel, 8, 35, 54n, 58–9, 78, 109, 201n
Bradshaw, David, 33
Braidotti, Rosi, 13, 18–21, 52–3, 61–77, 101–8, 122, 129n, 152, 168n, 183–4, 200n
Butler, Judith, 69–70, 98n, 104, 108

Calarco, Matthew, 137, 142, 153, 160, 163–4, 168n
Caughie, Pamela, 7–8, 10, 28–30, 36, 41, 60, 132, 138, 164n
'Character in Fiction', 13
Colebrook, Claire, 9, 13, 17, 24n, 75, 107, 129n
Coleridge, Samuel Taylor, 58, 60, 64, 96n
companion species, 142–3, 147, 150–2, 156–60
'Craftsmanship', 10, 30, 69, 184

Darwin, Charles, 40, 74, 168n
deconstruction, 7, 14–15, 163
Deleuze, Gilles, 3, 9, 11–21, 23n, 24n, 51–2, 67, 71–95, 106, 115–24, 127, 130n, 131n, 137–8, 146–7, 152–9, 162–3, 168n, 173, 176, 183, 186, 190–7, 199n, 201n
Derrida, Jacques, 7, 14–15, 24n, 137–48, 154, 160, 163, 166n, 168n
desire, 64, 76, 101–20, 123–4, 126–8, 128n, 131n, 137, 146, 155, 195–6
The Diary of Virginia Woolf, 32, 38, 42, 48, 56n, 101–2, 165n, 173, 190–1
différance, 15, 24n
'The Duchess of Newcastle', 42
Duns Scotus, John, 193, 201n
Dürer, Albrecht, 47–8

eco-criticism, 22n, 200n
'Evening Over Sussex', 125–6

feminism, 7–8, 58–76, 197n
Flush, 132–64, 165n, 166n, 167n, 168n
Forster, E. M., 43–4
Foucault, Michel, 9, 24n
free indirect discourse, 92, 100n, 145, 155
Freud, Sigmund, 58, 78, 120

Geology, 39–40
Goldman, Jane, 1, 6, 52, 54n, 57n, 66, 82, 88, 94–5, 138, 167n, 198n

Grosz, Elizabeth, 13, 15, 63, 74, 76, 188, 194
Guattari, Félix *see* Deleuze, Gilles

haecceity, 17, 154, 189–92, 196, 201n
Haraway, Donna, 142–3, 148–60, 163–4, 165n
Heidegger, Martin, 5–6, 15, 142
'How it Strikes a Contemporary', 7
Hussey, Mark, 1, 28, 55n

Ibsen, Henrik, 43
immanence, 2–4, 12–13, 76, 106–7, 181–3, 192–7
'Impressions at Bayreuth', 47
intra-action, 174–80, 184–91, 196–7

Jacob's Room, 39, 53

Kafka, Franz, 16, 80
Keats, John, 48, 69
Kristeva, Julia, 7, 24n, 60, 98n

Lacan, Jacques, 7, 24n, 137, 166n
Latour, Bruno, 167n, 200n
Lawrence, D. H., 16, 37, 42, 45–6, 115
The Letters of Virginia Woolf, 2, 32, 38–9, 41–2, 47–8, 114, 116, 132
Levinas, Emmanuel, 166n
'Life and the Novelist', 42
life itself, 13, 180–6, 189, 194, 197

Mansfield, Katherine, 154, 165n
Marxism, 11–12, 137
materialism, 3–4, 50, 119, 152, 185–6, 192, 200n
Minow-Pinkney, Makiko, 7–8, 14, 60, 88, 104, 125
Moi, Toril, 7–8, 60
'Monday or Tuesday', 126–7
Mrs Dalloway, 17, 32, 50, 190–1, 199n, 201n

naturecultures, 150, 163, 167n, 189
'The New Biography', 26–31, 42, 50, 53n
new materialisms, 11–13, 23n
Nietzsche, Friedrich, 5, 14–15, 23n, 24n
Night and Day, 33–7
'The Novels of E. M. Forster', 43–4

'On Not Knowing Greek', 33
Orlando, 17, 27, 30, 45–6, 101–28, 195–6

The Pargiters, 27–9
physics, 171–6, 179
Plato, 58, 172

posthumanism, 12–13, 171, 174, 177, 188–90
postmodernism, 4–5, 7–11, 50–1, 62
poststructuralism, 4–5, 7–12, 14, 41, 59–60
'Professions for Women', 66
Proust, Marcel, 16, 59, 123
psukhē, 181–2
psychoanalytic theory, 5, 8–9, 58, 76–8, 82–3, 106–7, 115–18, 154

queer theory, 8, 30, 102, 107–9, 113–16, 119, 122–8, 128n, 129n, 130n, 123–4

rhizome, 84–7, 93–6, 106
A Room of One's Own, 11, 13, 32, 42, 58–75, 81–2, 74, 89, 93, 116, 150, 159, 165n, 168n, 183, 197n
Russell, Bertrand, 6, 131n, 171, 201n

Sackville-West, Vita, 2, 38, 42, 101–3, 105–6, 108–9, 124
scholasticism, 193–4, 201n
Sedgwick, Eve Kosofsky, 108
sexual difference, 61–77, 81, 88, 92–3, 96n, 103–4, 107
sexuality, 102–16, 119, 122, 188
'A Simple Melody', 191
'Sketch of the Past', 1–3, 37–9, 44–5, 56n, 78–9, 189
smooth/striated spaces, 89–91
Spinoza, Baruch, 15, 23n, 193–4
'The Sun and the Fish', 45–6

Thacker, Eugene, 181, 193–4
thing theory/thing-power, 184, 186,199n
'"This is the House of Commons"', 33
Three Guineas, 13, 17, 97n, 159
To the Lighthouse, 31, 45, 75–96, 113, 123, 156, 158, 173–5

virtual, 52, 93, 192, 195
vitalism, 12–14, 106–7, 116, 174, 182, 184–6, 191–2, 200n
The Voyage Out, 16, 33–4

The Waves, 17, 50, 63, 146, 171–97, 200n
Whitworth, Michael, 36–7, 100n, 172, 199n
'The Widow and the Parrott', 136
'Women Novelists', 65
Woolf, Virginia *see individual works by title*

The Years, 28, 167n, 172

Žižek, Slavoj, 137

EU representative:
Easy Access System Europe
Mustamäe tee 50, 10621 Tallinn, Estonia
Gpsr.requests@easproject.com